C000001984

TORT LAW

TORT LAW

Kate Smith

Hall and Stott Publishing Ltd
27 Witney Close
Saltford
BS31 3DX

© Kate Smith 2021

The moral rights of the author have been asserted

All rights reserved. No part of this publication may be reproduced, stored in a retrieval system, or transmitted, in any form or by any means, without the prior written permission of the copyright holder, application for which should be addressed to the publisher, or as expressly permitted by law, by licence or under terms agreed with the appropriate reprographics rights organisation.

Contains public sector information licensed under the Open Government Licence v3.0.

British Library Cataloguing in Publication Data

ISBN 978 1 9162431 5 6

Typeset by Style Photosetting Ltd, Mayfield, East Sussex

PREFACE

I want this book to give students access to the kind of depth plus accessibility that I couldn't always find when I was studying tort for the first time, way back in the dark ages (circa the 1990s). I think if someone had made clear from the start that tort can be (a) like a black comedy, (b) clear as mud, and (c) both rules-driven and at the same time reliant on that dreaded term, 'common sense', I might have got the measure of it more quickly. I hope this book helps you, and that you enjoy it, wherever you intend to take your study of tort.

Special thanks to both Sue Hall and David Stott for their support and patience in the writing of this book. You are the dream team to work with.

Kate Smith
Hove, East Sussex
May 2021

CONTENTS

Preface   v
Table of Cases   xv
Table of Legislation   xxv

1   Introduction to Tort Law   **1**

1.1   Introduction   1
1.2   What is tort?   1
1.3   What is tort not?   2
       1.3.1   Criminal law   2
       1.3.2   Contract law   3
       1.3.3   Land law   3
1.4   Torts we will examine   4
1.5   The torts in outline   4
1.6   The significance of policy   5
       1.6.1   Floodgates   6
       1.6.2   Other policy considerations   7
1.7   Tort terminology, key terms and phrases   7
       1.7.1   Claimant and defendant   7
       1.7.2   Loss, damage, damages   8
       1.7.3   Tortious not tortuous   8
       1.7.4   Fault liability and strict liability   8
       1.7.5   Actionable *per se*   8
1.8   Further reading   9

2   General Negligence – Loss and Duty of Care   **11**

2.1   Scope of this chapter   11
2.2   What is Negligence?   11
2.3   The Negligence sequence   12
       PART I   LOSS/DAMAGE AND DUTY   12
2.4   Loss/damage   12
       2.4.1   The types of recoverable or recognisable loss/damage 12
       2.4.2   Types of loss that may not be recoverable   14
2.5   Duty of care   15
       2.5.1   Expansion and contraction   16
       2.5.2   *Caparo v Dickman*   17
       2.5.3   What did the stages mean?   17
       2.5.4   *Caparo* revisited: the incremental approach   18
       2.5.5   *Michael and Robinson*   19

	2.5.6	Where do we go from here?	20
2.6	Special duty situations		21
	2.6.1	Omissions: the general rule	21
	2.6.2	Liability for acts of third parties	24
	2.6.3	Public bodies, including the emergency services	27
2.7	Consolidation and reflection		33
2.8	Further reading		33
	PART II PSYCHIATRIC HARM AND ECONOMIC LOSS		36
2.9	Duty of care where the loss/damage is psychiatric harm		36
	2.9.1	What is psychiatric harm?	36
	2.9.2	Why is the court reluctant to impose a duty?	36
	2.9.3	The process for establishing a duty of care	37
	2.9.4	Categorising the claimant: primary and secondary claimants/ victims	37
	2.9.5	Conclusion	43
2.10	Pure economic loss and duty of care		44
	2.10.1	The current position	45
	2.10.2	Summary so far	47
	2.10.3	Extension of the principle to incorporate not just negligent advice but the negligent provision of services	48
2.11	Further reading		48
3	**General Negligence – Breach**		**53**
3.1	Introduction		53
3.2	The Negligence sequence – breach		53
3.3	Setting the standard – the so-called 'reasonable person'		54
	3.3.1	An objective standard	54
	3.3.2	Is the objective standard ever lowered, ie subjective?	55
	3.3.3	The standard for professionals acting in their professional capacity	57
3.4	Establishing breach – question of fact		58
3.5	Factors the court may take into account in determining whether there has been a breach		58
	3.5.1	Likelihood of harm	58
	3.5.2	Potential seriousness of injury	58
	3.5.3	Common practice	59
	3.5.4	The practicality of taking precautions	60
	3.5.5	Foresight not hindsight	60
	3.5.6	Social utility/value of the activity	61
	3.5.7	Balancing the factors	61
3.6	*Res ipsa loquitur*		62
3.7	Further reading		63
4	**General Negligence – Causation**		**67**
4.1	Introduction		67
4.2	The Negligence sequence – causation		68
4.3	Factual causation – the 'but for' test		68

	4.3.1 Problems with the but for test	70
	4.3.2 So how do we determine factual causation?	75
4.4	Legal causation	77
4.5	Intervening events – *novus actus interveniens*	77
	4.5.1 Acts of the claimant	77
	4.5.2 Acts of third parties	79
	4.5.3 Acts of God/natural events	80
4.6	Further reading	80

5   General Negligence – Remoteness   85

5.1	Introduction	85
5.2	The Negligence sequence – remoteness	86
5.3	The test of reasonable foreseeability	86
5.4	The same kind or type of harm – extent need not be foreseen	87
	5.4.1 A note on practicalities and procedure	87
	5.4.2 Extent need not be foreseen – examples	88
5.5	The same kind or type of harm – narrow and wide view	88
5.6	No need to foresee the precise way in which the damage occurs	89
5.7	Consolidation	90
5.8	The claimant's impecuniosity	90
5.9	Further reading	91

6   General Negligence – Defences and Remedies   95

6.1	Scope of this chapter	95
6.2	Where in the Negligence sequence do defences and remedies fit?	95
6.3	*Volenti* (or consent)	96
	6.3.1 The elements of *volenti*	96
	6.3.2 Other examples of *volenti*	98
6.4	*Ex turpi* or illegality	98
	6.4.1 The elements of *ex turpi*	98
	6.4.2 In what circumstances will this defence actually work?	99
	6.4.3 Has the defence evolved or changed over time?	100
6.5	Contributory negligence	100
	6.5.1 The elements of contributory negligence	101
	6.5.2 Did the claimant fail to exercise reasonable care for their own safety?	101
6.6	Remedies	102
6.7	Further reading	102

7   Clinical Negligence   107

7.1	Scope of this chapter – old and new	107
7.2	Overlaps with criminal law	107
7.3	Loss/damage	108
7.4	Duty of care	108
7.5	Breach of duty	109
	7.5.1 Setting the standard	109
	7.5.2 Breach of that standard	109

7.6	Causation	117
	7.6.1 A reminder – factual causation	117
	7.6.2 A reminder – legal causation	117
7.7	The other elements in the Clinical Negligence sequence	118
7.8	Apportionment	118
7.9	Further reading	118

8 Employers' Primary Liability and Vicarious Liability 121

8.1	Introduction and scope	121
8.2	Structure of an employers' primary liability claim	122
8.3	Damage/loss	122
8.4	Is the claimant an employee of the defendant?	123
8.5	Employers' duty of care	124
	8.5.1 Employers' duty to provide safe and competent fellow employees	125
	8.5.2 Employers' duty to provide a safe place of work	127
	8.5.3 Employers' duty to provide a safe system of work	128
	8.5.4 Employers' duty to take reasonable care to ensure the safety of staff is not an absolute duty	129
8.6	Breach of duty	130
8.7	Causation	130
8.8	Remoteness	131
8.9	Defences	131
	8.9.1 *Volenti*/consent	131
	8.9.2 Contributory negligence	131
8.10	Vicarious liability	132
	8.10.1 Rationale for vicarious liability	132
	8.10.2 Who can sue?	133
	8.10.3 Elements of vicarious liability	133
8.11	Further reading	138

9 Product Liability 141

9.1	Introduction	141
9.2	Claims under the CPA 1987 for defective products	142
	9.2.1 Who can sue and be sued?	142
	9.2.2 What damage can the claimant claim for?	144
	9.2.3 What is a 'product'?	144
	9.2.4 What is a 'defect'?	145
	9.2.5 Causation	148
	9.2.6 Limitation period	149
	9.2.7 Defences	149
	9.2.8 Summary of structure of a claim under CPA 1987	151
9.3	Claims in Negligence	151
	9.3.1 Damage	151
	9.3.2 Duty	151
	9.3.3 Breach	152
	9.3.4 Causation, remoteness and defences	152

| | 9.3.5 | Design defects | 152 |
| 9.4 | | Further reading | 153 |

10   Occupiers' Liability   157

10.1		Introduction	157
10.2		Differences between occupiers' liability and General Negligence	158
10.3		Categories of claimant and terminology	159
	10.3.1	Occupier	159
	10.3.2	Visitor	160
	10.3.3	Premises	162
10.4		Claims under the OLA 1957	163
	10.4.1	Which Act?	163
	10.4.2	Duty of care	163
	10.4.3	Breach – setting the standard	163
	10.4.4	Defences and attempts to exclude	169
10.5		Claims under the OLA 1984	170
	10.5.1	How do we define non-visitor or trespasser?	170
	10.5.2	Background to the OLA 1984	171
	10.5.3	Duty of care under the OLA 1984	171
	10.5.4	Breach	173
	10.5.5	Defences	174
	10.5.6	Do claims under the OLA 1984 ever succeed?	175
10.6		Differences between the OLA 1957 and the OLA 1984	176
10.7		Further reading	177

11   Defamation   181

11.1		Defamation – definition and background	181
11.2		Libel and slander	182
	11.2.1	Libel	182
	11.2.2	Slander	183
	11.2.3	Does the distinction between libel and slander matter?	183
	11.2.4	Difference between defamation and mere abuse	183
11.3		Structure of a claim	184
	11.3.1	Who can and cannot sue?	184
	11.3.2	The requirement of serious harm	185
11.4		Elements of defamation	186
	11.4.1	A defamatory statement was made	186
	11.4.2	The statement referred to the claimant	190
	11.4.3	The statement was published to a third party	192
11.5		Defences	193
	11.5.1	Truth	193
	11.5.2	More than one statement made?	194
	11.5.3	Honest opinion	194
	11.5.4	Privilege	195
	11.5.5	Publication on a matter of public interest	197
	11.5.6	Distributors, including operators of websites	199
	11.5.7	Offer of amends	200

11.6	Remedies: damages and injunctions	201
11.7	Further reading	202

12   Nuisance and the Rule in *Rylands v Fletcher*   205

12.1	What is nuisance?	205
	12.1.1 What interests does nuisance protect?	205
	12.1.2 Remedies	206
	12.1.3 Order of play	206
12.2	Private nuisance	206
	12.2.1 What can the claimant claim for?	207
	12.2.2 Structure of a private nuisance claim	208
	12.2.3 Other elements of the claim	209
	12.2.4 Defences	212
	12.2.5 Remedies	214
12.3	The rule in *Rylands v Fletcher*	214
	12.3.1 Strict liability	215
	12.3.2 Who can sue and be sued?	215
	12.3.3 Loss/damage and remedies	215
	12.3.4 Elements of the tort	215
	12.3.5 Defences	217
12.4	Public nuisance	217
	12.4.1 What is public nuisance?	217
	12.4.2 Structure of a public nuisance claim	218
	12.4.3 Elements of the tort	218
	12.4.4 Defences and remedies	219
12.5	Further reading	220

13   Trespass to the Person   223

13.1	Introduction and scope	223
13.2	Differences between trespass and Negligence	223
13.3	Trespass to the person overview	224
	13.3.1 Actionable *per se*	224
	13.3.2 What links the torts?	224
13.4	Assault	225
	13.4.1 Intention or recklessness	225
	13.4.2 Reasonable apprehension	226
	13.4.3 Defences	227
13.5	Battery	228
	13.5.1 Intentional application of force	228
	13.5.2 Direct and immediate force (or indirect force)	229
	13.5.3 Defences	229
13.6	False imprisonment	230
	13.6.1 Intention to completely restrict the claimant's liberty	230
	13.6.2 Defences	231
13.7	The tort in *Wilkinson v Downton*	233
13.8	Further reading	234

14   Revision and Consolidation

14   Revision and Consolidation   239

Chapter 1: Introduction to Tort Law   239
Chapter 2: General Negligence – Loss and Duty of Care   240
Chapter 3: General Negligence – Breach   243
Chapter 4: General Negligence – Causation   244
Chapter 5: General Negligence – Remoteness   245
Chapter 6: General Negligence – Defences and Remedies   246
Chapter 7: Clinical Negligence   247
Chapter 8: Employers' Primary Liability and Vicarious Liability   248
Chapter 9: Product Liability   249
Chapter 10: Occupiers' Liability   250
Chapter 11: Defamation   251
Chapter 12: Nuisance and the Rule in *Rylands v Fletcher*   252
Chapter 13: Trespass to the Person   253
Guidance on Answering MCQs, Essay Questions and Problem Questions 254
General Exam Guidance Top Tips   256

Index   257

TABLE OF CASES

A

A and Others v National Blood Authority [2001] 3 All ER 289   146
A v National Blood Authority [2001] 3 All ER 289   145
A, Re (conjoined twins) [2001] 2 WLR 480   233
Abouzaid v Mothercare (UK) Ltd [2000] EWCA Civ 348   146
AC Billings & Sons Ltd v Riden [1958] AC 240   54
Adam v Ward [1917] AC 309   196
Adams v Ursell [1913] 1 Ch 269   213
AG v Hastings Corporation (1950) SJ 225   219
Alcock v Chief Constable of South Yorkshire Police [1992] 1 AC 310   38, 40
Alexander v North Eastern Railway Co (1865) 6 B&S 340   193
Al-Fagih v HH Saudi Research & Marketing (UK) Ltd [2002] EWCA Civ 1634   190
Allen v Gulf Oil Refining [1981] 1 All ER 353   213
Allied Maples Group v Simmons & Simmons [1995] 1 WLR 1602   75
Allsop v Church of England Newspaper Ltd [1972] 2 QB 161   189
Ames v Spamhaus [2015] EWHC 127 (QB)   185
Andreae v Selfridge and Co Ltd [1938] Ch 1   212
Anns v London Borough of Merton [1978] AC 728   16
Applause Stores Productions Ltd and Another v Raphael [2008] EWHC 1781 (QB)   182
Armes v Nottinghamshire County Council [2017] UKSC 60   136
Ashton v Turner [1981] 1 QB 137   98
Aspro Travel Ltd v Owners Abroad Group plc [1996] 1 WLR 132   192
Attorney General v PYA Quarries [1957] 2 QB 169   217
Ayres v Odedra [2013] EWHC 40 (QB)   102

B

Bailey v Ministry of Defence [2008] EWCA Civ 883   71
Baker v Quantum Clothing Group Ltd [2011] UKSC 17   127
Bamford v Turnley (1862) 122 ER 25   206
Banca Nazionale del Lavaro SPA v Playboy Club London Ltd [2018] UKSC 43   46
Barber v Somerset County Council [2004] UKHL 13   122
Barclays Bank v Various Claimants [2020] UKSC 13   134
Barker v Corus Ltd [2006] UKHL 20   73
Barnett v Chelsea and Kensington Hospital [1969] 1 QB 428   69
Barrett v Ministry of Defence [1995] 1 WLR 1217   23
Bayley v George Eliot Hospital [2017] EWHC 3398 (QB)   116
Berkoff v Burchill [1996] 4 All ER 1008   184

Bird v Jones [1845] 7 QB 742   230
Black v Fife Coal Ltd [1912] AC 149   126
Bolam v Friern Hospital Management Committee [1957] 1 WLR 583   57, 109, 110
Bolitho v City and Hackney Health Authority [1998] AC 232   59, 111, 114
Bolton v Stone [1951] AC 850   58
Bonnington Castings Ltd v Wardlaw [1956] AC 613   71
Bottomley v Secretary and Members of Todmorden Cricket Club (2003) The Times, 13 November   60
Bowater v Rowley Regis Corporation [1944] KB 476   131
Bradford v Robinson Rentals Ltd [1967] 1 WLR 337   88
British Chiropractic Association v Singh [2010] EWCA Civ 35   197
British Railways Board v Herrington [1972] AC 877   170, 171
Bull and Another v Devon Area Health Authority (1993) 4 Med LR 117   108
Busby v Berkshire Bed Co Ltd [2018] EWHC 2976 (QB)   148
Butt v Secretary of State for the Home Department [2017] EWHC 2619 (QB)   194
Bux v Slough Metals Ltd [1973] 1 WLR 1358   121
Byrne v Dean [1937] 1 KB 818   190

C

Calgarth, The [1927] P 93 Coram   161
Cambridge Water Co Ltd v Eastern Counties Leather Plc [1994] 2 AC 264   216
Caparo Industries plc v Dickman [1990] 2 AC 605   17, 47
Capital & Counties plc v Hampshire County Council [1997] QB 1004   24, 29
Cassidy v Daily Mirror Newspapers Ltd [1929] 2 KB 331   189
Cassidy v Ministry of Health [1951] 2 KB 343   62, 108
Chadwick v British Transport Commission [1967] 2 All ER 945   39
Charleston v News Group Newspapers Ltd [1995] 2 All ER 313   188
Chatterton v Gerson [1981] QB 432   232
Chester v Afshar [2005] 1 AC 134   74
Clark Fixing Ltd v Dudley Metropolitan Borough Council [2001] EWCA Civ 1898   27
Clifford v Charles Challen and Son Ltd [1953] AC 643   129
CN & GN v Poole Borough Council [2019] UKSC 25   28
Cockroft v Smith [1705] 11 Mod 43   233
Collier v Anglian Water Authority (1983) The Times, 26 March   160
Collins v Wilcock [1984] 1 WLR 1172   225
Colour Quest Ltd v Total Downstream UK Plc [2009] EWHC 823 (Comm)   219
Commissioner of the Police of the Metropolis v DSD and Another [2018] UKSC 11   32
Condon v Basi [1985] 1 WLR 866   98
Cooke & Another v MGN Ltd [2014] EWHC 2831 (QB)   185
Cooper v Turrell [2011] EWHC 3269 (QB)   183
Corr v IBC Vehicles Ltd [2008] 2 WLR 499   79, 89
Costello v Chief Constable of Northumbria Police [1999] 1 All ER 550   23
Coventry v Lawrence (No 2) [2014] UKSC 46   209, 213
Cox v Ministry of Justice [2016] UKSC 10   136
Cruise and Kidman v Express Newspapers plc [1999] QB 931   194
Cullin v London Fire and Civil Defence Authority [1999] PIQR 314   39

D

Dann v Hamilton [1939] 1 KB 509   97, 131

Darby v National Trust [2001] EWCA Civ 189	161, 167
Darnley v Croydon Health Services NHS Trust [2018] UKSC 50	21
Davis Contractors v Fareham Urban District Council [1956] AC 696	54
De Freitas v O'Brien [1995] EWCA Civ 28	111
Dennis v Ministry of Defence [2003] EWHC 793 (QB)	214
Dobson v Thames Water Utilities Ltd [2009] EWCA Civ 28	208
Dodwell v Burford (1670) 1 Mod 24	229
Donoghue v Folkestone Properties Ltd [2003] 3 All ER 110	173
Donoghue v Stevenson [1932] AC 562	16
Doughty v Turner Manufacturing Co Ltd [1964] 1 QB 518	89
DPP v K (A Minor) [1990] 1 WLR 1067	229
Dunn v Birmingham Canal Co (1872) LR 8 QB	217

E

Economou v De Freitas [2018] EWCA Civ 2591	197, 199
Edwards v Railways Executive [1952] AC 737	162
English Heritage v Taylor [2016] EWCA Civ 448	167
Esegbona v King's College Hospital Foundation NHS Trust [2019] EWHC 77 (QB)	231
Euro-Diam Ltd v Bathurst [1990] 1 QB 1	98

F

F, Re (Mental Patient: Sterilization) [1990] 2 AC 1	229
Fagan v Metropolitan Police Commissioner [1969] 1 QB 439	228
Fairchild v Glenhaven Funeral Services Ltd [2003] 1 AC 32	73
Fearn & Others v The Board of Trustees of the Tate Gallery [2020] EWCA Civ 104	207
Fitzgerald v Lane & Patel [1989] 1 AC 328	55, 118
Flood v Times Newspapers Ltd [2012] UKSC 11	198
Froom v Butcher [1976] 1 QB 286	101
Frost v Chief Constable of South Yorkshire [1999] 2 AC 455 (PTSD)	36

G

Galli-Atkinson v Seghal [2013] EWCA Civ 679	43
Geary v Wetherspoons plc [2011] EWHC 1506 (QB)	169
Gee & Others v DePuy International Ltd [2018] EWHC 1208 (QB)	147
General Cleaning Contractors Ltd v Christmas [1954] AC 180	128
Giles v Walker (1890) 24 QBD 656	215
Glass v Cambridge Health Authority [1995] 6 Med LR 91	63
Godfrey v Demon Internet Ltd [2001] QB 201	182, 192
Goldman v Hargrave [1967] 1 AC 645	24
Gouldsmith v Mid Staffordshire General Hospitals NHS Trust [2007] EWCA Civ 397	115
Graham v Commercial Bodyworks Ltd [2015] EWCA Civ 47	126
Gray v Thames Trains Ltd [2009] UKHL 33	79, 100
Gregg v Scott [2005] UKHL 2	75
Grobbelaar v News Group Newspapers Ltd [2002] UKHL 40	102, 193
Gunapathy Muniandy v Khoo and Others [2001] SGHC 165	114
Gwilliam v West Hertfordshire Hospitals NHS Trust [2002] EWCA Civ 1041	163, 168

H

Haley v London Electricity Board [1965] AC 778	164
Hall v Brooklands Auto-Racing Club [1933] 1 KB 205	54
Hamilton v News Group Newspapers Ltd [2020] EWHC 59 (QB)	186
Harris v Birkenhead Corporation [1976] 1 WLR 279	160
Harrison v Lawrence Murphy & Co, The Chartered Secretary, 1 March 1998	126
Harvey v French (1832) 1 Cr & M 11	187
Haseldine v Daw [1941] 2 KB 343	168
Haynes v Harwood [1936] 1 KB 146	27
Hedley Byrne & Co Ltd v Heller & Partners Ltd [1964] AC 465	44
Henderson v Dorset Healthcare University NHS Foundation Trust [2020] UKSC 43	100
Herald of Free Enterprise, Re (1987) The Independent, 18 December	59
Hicks v Young [2015] EWHC 1144 (QB)	101
Hill v Chief Constable of West Yorkshire [1989] AC 53	25
Hollywood Silver Fox Farm v Emmett [1936] 2 KB 468	211
Home Office v Dorset Yacht Co Ltd [1970] AC 1004	26
Hotson v East Berkshire Health Authority [1987] AC 750	75
Hubbard v Pitt [1976] 1 QB 142	208
Hucks v Cole [1993] 4 Med LR 393	114
Hudson v Ridge Manufacturing Company Ltd [1957] 2 QB 348	126
Hughes v Lord Advocate [1963] AC 837	89
Hulton v Jones [1910] AC 20	191
Humber Oil Terminal Trustee Ltd v Sivand [1998] CLC 751	80
Hunter v Canary Wharf Ltd [1997] 2 All ER 426	207
HXA & SXA v Surrey County Council [2021] EWHC 250 (QB)	29

I

ICI Ltd v Shatwell [1965] AC 656	131
Iqbal v Prison Officers Association [2009] EWCA Civ 1312	225

J

J v North Lincolnshire County Council [2000] LGR 269	62
Janvier v Sweeney [1919] 2 KB 316	233
JGE v Trustees of the Portsmouth Roman Catholic Diocesan Trust [2012] EWCA Civ 938	135
Jobling v Associated Dairies Ltd [1982] AC 794	80
John v Central Manchester and Manchester Children's University Hospitals NHS Trust Foundation Trust [2016] EWHC 407 (QB)	72
John v Mirror Group Newspapers Ltd [1996] 2 All ER 35	201
Johnston v NEI Intl Combustion Ltd [2007] UKHL 39	87
Jolley v Sutton London Borough Council [2000] 1 WLR 1082	165
Jones v Livox Quarries Ltd [1952] 2 QB 608	101

K

Kapfunde v Abbey National plc (1998) 46 BMLR 176	108
Kemsley v Foot [1952] AC 345	195
Kennaway v Thompson [1981] QB 88	211
Kennedy v Cordia (Services) LLP [2016] UKSC 6	127

Kent v Griffiths [2000] 2 All ER 474 — 30
Knightley v Johns [1982] 1 WLR 349 — 79
Knupffer v London Express Newspaper Ltd [1944] AC 116 — 192

L

Lachaux v Independent Print Ltd & Another [2019] UKSC 27 — 186
Lagden v O'Connor [2004] 1 AC 1067 — 90
Lane v Holloway [1967] 3 WLR 1003 — 233
Latimer v AEC Ltd [1953] AC 643 — 60
Laverton v Kiapasha [2002] EWCA Civ 1656 — 164
Leakey v National Trust [1980] 1 All ER 17 — 209
Liesbosch Dredger v SS Edison [1933] AC 449 — 90
Lillie and Reed v Newcastle City Council & Others [2002] EWHC 1600 (QB) — 196
Lister v Hesley Hall [2002] 1 AC 215 — 136
Livingstone v Ministry of Defence [1984] NILR 336 — 228
London Artists v Littler [1969] 2 QB 375 — 198

M

Mahon v Osborne [1939] 1 All ER 535 — 62
Mansfield v Weetabix Ltd [1998] EWCA Civ 1352 — 56
Marriott v West Midlands RHA [1999] Lloyd's Rep Med 23 — 112
Massey v Crown Life [1977] EWCA Civ 12 — 124
Maynard v West Midlands Regional Health Authority [1985] 1 All ER 635 — 111
McDermid v Nash Dredging [1987] 2 All ER 878 — 124
McFarlane v EE Caledonia [1994] 2 All ER 1 — 38
McFarlane v Tayside Health Board [2000] 2 AC 59 — 54
McGhee v National Coal Board [1973] 1 WLR 1 — 72
McGuinn v Lewisham and Greenwich NHS Trust [2017] EWHC 88 (QB) — 113
McKenna v British Aluminium [2002] Env LR 30 — 208
McKew v Holland and Hannen and Cubitts (Scotland) Ltd [1969] 3 All ER 1621 — 78
McKie v Swindon College [2011] EWHC 469 (QB) — 48
McKinnon Industries v Walker [1951] 3 DLR 577 — 211
McLoughlin v O'Brian [1983] 1 AC 410 — 40, 42
McManus v Beckham [2002] EWCA Civ 939 — 183
McWilliams v Sir William Arrol [1962] 1 WLR 295 — 130
Meah v McCreamer (No 1) [1985] 1 All ER 367 — 80
Meering v Grahame-White Aviation (1919) 122 LT 44 — 231
Michael v Chief Constable of South Wales [2015] UKSC 2 — 19
Mitchell v Darley Main Colliery [1886] App Cas 12 — 208
Mitchell v Glasgow City Council [2009] 1 AC 874 — 26
Mohamud v WM Morrison Supermarkets Plc [2016] UKSC 11 — 137
Monroe v Hopkins [2017] EWHC 433 (QB) — 185
Monson v Madame Tussauds Ltd [1894] 1 QB 671 — 183
Montgomery v Lanarkshire Health Board [2015] UKSC 11 — 115, 116
Morris v Murray [1991] 2 WLR 195 — 97
Murphy v Brentwood [1991] 1 AC 398 — 16
Murray v Ministry of Defence [1988] 2 All ER 521 — 231
Musgrove v Pandelis [1919] 2 KB 43 — 216

N

Nettleship v Weston [1971] 2 QB 691   55
Network Rail Infrastructure Ltd v Morris [2004] EWCA Civ 172   212
Network Rail Infrastructure Ltd v Williams and Another [2018] EWCA Civ 1514   5, 208
Newstead v London Express Newspaper Ltd [1940] 1 KB 377   191
Nichols v Marsland (1876) 2 Ex D 1   217
North Glamorgan NHS Trust v Walters [2002] EWCA Civ 1792   41
Nyang v G4S Care & Justice Services Ltd and Others [2013] EWHC 3946 (QB)   69

O

O'Shea v MGN Ltd [2001] EMLR 40   191
Ogwo v Taylor [1987] 3 All ER 961   40, 166
Orange v Chief Constable of West Yorkshire Police [2002] QB 347   23
Orchard v Lee [2009] EWCA Civ 295   56
Overseas Tankship (UK) Ltd v Morts Dock and Engineering Co Ltd (The Wagon Mound No 1) [1961] UKPC 2   86

P

Page v Smith [1996] 1 AC 155   36, 38, 87, 89
Palmer v Tees Health Authority [1999] EWCA Civ 1533   25
Paris v Stepney Borough Council [1951] AC 367   59, 129
Patel v Mirza [2016] UKSC 42   100
Pearce v United Bristol Healthcare NHS Trust [1999] EWCA Civ 865   115
Pearson v Coleman Bros [1948] 2 KB 359   161
Perry v Harris [2008] EWCA Civ 907   59
Phipps v Rochester Corporation [1955] 1 QB 450   165
Pitts v Hunt [1991] 1 QB 24   99
Polemis, Re [1921] 3 KB 560   87
Pollard v Tesco Stores Ltd [2006] EWCA Civ 393   146
Pollock v Cahill [2015] EWHC 2260 (QB)   164
Prendergast v Sam and Dee Ltd (1989) 1 Med LR 36   118

Q

Qualcast v Haynes [1959] AC 743   128

R

R v Ireland [1998] 3 WLR 534   227
R v Meade and Belt [1823] 1 Lew CC 184   227
R v Rimmington [2005] UKHL 63   219
R v St George [1840] 9 C&P 483   226
Ratcliff v McConnell [1997] EWCA Civ 2679   174
RE (A minor by her mother and Litigation Friend LE) and Others v Calderdale & Huddersfield NHS Foundation Trust [2017] EWHC 824 (QB)   42
Reachlocal UK Ltd v Bennett [2014] EWHC 3405 (QB)   183
Ready Mixed Concrete Ltd v Minister of Pensions [1968] 2 QB 497   123
Reaney v University Hospital of North Staffordshire NHS Trust [2015] EWCA Civ 1119   88
Reeves v Commissioner of Police for the Metropolis [2000] 3 All ER 897   23

Rehill v Rider Holdings Ltd [2014] EWCA Civ 42 — 101
Reilly v Merseyside HA [1995] 6 Med LR 246 — 36
Revill v Newbery [1996] QB 567 — 175
Reynolds v Strutt and Parker LLP [2011] EWHC 2263 (Ch) — 101
Reynolds v Times Newspapers Ltd [2001] 2 AC 127 — 197
Rhind v Astbury Water Park Ltd [2004] EWCA Civ 756 — 172
Rhodes v OPO (by his litigation friend BHM) and Another [2015] UKSC 32 — 234
Richardson v Facebook [2015] EWHC 3154 (QB) — 193
Richardson v London Rubber Company Products Ltd [2000] Lloyd's Rep Med 280 — 146
Rickards v Lothian [1913] AC 263 — 216
Rigby v Chief Constable of Northamptonshire [1985] 2 All ER 985 — 32, 109
Robert Addie & Son (Collieries) Ltd v Dumbreck [1929] AC 358 — 170
Roberts v Ramsbottom [1980] 1 WLR 823 — 56
Robinson v Chief Constable of West Yorkshire [2018] UKSC 4 — 19
Robinson v Kilvert (1889) 41 ChD 88 — 211
Robinson v The Post Office [1974] 2 All ER 737 — 79
Roe v Minister of Health [1954] 2 All ER 131 — 60
Roles v Nathan [1963] 1 WLR 1117 — 166
Rose v Miles (1815) 4 M & S 101 — 219
Rylands v Fletcher (1868) LR 3 HL 330 — 214

S

Salmon v Seafarer Restaurants Ltd [1983] 3 All ER 729 — 166
Saunders v Edwards [1987] 1 WLR 1116 — 99
Savage v Fairclough [2000] Env LR 183 — 219
Scott v London and St Katherine Docks & Co (1865) 3 H & C 596 — 62
Scott v Shepherd (1773) 2 BI R 892 — 229
Scout Association v Barnes [2010] EWCA Civ 1476 — 61
Sherlock v Chester City Council [2004] EWCA Civ 201 — 131
Sidaway v Bethlem Royal Hospital [1985] AC 871 — 115
Sienkiewicz v Greif (UK) Ltd [2011] UKSC 10 — 73
Sim v Stretch [1936] 2 All ER 1237 — 181
Simkiss v Rhondda Borough Council (1983) 81 LGR 460 — 165
Sion v Hampstead Health Authority (1994) 5 Med LR 170 — 41
Smith v Charles Baker & Sons [1891] AC 325 — 96, 131
Smith v Crossley Bros [1951] 95 SJ 655 — 126
Smith v Eric S Bush [1990] 1 AC 831 — 46, 47
Smith v Finch [2009] EWHC 53 (QB) — 101
Smith v Leech Brain and Co Ltd [1962] 2 QB 405 — 88
Smith v Littlewoods Organisation Ltd [1987] AC 241 — 22
Snook v Mannion [1982] Crim L Rev 601 — 162
Spartan Steel and Alloys Ltd v Martin & Co (Contractors) Ltd [1973] 1 QB 27 — 5, 15
Speed v Thomas Swift Co Ltd [1943] KB 557 — 128
Spencer v Wincanton Holdings Ltd [2009] EWCA Civ 1404 — 78
Spring v Guardian Assurance Plc [1995] 2 AC 296 — 48, 75
St Helen's Smelting Co v Tipping (1865) 11 HL Cas 642 — 207
Stansbie v Troman [1948] 2 KB 48 — 25
Stanton v Collinson [2010] EWCA Civ 81 — 101

Steel and Another v NRAM Ltd (Scotland) [2018] UKSC 13   45
Stephens v Myers [1830] 4 C&P 349   226
Stocker v Stocker [2019] UKSC 17   187
Stone v Taffe [1974] 1 WLR 1575   161
Stovin v Wise [1996] UKHL 15   22
Sturges v Bridgman (1879) 11 Ch D 852   210, 211
Sunny Metal and Engineering Pte Ltd v Ng Khim Ming Eric [2007] SGCA 36,
    (2007) 113 Con LR 112   85
Swinney v Chief Constable of Northumbria (No 2) (1999) The Times, 25 May   25

T

Taaffe v East of England Ambulance Service NHS Trust [2012] EWHC 1335 (QB)   113
Taylor v A Novo (UK) Ltd [2013] EWCA Civ 194   43
Tedstone v Bourne Leisure Ltd [2008] EWCA Civ 654   164
Theaker v Richardson [1962] 1 WLR 151   192
Thomas v National Union of Mineworkers (South Wales Area) [1986] Ch 20   208, 227
Tinsley v Milligan [1994] 1 AC 340   99
Titchener v British Railway Board [1983] 1 WLR 1427   174
Tolley v JS Fry & Sons Ltd [1931] AC 33   189
Tomlinson v Congleton Borough Council [2004] 1 AC 46   61, 158, 161, 172
Transco plc v Stockport MBC [2003] UKHL 61   206, 215, 216
Tremain v Pike [1969] 1 WLR 1556   89

V

Vacwell Engineering Co Ltd v BDH Chemicals Ltd [1971] 1 QB 88   88
Van Colle v Chief Constable of South Hertfordshire Police [2008] UKHL 50   32
Various Claimants v Institute of the Brothers of the Christian Schools [2012] UKSC 56   135
Vernon Knight Associates v Cornwall County Council [2013] EWCA Civ 950   209
Vernon v Bosley (No 1) [1997] 1 All ER 577   36
Victorian Railway Commissioners v James & Mary Coultas (1888) 13 App Cas 222   36

W

W v Sanofi Pasteur (Case C-621/15)   148
Wainwright v Home Office [2003] UKHL 53   233
Walker v Northumberland County Council [1995] 1 All ER 737   122
Walker v The Commissioner of the Police of the Metropolis [2014] EWCA Civ 897   231
Wandsworth London Borough Council v Railtrack plc [2001] All ER 410   218
Ward v London County Council [1938] 2 All ER 341   61
Warner Holidays Ltd v Secretary of State for Social Services [1983] ICR 440   123
Watson v British Boxing Board of Control Ltd [2001] QB 1134   59
Watson v Croft-Promo Sport Ltd [2009] EWCA Civ 15   214
Watt v Hertfordshire County Council [1954] 1 WLR 835   61
Webster v Burton Hospitals NHS Foundation Trust [2017] EWCA Civ 62   116
West Bromwich Albion FC v El-Safty [2006] EWCA Civ 1299   108
Wheat v Lacon & Co Ltd [1966] AC 552   160
Wheeler v JJ Saunders Ltd [1995] 3 WLR 466   213
White v Chief Constable of South Yorkshire [1998] UKHL 45   38
White v J & F Stone (Lighting and Radio) Ltd [1939] 2 KB 827   192

White v Jones [1995] UKHL 5   48
Whitehouse v Jordan [1981] 1 All ER 267   113
Wieland v Cyril Lord Carpets Ltd [1969] 3 All ER 1006   79
Wild v Southend University Hospital NHS Foundation Trust [2014] EWHC 4053 (QB)   42
Wilkes v DePuy International Ltd [2017] 3 All ER 589   147
Wilkinson v Downton [1897] EWHC 1 (QB)   233
Williams v MGN Ltd [2009] EWHC 3150 (QB)   187
Williams v The Bermuda Hospitals Board [2016] UKPC 4   71
Wilsher v Essex Area Health Authority [1988] 1 AC 1074   54, 70, 109
Wilson v Pringle [1987] QB 237   229
Wilson v Tyneside Cleaning Co [1958] 2 QB 110   127
Wilsons and Clyde Coal Co Ltd v English [1938] AC 57   122, 124
Winter v Cardiff Rural District Council [1950] 1 All ER 819   125
WM Morrisons Supermarkets plc v Various Claimants [2020] UKSC 12   137
Wong v Parkside Health NHS Trust [2003] 3 All ER 932   233
Woods v Durable Suites Ltd [1953] 1 WLR 857   129
Woodward v Mayor of Hastings [1945] KB 174   168
Worlsey v Tambrands [2000] PIQR P95   154

Y

Yorkshire Traction Co Ltd v Walter Searby [2003] EWCA Civ 1856   128
Young v Kent County Council [2015] EWHC 1342 (QB)   175
Yousopoff v MGM (1934) 50 TLR 581   190
Yuen Kun-Yeu v Attorney General of Hong Kong [1988] AC 175, PC   21

TABLE OF LEGISLATION

Broadcasting Act 1990 182

Civil Liability (Contribution) Act 1978
  s 1(1) 73
Consumer Protection Act 1987 141, 142, 145, 147,
  148, 150–152, 154, 155, 249
  s 1(2) 143, 151
  s 2(1) 142, 143, 151
  s 2(2)(a)–(c) 143
  s 2(3) 143
  s 2(3)(a)–(c) 143
  s 2(5) 143
  s 3 145, 146
  s 3(1) 145, 151
  s 3(2) 152
  s 3(2)(a) 145, 148, 151
  s 3(2)(b) 145, 148, 151
  s 3(2)(c) 145, 148, 151
  s 4 150
  s 4(1)(a)–(d) 148, 149, 151
  s 4(1)(e) 148, 149, 150, 151
  s 4(1)(f) 148, 149, 151
  s 5(1) 144, 151
  s 5(2) 144, 151
  s 5(3) 144
  s 5(3)(a), (b) 144
  s 5(4) 144, 151
  s 45 144, 151
Consumer Rights Act 2015 44
Corporate Manslaughter and Corporate Homicide
  Act 2007 108, 142
Criminal Law Act 1967
  s 3(1) 232

Defamation Act 1996
  s 1 199

Defamation Act 1996 – *continued*
  s 1(3)(d) 200
  s 2 200
  s 3 200
  s 4 200, 201
  s 15 196
  Sch 1, Pt I 196
Defamation Act 2013 181, 182, 185, 190, 193, 198,
  202
  s 1 199
  s 1(1) 185
  s 1(2) 185
  s 2(1) 193
  s 2(2) 194
  s 2(3) 194
  s 2(4) 193
  s 3 194
  s 3(3) 195
  s 3(4)(a) 195
  s 3(4)(b) 195
  s 4 197, 204
  s 4(1) 198
  s 4(1)(a) 198, 199
  s 4(1)(b) 198, 199
  s 4(2) 198
  s 5 200
  s 5(2) 200
  s 5(11) 200
  s 6 197
  s 6(2) 197
  s 8 192
  s 9 185
  s 10(1) 200
  s 11 184, 202
Defamation (Operators of Websites) Regulations
  2013 200

Employers' Liability (Compulsory Insurance) Act 1969 121
Employers' Liability (Compulsory Insurance) Regulations 1998 121
Employer's Liability (Defective Equipment) Act 1969 128
Environmental Protection Act 1990 206
European Convention on Human Rights
    Article 2 32
    Article 3 32
    Article 6 208
    Article 8 182, 208
    Article 10 182, 191

Factories Act 1937 131
Fatal Accidents Act 1976 141, 142

Human Rights Act 1998 32, 182, 208

Law Reform (Contributory Negligence) Act 1945
    s 1(1) 101, 213, 246

Mental Capacity Act 2005 232

Occupiers' Liability Act 1957 157, 159, 160, 162–164, 169–171, 173–176, 178, 180, 250, 251
    s 1(1) 172
    s 1(2) 159, 160
    s 1(3)(a) 162
    s 2(1) 163, 169, 170, 176, 177
    s 2(2) 163, 166, 173, 176
    s 2(3) 169, 177

Occupiers' Liability Act 1957 – *continued*
    s 2(3)(a) 165, 177
    s 2(3)(b) 165, 166, 177
    s 2(4)(a) 166, 173, 174, 177
    s 2(4)(b) 167, 168, 169
    s 2(5) 169
    s 2(6) 162
    s 5(1) 161
Occupiers' Liability Act 1984 157, 159, 163, 169–176, 178, 179, 250, 251
    s 1(2) 162
    s 1(3)(a) 171, 172, 176
    s 1(3)(b) 171, 172, 173, 176
    s 1(3)(c) 171, 172, 173, 176
    s 1(4) 173, 176
    s 1(5) 173, 174, 177
    s 1(8) 170, 176

Police and Criminal Evidence Act 1984 232
Product Liability Directive (85/374/EEC) 152
Protection from Harassment Act 1997 4

Road Traffic Act 1988 99
    s 149 97

Suicide Act 1961 108

Theatres Act 1968 182

Unfair Contract Terms Act 1977 44, 47
    s 1(1)(c) 170
    s 2(1) 170, 177
    s 2(2) 170, 177

chapter 1

Introduction to Tort Law

study points

After reading this chapter, you will be able to understand:

- what is meant by the term 'tort'
- how tort can be defined by what it is and what it is not
- the scope and breadth of the torts that we'll be looking at throughout this book
- some of the key terms and phrases.

1.1 Introduction

If you've ever bought a newspaper and read it, chances are you will have some concept of contract law (you bought the newspaper, there's your contract) and criminal law (perhaps you read the front page about a burglary or a murder). But tort law as a concept might not feel so familiar. It's that word 'tort'. A cake? Something pulled tight? The thing the teacher did last week? This chapter should clarify things: it will explore what tort law is, what it isn't, the different types of torts covered in this book, and some of the key terms you'll need. In short, tort law is a fascinating subject and it's everywhere you look. In fact, they say you're never more than 6 feet away from a tort …*

(*Do you smell a rat?)

1.2 What is tort?

The word tort derives from the Old French for *wrong*, via Latin and Medieval Latin (*tortum*: something twisted; *torquere*: to twist). For legal purposes, a tort is simply **a civil wrong, for which the law provides a remedy**. The last part of this definition ('for which the law provides a remedy') is an important clarification, in that not every civil wrong you might be able to think of would be classified as a tort for which the law might provide a remedy.

So which civil wrongs are torts? We can examine a list of these, and we will in a moment, but you may be wondering what it is that connects these apparently disparate torts. The simplest answer is to think of tort law as a residual or bucket category, holding those civil wrongs not caught by other areas of civil law, such as land law or contract law. This is how Negligence, a tort, can sit with other torts, such as nuisance and defamation, though the three are very different in character and in terms of the interests they protect. Therefore, one way to get at what tort is, is to think a little more about what it is not.

What's the point of it all?

You might be wondering what the purpose of tort law is. Beyond the most important aim of providing a remedy for a claimant who has been wronged in a civil law setting, can you think of other purposes? All of the following have judicial and/or academic support – you may feel some are more important than others:

(1) *To compensate* those who have been wronged – though note that not every type of harm that the claimant has sustained can be remedied in tort. For example, Negligence only recognises certain types of harm (or damage or loss – we use these terms interchangeably) and not others. You can't claim for upset, grief or irritation.

(2) *To deter* – this can be measured in terms of exemplary damages (albeit only rarely available). It can also be said to be reflected in other ways. For example, making an employer potentially liable in Negligence to its employees ensures that the employer works hard to maintain high standards (to avoid being sued).

(3) *Striking a balance between competing interests and rights* – we see this perhaps most obviously in the tort of private nuisance where the court seeks to allow, so far as is reasonable, the defendant freely to carry out activities on their land, whilst also seeking to provide the claimant with the right to enjoy their own land without interference.

(4) *As an alternative to statutory compensation.*

1.3 What is tort not?

Tort can be distinguished from other areas of law. Let's take a look at the most important of these.

1.3.1 Criminal law

Criminal law is a type of public law (whereas tort is private, ie usually an action between two private individuals or bodies). Criminal cases are brought on behalf of the Crown; hence criminal cases are cited as *R v Name of Defendant* (meaning Regina against the individual). Tort law, being a branch of civil law, has different aims. The principal aim in tort law is for the claimant to be compensated, ie to receive monetary damages for the loss or damage caused to them by the defendant (whereas, in criminal law, the emphasis is on punishment of the offender). As such, tort law citations will look like this: *Name of Claimant v Name of Defendant*. (We'll look at tort terminology in more detail below at **1.7**.)

The remedies available are different in respect of the two types of law. In criminal law, we are not dealing with remedies so much as sanctions, and these might include a fine, imprisonment, etc. In tort law, the claimant will usually be seeking some kind of remedy, and if not damages, as mentioned above, the other key remedy sought will normally be an equitable remedy known as an injunction, which might be full or partial. An injunction is an order that stops or limits an activity. As we'll discover, injunctions are only available for certain torts, for example defamation and nuisance.

The final key difference between criminal law and tort law is as to the standard of proof. Criminal law is based on the criminal standard of proof, so that the judge or jury in a criminal case must be sure beyond reasonable doubt before finding a defendant guilty. In tort law, because it is a branch of civil law, the standard of proof is the lower, civil standard. The judge (there being no jury) will need to be persuaded on the balance of probabilities, ie they must feel that it is 'more likely than not' that the claimant's version of events is to be believed in order for the claimant to succeed. We don't talk about a defendant in a tort action being guilty. Instead, we are concerned with their liability.

1.3.2 Contract law

Whilst there are some overlaps between contract law and tort law, in that both are types of civil law, at heart they are very different. Contract law disputes arise where there have been breaches of contract, ie duties and obligations voluntarily undertaken between parties. Tort law, by contrast, regulates our conduct whether we voluntarily agree or not. Such duties are not (normally) imposed by contract so much as by society.

example

Tom, a car driver, carelessly pulls out at a junction without looking. He knocks over Sadiq, a pedestrian, causing him injury.

In this simple example, it is likely that Sadiq will be able to sue Tom in the tort of Negligence, because Tom owed Sadiq a legal duty to take care. It's not that Tom and Sadiq signed a contract to this effect – in fact they are strangers – but rather, the court would say that Tom owes a tortious legal duty to take care of anyone who might feasibly make up the class of person using the road that he's driving on, including other drivers, cyclists and pedestrians. This duty attaches to the task – driving – and is separate from any contract between the parties.

1.3.3 Land law

Land law, another branch of civil law, is primarily concerned with the ownership and control of land, and with its transfer or acquisition. In contrast, whilst we do have so-called land torts, such as nuisance and trespass to land, generally speaking a claimant will be more concerned with any infringement of their use and enjoyment of that land arising out of, for example, the noise emanating from the defendant's house (a classic nuisance action) than with ownership of land *per se*. Again, there are some overlaps between land law and tort law; for example, tort lawyers utilise a defence called prescription – a form of acquiescence – as a defence to a nuisance action.

1.4   Torts we will examine

Now we're a little clearer on the nature of tort, partly by reference to what it's not, let's turn to the torts we'll be studying. This is best expressed as a table, with the name of the tort and the interest(s) that that tort protects, in other words, the heads of loss for which you would sue as a claimant affected by the defendant's tortious conduct towards you. If this appears at first glance as a disparate list of civil wrongs, that's because it is! (Remember that concept of the residual or bucket category.) You may be able to spot some connections between some of the torts, however.

Table 1.1   Protected interests

Tort	Interests protected
General Negligence	Bodily integrity, property, finances
Clinical Negligence	Bodily integrity, property, finances
Employers' Liability	Bodily integrity, property, finances
Occupiers' Liability	Bodily integrity, sometimes property
Product Liability	Bodily integrity and property
Trespass to the Person	Body (and mind), liberty
Defamation	Reputation
Nuisance	Use and enjoyment of land, property, sometimes other losses

Torts that haven't made the list

There are many more torts than we have space to study here; in fact there are more than 30 recognised in English law. Here are some of the more common torts that we don't cover in this book:

- abuse of judicial process
- breach of statutory duty (we touch on this in passing)
- deceit (which is related to but not the same as defamation)
- harassment (a statutory tort created by the Protection from Harassment Act 1997)
- malicious falsehood (again sometimes an alternative to defamation)
- misuse of private information (this is mentioned in a case discussed in **Chapter 8** on vicarious liability – can you spot it?)
- trespass to land and trespass to goods
- passing off.

1.5   The torts in outline

The list set out at **Table 1.1** above represents the torts that we'll look at in this book, and the order in which we'll do that.

The first five torts on the list, from General Negligence to Product Liability, are all types or variations of Negligence (negligence being legal-speak for carelessness). This means that once you are clear on the elements of a Negligence claim, the basic principles remain broadly the same within those five torts. Acts of Trespass to the Person (which is the generic term for three specific torts, namely assault, battery and false imprisonment) are crimes as well as torts, so you'll notice that some of the authorities we rely on are actually imported from criminal law. Defamation (the generic term for two torts, namely libel and slander) is very different from the other torts, in terms of the interest it protects and the legal structure we use when discussing or advising on it. Most lawyers who practise defamation do little else as it is a highly specialised and sometimes technical area.

Finally, Nuisance (the generic term for three torts, namely private nuisance, public nuisance and the rule in *Rylands v Fletcher*) is the oldest tort, and this is reflected in some of the archaic language that underpins it. For example, you can claim in private nuisance for 'sensible personal discomfort', which means something the defendant does on their land that adversely affects a claimant's sense of smell, hearing or taste. On the other hand, private nuisance is also current, and evolving, with a case concerning the spread of Japanese knotweed having been heard fairly recently in the Court of Appeal (see *Network Rail Infrastructure Ltd v Williams and Another* [2018] EWCA Civ 1514, discussed as part of private nuisance in **Chapter 12**).

1.6 The significance of policy

Before we move on to tort terminology, it's important to be aware of what we mean by the term 'policy' in a tortious context and why it's relevant to many torts, especially Negligence. Tort law is decided on the basis of precedent and the application of statute, yet policy has clearly played its part in many landmark judgments. So what is policy? It can best be defined as the non-legal considerations, whether social, political or economic (or a combination), that the court takes into account when having regard to the effect its decisions will have. Policy considerations can work for or against either party, and they can narrow or broaden the scope of claims depending on the legal climate at any time.

Rather than list every possible policy consideration here, it makes sense to highlight the most important consideration, a policy term called 'floodgates' (see below at **1.6.1**), and to explore the rest as and when they arise in the case law.

Do look out for the mention of policy in judgments. Some judges will refer overtly to the term, citing policy as the reason why a claim might fail or succeed. (For an illuminating and entertaining example, read Lord Denning's judgment in *Spartan Steel and Alloys Ltd v Martin & Co (Contractors) Ltd* [1973] 1 QB 27, which we will look at when we consider pure economic loss in **Chapter 2**.) Often, however, the judgments do not make their policy considerations explicit, and, as lawyers, we have to learn to read between the lines, reconciling ostensibly strange decisions on the basis of policy.

1.6.1 Floodgates

This is probably the most frequently cited policy consideration. It refers to the courts' concern that to allow one claim would be to open the floodgates to a deluge of claims which would overwhelm the courts, and therefore effectively thwart their attempts to deal fairly with the most important cases. It tends to arise where the potential class of claimant is very wide.

A clear example of floodgates being used as a judicial obstacle to limit claims arises in the context of Negligence claims where the loss suffered is psychiatric harm (defined as a recognised form of psychiatric illness, such as post-traumatic stress disorder, clinical depression and so on) in the absence of any physical harm (see **Chapter 2**).

example

Bryony and two friends, Charlie and Dylan, are walking down the street past a house being rebuilt by a team of builders. Charlie and Dylan, themselves builders, go close to the scaffolding to take a closer look at the quality of the build. At that moment, due to the negligence of one of the builders, some bricks fall from the scaffolding, narrowly missing Charlie but glancing Dylan's head, causing him concussion. Both Charlie and Dylan sustain psychiatric harm. Bryony also sustains psychiatric harm as a result of what she saw.

This scenario does raise the issue of floodgates but not for all of the potential claimants. Can you work out which claim the court might seek to prevent?

The answer – and we will look more closely at the mechanics of this in Chapter 2 – is that Dylan is the most likely to succeed in his Negligence action against the builder because he suffered both personal injury and psychiatric harm. Charlie is likely also to be able to claim, because although he wasn't himself physically injured, objectively it would appear that physical harm was reasonably foreseeable in this situation. For both, there is no danger of floodgates because they belong to a small and finite class of people caught up in the incident itself.

Bryony, on the other hand, will struggle to succeed in her claim because she was neither physically hurt, nor was it reasonably foreseeable that she might be. She was not intimately caught up in the incident though she witnessed it. The court would say that the floodgates concern arises with her claim. Why? Because if she is allowed to succeed, where would the courts draw the line? What about everyone else walking down the street at that moment who might have seen or heard something? What about the people Bryony told later that day, and the people who later read the local newspaper article about the incident? Should they be able to claim? Can you see the potential for floodgates here, with the class of claimants getting very wide, and further removed from the negligent incident itself?

For this reason, as we will see, the courts have put mechanisms or obstacles in place whereby claimants like Bryony, classified as 'secondary victims', can only claim for their loss if they can satisfy a number of stringent criteria. You might feel this is unfair, but the courts would say that they exist to deal with the most pressing Negligence claims, and in particular those claimants who suffer physical injury and/or were in the 'zone of danger' at the time. So the concept of floodgates is a judicial control mechanism that controls and limits the numbers of Negligence claims allowed to succeed.

1.6.2 Other policy considerations

The other policy considerations you are likely to come across frequently as you read into the case law are as follows:

- *Crushing liability* (see especially on pure economic loss (**Chapter 2**) and remoteness (**Chapter 5**)). This would be where the defendant is held financially responsible disproportionately to the wrong they have caused.
- *Insurance.* The courts are more likely to find a defendant liable where they are insured because they will have the financial means to pay out for exactly the eventuality that is envisaged by virtue of the insurance. We see this often in tort, especially connected with those activities for which insurance is compulsory (driving, being an employer, and so on). Sometimes, the claimant will be insured; a reason why the court may decide not to make the defendant liable.
- *Defensive practices.* We see this most often where the court arguably tries to protect public bodies or professionals so as to ensure that they don't feel fettered through fear of litigation and can do their work/carry out investigations freely. See if you can find reference to this in the case law, particularly as regards the police (see **Chapter 2**) and the medical profession (see **Chapter 7**).

There are many other policy considerations, including *deterrence* and *justice*, but the above are the most important for our purposes.

1.7 Tort terminology, key terms and phrases

Think of this section as a basic phrasebook that you might have reference to when you're in a foreign country trying to make sense of what you're hearing or reading. Some of these key terms and phrases may feel abstract until we start to apply them to real situations or read about them in cases, some of which you may already be familiar with, but either way hopefully they will provide a useful foundation as you move through this book.

1.7.1 Claimant and defendant

The person bringing the claim is the claimant (formerly known as the plaintiff, as seen in older cases pre-dating the Woolf reforms in 2000). The person or legal body (such as an NHS Trust, etc) against whom the claim is brought is the defendant, or the tortfeasor. When you read cases – also known as authorities, though an authority is *any* legal source you are relying upon, whether that be a case, an excerpt from a statute or possibly an academic authority – the name of the claimant appears first followed by the defendant's name. The 'v' separating them is pronounced 'and' rather than 'versus' or 'against'. The only time the order of the names might be different is on appeal, where the appellant's name goes first, meaning whichever party is appealing (claimant or defendant).

1.7.2 Loss, damage, damages

You may read about a claimant claiming damages for their damage. What does that mean? Simply that the claimant is seeking monetary compensation, known as damages, from the defendant for their loss (also known as damage or harm). This would typically arise in a Negligence claim where, as a result of the defendant's careless act or omission, the claimant is injured/suffers loss. Let's say the careless act in question is driving. A claimant knocked down by a negligent defendant driver may suffer personal injury, such as a broken leg, and also possibly psychiatric harm such as post-traumatic stress disorder, property damage, which could be a damaged watch or mobile phone, and consequential economic loss, which is financial loss flowing from the damage to their person or property, typically time off work for which they are not paid.

1.7.3 Tortious not tortuous

Tort may sometimes feel tortuous, but if we're talking liability, the correct term is tortious. And while we're on the subject of liability, use liability and not guilt when you're advising on whether the defendant committed the tort. Similarly, the words liable and libel are not interchangeable. A defendant may be liable in libel but not libel in liable!

1.7.4 Fault liability and strict liability

Most torts require a claimant to prove that the defendant was in some way at fault in committing the tort. This means proving, on the balance of probabilities, that the tortfeasor intentionally carried out the act that constitutes the tort (required for certain torts such as trespass to the person) or that they negligently acted or omitted to act (required for certain torts such as Negligence).

However, a few torts are known as strict liability torts. These are torts that do not require proof of fault on the part of the defendant and are deemed to be made out as soon as the relevant act or omission has occurred, regardless of what the defendant intended or how careful they were. Examples of such torts for our purposes would be some types of nuisance and product liability under statute. This is not to say that the defendant in such circumstances is automatically liable (a concept closer to a term called absolute liability); they may have a defence.

Vicarious liability is not a tort but a mechanism, and this imposes strict liability on employers for the torts of their employees (see **Chapter 8**).

1.7.5 Actionable *per se*

Most torts require proof of loss, for example Negligence, which is not actionable unless the claimant has sustained some form of recognisable loss. Some torts, however, are actionable without proof of loss and we say that these are actionable *per se* (of themselves). An example of such a tort would be trespass to the person. Having said that, whilst you can, in theory, bring an action for, say, battery, a form of trespass to the person, without having suffered any quantifiable loss, ultimately you might choose not to, as the costs and time and inconvenience of bringing the matter to court might well outweigh the nominal damages you might receive if successful.

1.8 Further reading

R Bagshaw, 'Responsibility and Fault' (2000) 116 LQR 321–23.
V Corbett, 'The promotion of human dignity: a theory of tort law' (2017) 58 Irish Jurist 121–52.
J McEldowney, 'Tort Law and Human Rights' (2003) 22 CJQ 213–16

summary

- A tort is a civil wrong for which the law provides a remedy.
- There is nothing much to connect the torts apart from some overlaps as to the interests they protect and the fact they fit into a residual category of civil wrongs not dealt with by other types of civil law.
- The claimant is the party bringing the action and the defendant or tortfeasor is the party defending it.
- Most (but not all) torts require some kind of fault to be proven and for the claimant to have suffered recognisable loss.
- Policy underpins much of tort law.

test your knowledge

Have a go at these multiple choice questions (MCQs):

Question 1

A man is injured as a result of being run over by a careless motorcyclist. The man suffers personal injury and has to take 6 weeks off work to recover from his injuries. His work only pays him 4 weeks of sick pay. The man succeeds in his Negligence action against the motorcyclist.

Which one of the following options best describes what the man will be able to claim for in terms of his financial loss?

A   He will be able to claim for 6 weeks of lost salary, as this is consequential economic loss.

B   He will be able to claim for 4 weeks of lost salary, as this is consequential economic loss.

C   He will be able to claim for 2 weeks of lost salary, as this is consequential economic loss.

D   He will be able to claim for 6 weeks of lost salary, as this flowed from the injury to his person.

E   He will not be able to claim for any lost salary, as he was back at work after 6 weeks.

Answer

The correct answer is option C. Consequential economic loss refers to financial loss flowing from injury to your person or your property, but you can only claim for what you have actually lost.

Question 2

A junior solicitor has been asked to give a presentation outlining some of the key terminology used in tort law.

Which one of the following is completely accurate as to tort terminology?

A   A tort is a civil wrong; the standard of proof used is the balance of probabilities; the tortfeasor is the also known as the defendant.

B   A tort is a civil wrong; all civil wrongs are torts; the standard of proof used is the balance of probabilities.

C   The tortfeasor is the party bringing the action; a tort is a civil wrong; the standard of proof used is beyond reasonable doubt.

D   A tort is a civil wrong; the standard of proof used is beyond reasonable doubt; the usual remedies are damages or an injunction.

E   The usual remedies are damages or an injunction; all civil wrongs are torts; the standard of proof used is the balance of probabilities.

Answer

The correct answer is option A: the others all contain at least one inaccuracy.

Question 3

You are reading a judgment in which the judge discusses policy as being one of the factors influencing her decision.

Which one of the following provides the most accurate definition of policy?

A   Policy is where the courts limit the number of claims allowed through the courts.

B   Policy refers to the courts using their own political persuasions to determine the outcome.

C   Policy is where the courts consider the floodgates argument.

D   Policy refers to the non-legal considerations underpinning a decision, such as the social, political and economic factors that might have a bearing on future cases.

E   Policy refers to the legal considerations underpinning a decision, such as the social, political and economic factors that might have a bearing on future cases.

Answer

The correct answer is option D. Policy is not a legal consideration as such. Option C gives an example of policy but the question doesn't ask for this. Option A is incorrect in that policy can favour either a claimant or a defendant.

2 General Negligence – Loss and Duty of Care

After reading this chapter, you will be able to:

- define the tort of General Negligence
- understand the types of loss/damage for which a claimant can claim
- appreciate the Negligence sequence and where the concept of duty of care fits within that
- understand the current law relating to duty of care
- answer questions on duty where the loss/damage is more complex.

2.1 Scope of this chapter

There's no getting around it, this chapter is a *big one*. But then it's doing some heavy lifting: it first of all defines Negligence and introduces the concept of the Negligence sequence. Secondly, it outlines the first and second elements in the sequence, namely (1) loss or damage and (2) duty of care. Once you feel comfortable with these principles, the various types of duty situations we'll explore should feel, if not straightforward, then much clearer. You'll find that when we move onto the next chapter (Breach of Duty), you'll have a firm grasp of the basics in terms of law and structure. So, think of this first chapter as an exercise in getting the corners and the edges of the jigsaw in place before we fill in the rest.

2.2 What is Negligence?

Negligence is really just legal-speak for carelessness. It is a tort, a civil wrong, that provides a remedy (normally damages) where loss or damage is caused to a claimant by the defendant tortfeasor's carelessness, specifically by their breach of a legal duty imposed on them to take care.

example

James is not paying attention as he pulls out of a junction in his car. As a result, he knocks over a cyclist, Sandra, who suffers a broken leg and damage to her expensive bike. She has to take six weeks off work to recover.

This is a classic example of a Negligence claim in the context of a road traffic accident (or RTA). Sandra, the claimant, may bring an action in Negligence against James, the defendant. On the facts here, the claim is likely to succeed in that all the elements are satisfied (for a discussion of the elements of a Negligence claim, and as to the Negligence sequence, see below).

Sandra suffers recognisable forms of loss/damage, namely personal injury, property damage (to her bike) and consequential economic loss. (For types of recognised loss/damage, see below at **2.4.1**.) James owes her a duty of care which he breaches, causing her loss which is reasonably foreseeable. There are no obvious defences applicable here.

The above is a whole Negligence claim in a nutshell. Over the course of this chapter and the subsequent chapters, we'll break that down into bite-sized chunks.

2.3 The Negligence sequence

Loss/Damage – Duty – Breach – Causation – Remoteness – Defences – Remedies

Figure 2.1   The Negligence sequence

The claimant has to prove a number of elements against the defendant in order to win their claim. They must prove those elements on the balance of probabilities (of course) and in a certain order. Why? Because each element is dependent on the next. That means that if there is no damage, or rather if the claimant has not suffered damage of a recognisable kind, then the claim ends there. It's the damage that kickstarts the claim. If there is damage, but no duty was owed by the defendant, the claim ends there. If there was damage, and a duty was owed, but that duty wasn't breached, the claim ends there, and so on. Where you read of judges discussing, say, breach, in a case where they have already decided there was no duty, then that would be *obiter* (which is possibly persuasive for future claims but not binding).

With that in mind, we're going to look first at loss/damage and then at duty.

PART I   LOSS/DAMAGE AND DUTY

2.4 Loss/damage

Damages in Negligence are intended to put the claimant in the position they would have been had the tort not been committed. (Some say it is backwards-looking for that reason, as opposed to contract law, which aims to put the claimant in the position they would have been had the contract been fulfilled.)

2.4.1 The types of recoverable or recognisable loss/damage

When we say 'recoverable' or 'recognisable', we mean those types of loss in respect of which the court will often impose a duty of care on the defendant. This isn't to say the claimant has won the claim, not yet. Rather, they have jumped the first hurdle and are setting up for the second.

The types of loss or damage (and we use those terms interchangeably here) that are recoverable in Negligence are as follows:

Personal injury

This is very common in general Negligence. You might say it's what general Negligence was primarily 'invented' for – to compensate those who have sustained personal injury. Personal injury can be both physical and psychiatric, and whilst it's usually relatively straightforward to prove that a duty ought to be imposed on the defendant in relation to personal/physical injury, it's not so straightforward where that loss is psychiatric. At **2.9** we'll discuss the circumstances in which a duty of care would and would not be imposed in respect of psychiatric loss (such as post-traumatic stress disorder). Clue: it's dictated by policy, so look back to **1.6** for a reminder of what this means.

There are various ways of calculating or quantifying loss in personal injury claims, but it would be outside the scope of this book to look in detail at those here. Suffice to say, the court will compensate a claimant for their 'pain, suffering and loss of amenity', a stock phrase that takes into account, among other things, the reduced ability of the claimant to do what they used to do, where appropriate. The court can compensate for future loss of earnings, using specific formulae, the rationale being that it is not speculating but calculating, and it will also provide a lump sum of damages dependent on the body part affected. For example, injury to a thumb would generally be worth less than, say, injury to a knee ... unless that thumb was insured for a large sum of money, as was, for example, the thumb of Mark King, the slap-bass player from the band Level 42.

There is a very useful (but gruesome!) series of books on quantifying damage by Kemp & Kemp, which list body parts and their relative worth. If you're lucky you'll get to peruse them one day.

Property damage

This might be damage to your vehicle, your watch, your antique vase, your pet (animals are property in tort law), your house – potentially anything damaged as a result of the defendant's breach of their duty.

Consequential economic loss

Consequential economic loss is financial loss flowing from damage to your person or property. So, in our example above at **2.2**, Sandra's consequential economic loss would be any money she loses as a result of having to take time off work. (Note if she received full sick pay for that period, she would not be able to claim because she would not have lost any income.) Such loss might also include other costs such as physiotherapy fees, equipment required, travel costs to and from treatment, and so on.

In practice, often consequential economic loss is considered a facet of personal injury loss, but for our purposes we keep them separate so as to distinguish them from what we call pure economic loss (see below at **2.4.2**). In any event, as you're not being asked, at this stage, to quantify the loss, the semantic difference is of little consequence, though it hopefully keeps things clear and simple.

2.4.2 Types of loss that may not be recoverable

The court will not impose a duty of care in relation to all types of damage or loss. You cannot claim in Negligence for, say, irritation or annoyance, or for types of loss that aren't recognisable in Negligence but might be in other torts, such as libel (see **Chapter 11** (Defamation)) or 'sensible personal discomfort' (see **Chapter 12** (Nuisance)).

Psychiatric harm

As mentioned already, the claimant may struggle to show that psychiatric harm is recoverable, where that harm is remote or removed from the physical damage. So, for example, a claimant injured in a road traffic accident who sustains, as a result, personal injury and also a form of post-traumatic stress disorder will find it easy to prove that the defendant ought to owe a duty of care in relation to both. But the bystander who watches that road traffic accident from a safe distance away, and as a result sustains some form of psychiatric harm, will find it difficult to establish that a duty ought to be imposed in respect of that damage, because the court will be concerned in particular about 'floodgates' – a policy concern that would effectively open the floodgates to similar claims if not controlled. Where that same claimant has a connection to the person in the car – for example, the woman in the car is the claimant's mother – then that is different: now the court is more likely to impose a duty because the pool of possible claimants is instantly reduced to a finite, manageable number.

We'll look in more detail at psychiatric harm and establishing a duty of care in Part II (at **2.9**).

Pure economic loss

The court will not normally impose a duty of care for what we call 'pure economic loss'. There are exceptions to that general rule which we'll look at when we consider negligent misstatement (below at **2.10**). If consequential economic loss is financial loss flowing from damage to the claimant's person or property, pure economic loss is financial loss that does *not* flow from such damage. It exists in and of itself.

example

Shahleena is driving to a job interview. On the way, she gets stuck in a traffic jam, due to a collision up ahead, caused by the negligent driving of Hugo. As a result, she misses the interview and fails to secure the job. Shahleena is sure that if she'd made it to the interview, she would have been offered the job with an increase on her current salary. She wants to sue Hugo in Negligence for the loss of salary she says he caused her.

Can you see that whilst Hugo, we are told, has been negligent, the type of loss caused to Shahleena is pure economic loss, in that it does not flow from damage to her person or property? What's more, it's speculative – another reason why the court might want to classify it as pure economic loss. For policy reasons, a duty of care is rarely imposed in respect of pure economic loss.

case example

***Spartan Steel and Alloys Ltd v Martin & Co (Contractors) Ltd* [1973] 1 QB 27**

The defendants negligently cut off power to the claimants' factory, thereby damaging beyond repair some steel 'melts' that were being processed. In respect of this property damage/loss, the court imposed a duty of care on the defendants (meaning the loss was recoverable). Further, the damaged melts would have been sold at a profit, and that loss of profit was also recoverable, as consequential economic loss.

However, the claimants also argued that, due to the electricity supply being cut off for a period of time, they were unable to make further melts and should be compensated for that too. The court disagreed, classifying this final head of loss as pure economic loss, for which the defendants did not owe a duty of care. Why? Because this financial loss did not flow, said the court, from damage to property, but as a result of the claimants' failure to mitigate their loss. Weren't they insured for just such an eventuality? Didn't they have a back-up generator? Couldn't they simply have 'worked harder the next day'? (Lord Denning's judgment is worth a read here.) In other words, there were strong policy reasons why it was not right that the claimants should be able to claim for this final head of loss.

As we'll see when we look at this again at **2.10**, sometimes what is classified as either consequential or pure economic loss is driven very much by policy considerations, as opposed to some hard and fast rule, as well as by the court's desire to see certain kinds of claim dealt with elsewhere, for example, in contract law rather than in tort.

We'll look in more detail at pure economic loss and the exceptions to the general rule that you can't recover for it in Part II (at **2.10**).

2.5 Duty of care

Once a claimant has established that they have suffered a recognisable form of loss, they must then prove that the defendant owed them a duty of care. So, what is a 'duty of care'? Essentially the defendant must be sufficiently legally proximate to the claimant whereby the defendant's carelessness carries legal consequences.

Perhaps this is best illustrated by way of example. Some relationships will always give rise to a duty of care, and these are fairly obvious: a driver owes a duty of care to other road users, a doctor owes a duty of care to their patients, an employer to its employees, and so on. This is a legal duty to take care imposed not by, for example, contract (we don't make a contract with every other road user each time we turn the ignition key in our car) but by the civil law of Negligence. We understand as citizens that if by our carelessness we fall below the standard that attaches to the task we are doing, whether that be driving, or performing surgery, or teaching, or giving advice, and we cause recognisable harm, we may be liable in Negligence, having breached our duty of care to a claimant.

But how far does this duty extend? Is it right that any potential defendant should owe a duty of care to any potential claimant in any given situation? Of course not, and the next case tackled this very issue.

Donoghue v Stevenson [1932] AC 562

In this seminal Negligence case, the claimant, Mrs Donoghue, had gone to a café in Paisley, Scotland, with her friend. The friend bought her a ginger beer float, which came in an opaque bottle. The claimant drank some of the ginger beer, and when she poured the remainder into her glass, she found the decomposed body of a snail. The claimant claimed that she had suffered personal injury (gastroenteritis) as a result of having drunk some of the ginger beer, but she was unable to sue the café owner in contract, as she had not bought the ginger beer herself. Instead, she sued the manufacturer of the ginger beer (who was based in Ireland) in tort. By a narrow majority, the House of Lords allowed her claim.

This was highly significant because, prior to this case, a duty of care had only arisen between manufacturer and consumer in limited situations which did not apply here. Indeed, in general, a duty of care had only arisen in limited recognised situations. Lord Atkin's famous 'neighbour principle' formulated, for the first time, a general principle relating to duty, and a template to be used in subsequent cases:

[I]n English law there must be, and is, some general conception of relations giving rise to a duty of care … You must take reasonable care to avoid acts or omissions which you can reasonably foresee would be likely to injure your neighbour. Who then, in law, is my neighbour? The answer seems to be – persons who are so closely and directly affected by my act that I ought reasonably to have them in contemplation as being so affected when I am directing my mind to the acts or omissions which are called into question.

Effectively, it was from this case that Negligence, as we understand it today, emerged.

2.5.1 Expansion and contraction

There followed a period of expansion and contraction as regards the test for the duty of care. Though the history is interesting, it is not necessary to go into too much detail here (though you may wish to look into this further). In summary, the 1970s saw a period of expansion, by which it is meant that a number of new duty situations were accepted, and so more claims were successful than before.

This reached its peak with a case called *Anns v London Borough of Merton* [1978] AC 728 (a case which was actually overruled in 1990 by the case of *Murphy v Brentwood* [1991] 1 AC 398). The court formulated a two-stage test which was heavily weighted in favour of a duty being imposed. It asked first whether the parties satisfied the requirements of the neighbour test (from *Donoghue*). If so, it asked whether there were any policy considerations which ought to negate such a duty being imposed. In other words, this was a test whose effect was: 'a duty will be owed *unless* …'.

2.5.2 *Caparo v Dickman*

Reservations about the emphasis of this test were discussed by the courts during the next few years, culminating in the case we'll look at now, *Caparo Industries plc v Dickman* [1990] 2 AC 605. This House of Lords case concerned economic loss and an area called 'negligent misstatement' (with regard to careless advice), an exception to the rule excluding claims where the loss is pure economic loss. We'll return to it in that context at **2.10**, but for now it is important for the impact it had and continues to have on the question of duty of care. It remains the leading case in this area.

The court in *Caparo* was keen to move away from attempts to make concrete a general principle of duty. It sought to move away from the position in *Anns*, and even in *Donoghue*, whereby foreseeability of damage was often enough for a duty to be imposed on the defendant, negated only if policy considerations were sufficiently compelling. Instead, the court favoured a return to 'the more traditional categorisation of different specific situations as guides to the existence, the scope and the limits of the varied duties of care which the law imposes' (Lord Bridge).

Lord Bridge also stated:

> … in addition to the *foreseeability of damage*, necessary ingredients in any situation giving rise to a duty of care are that there should exist between the party owing the duty and the party to whom it is owed a relationship characterised by the law as one of *'proximity' or 'neighbourhood'* and that the situation should be one in which *the court considers it fair, just and reasonable that the law should impose a duty* of a given scope on the one party for the benefit of another. (emphasis added)

From here, things get interesting. For many years, what most lawyers and academics took from this was that the court was expounding the virtues of a 'three-stage test', an inaccurate title as we shall see. For a duty to be imposed for a novel situation, it was said, the claimant must establish three things:

(1) The claimant's loss was reasonably foreseeable.
(2) There was a relationship of legal proximity between the claimant and the defendant.
(3) It was fair, just and reasonable to impose a duty of care on the defendant.

2.5.3 What did the stages mean?

Can you see that stage (1) was simply Lord Atkin's principle incorporated into this test?

Stage (2) was new, and difficult to define. Proximity didn't require geographical proximity (after all the claimant and defendant in *Donoghue* were in Scotland and Ireland respectively). Rather, it referred to some legal relationship between the parties, essentially some reason to make the defendant responsible for the claimant. As Lord Oliver stated in *Caparo*, proximity was 'a convenient expression so long as it is realised that it is no more than a label which embraces not a definable concept but merely a description of circumstances from which, pragmatically, the courts conclude that a duty of care exists'. However, *Caparo* itself told us very little about what kind of relationship or situation might give rise to the proximity requirement.

Stage (3) was the part enabling courts to consider policy. Arguably, this has often left the court with plenty of 'wriggle room' so as to find a duty or find against a duty even where stages (1) and (2) have been established. Relevant policy considerations might include floodgates (where the court chooses not to impose a duty), crushing liability (where the court chooses not to impose a duty), insurance (where the court might find against the party who is insured, which could be either claimant or defendant, on the basis that they're insured for exactly the eventuality that has arisen), defensive practices (where the court chooses not to impose a duty), and so on.

2.5.4 *Caparo* revisited: the incremental approach

It's fair to say that the notion of a three-stage test was something picked up and run with for many years, as if it were the answer to the question of duty for so-called novel situations, where it was unclear whether a duty ought to be owed. But, in fact, even within the judgment of *Caparo* itself, it is clear that this was never the court's intention. Recent cases have had cause to re-examine *Caparo* and its rationale, and they make for fascinating reading. It appears as though the judges in *Caparo* never intended the three so-called 'stages' to be seen as distinct, or even, perhaps, as stages at all. Look at what Lord Oliver says:

> I think it has to be recognised that to search for any single formula which will serve as a general test of liability is to pursue a will-o'-the wisp. The fact is that once one discards, as it is now clear one must, the concept of foreseeability of harm as the single exclusive test, even a prima facie test, of the existence of the duty of care, *the attempt to state some general principle which will determine liability in an infinite variety of circumstances serves not to clarify the law but merely to bedevil its development in a way which corresponds with practicality and common sense.* (emphasis added).

Further, Lord Bridge said that the concepts of proximity and fairness 'amount in effect to little more than convenient labels to attach to the features of different specific situations in which, on a detailed examination of all the circumstances, the law recognises pragmatically as giving rise to a duty of a given scope'. Lord Oliver suggested that the three stages were actually 'merely facets of the same thing'. You might say the approach to the issue of duty of care suggested here was always one of reverse-engineering: once the court concludes there is no duty, they work backwards from that result to justify how they got there, whether by justifying this on the basis of proximity or by reference to the notion of what's fair, just and reasonable.

2.5.5   *Michael* and *Robinson*

Two cases in particular have illuminated what was there all along in *Caparo*, and they give us perhaps the clearest indication of where we go from here in terms of determining the question of duty. Both cases concerned the duty owed by the police – something we will return to when we consider the question of duty as it relates to public bodies (see **2.6.3** below).

case example

Michael v Chief Constable of South Wales [2015] UKSC 2

Ms Michael called the police from her home in the early hours of 5 August 2009. Her mobile signal was picked up by Gwent police rather than South Wales police. She told the operator that her ex-partner had threatened to hit her. Later on in the conversation, she said he was going to come back and kill her, but there was a question mark over whether the operator had heard this. He told her that her call would be passed to South Wales police who would call her back.

The operator then relayed this information to his counterpart in the South Wales police, saying that the ex-partner had threatened to hit the claimant. (He did not mention the threat to kill.) This information was sent to the officers on patrol, but it had not been prioritised as needing an immediate response. Soon afterwards, Gwent police received another call from Ms Michael in which screaming was heard but then stopped. This call was graded as requiring an immediate response, but by the time officers arrived a few minutes later, Ms Michael had been murdered.

The estate of Ms Michael brought actions in Negligence against Gwent police and South Wales police. The Supreme Court considered four issues. The first two were as to whether the police owed a duty of care to Ms Michael on receiving the emergency call. It was decided by a majority that they did not. (Again, we will come back to the police in due course.) The third issue was as to whether the police should be held to have assumed responsibility to take reasonable care for Ms Michael's safety. (You might call this a proximity argument in the *Caparo* sense.) Lord Toulson, as part of the majority, rejected the argument that a duty was owed. Lord Kerr and Lady Hale disagreed strongly with the majority ruling to dismiss the appeal by Ms Michael's estate.

For our purposes, Lord Toulson in *Michael* makes an important point about Lord Bridge's discussion in *Caparo* (quoted above) on 'convenient labels'. He says: 'Paradoxically, this passage in Lord Bridge's speech has sometimes come to be treated as a blueprint for deciding cases, despite the pains which the author took to make clear that it was not intended to be any such thing.'

In *Robinson v Chief Constable of West Yorkshire* [2018] UKSC 4, the Supreme Court found that the police *did* owe a duty of care to the claimant, for their positive act, and did not have the perceived legal 'blanket immunity' which many had felt they were always or usually afforded. There is more to discuss here, and we will come back to it, as we will to *Michael*. For now, what was said by the Supreme Court about the issue of *Caparo* and duty is our focus. Lord Reed provided the leading judgment (Lady Hale and Lord Hodge in agreement). He said:

> … the proposition that there is a *Caparo* test which applies to all claims in the modern law of negligence, and that in consequence the court will only impose a duty of care where it considers it fair, just and reasonable to do so on the particular facts, is mistaken.

The correct approach, he said, and the

> whole point of the *Caparo* case… was to repudiate the idea that there is a single test which can be applied in all cases in order to determine whether a duty of care exists, and instead to adopt an *approach based*, in the manner characteristic of the common law, *on precedent, and on the development of the law incrementally and by analogy with established authorities*. (emphasis added)

2.5.6 Where do we go from here?

Lord Reed's judgment is very helpful, and in a sense it brings us back to where we started. When determining whether a duty of care ought to be imposed on the defendant for the loss sustained by the claimant, the starting point is always precedent. You might think of it in the form of a flowchart:

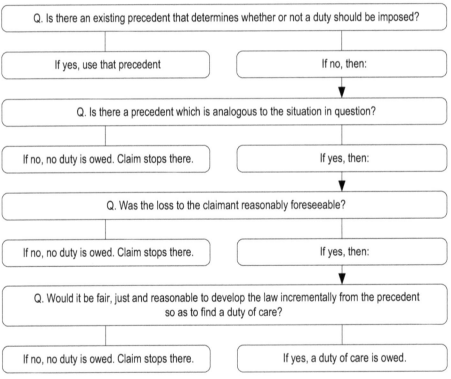

Figure 2.2   The current approach to duty

It should be remembered that most cases will fit a precedent, or be analogous to a precedent, and so determining duty for the most part will be, or should be, fairly straightforward.

Having said that, it can sometimes be difficult for the courts to ascertain whether a situation is actually novel, or whether it fits, or is analogous to, a precedent.

Darnley v Croydon Health Services NHS Trust [2018] UKSC 50

case example

The claimant presented at the Accident and Emergency department of a hospital with a serious head injury, having been driven there by a friend. He was incorrectly told by the receptionist that he would have to wait 4–5 hours to be seen. Distressed, the claimant decided to go home rather than wait. He went to bed but his condition deteriorated in the night. By the time he returned to hospital, he had sustained permanent brain damage.

The Court of Appeal found this to be a novel duty situation as to whether a hospital receptionist would owe a patient a duty of care concerning information about waiting times. The majority concluded that it would not be fair, just and reasonable to impose a duty.

However, on appeal, the Supreme Court found that this was not a novel situation at all. Lord Lloyd-Jones was very clear on this when he said:

> To my mind … the present case falls squarely within an established category of duty of care. It has long been established that such a duty is owed to those who provide and run a casualty department to persons presenting themselves complaining of illness or injury before they are treated or received into care in the hospital's wards.

He continued:

> While it is correct that no authority has been cited in these proceedings which deals specifically with misleading information provided by a receptionist in an A & E department causing physical injury, it is not necessary to address, in every instance where the precise factual situation has not previously been the subject of a reported judicial decision, whether it would be fair, just and reasonable to impose a duty of care. It is sufficient that the case falls within an established category in which the law imposes a duty.

Perhaps what this shows us is that, whilst the general principle now seems to be clearer in respect of the question of duty, the specifics are still open to interpretation. What is 'established'? If it is open to debate, as it was in *Darnley* (the Court of Appeal and the Supreme Court disagreeing), as to whether a situation is established or novel, then what hope do the lower courts have, where the situation isn't crystal clear, of being able to differentiate the one from the other?

2.6 Special duty situations

Having considered the basics as to establishing a duty of care, we now need to look at some special duty situations, where the rules can be slightly different or noteworthy, for reasons we'll explore as we go along. We'll look at how the question of duty is tackled as regards the following special duty situations:

- omissions
- acts of thirds parties
- public bodies, including the emergency services.

2.6.1 Omissions: the general rule

The general rule in Negligence is that there is no liability for an omission (*Yuen Kun-Yeu v Attorney General of Hong Kong* [1988] AC 175, PC). In other words, it is unlikely that the court will impose a duty of care on a defendant for not doing something. (Note that the situation is different in many civil law jurisdictions, where there is a positive duty to act even in respect of strangers.)

Lord Hoffmann, in *Stovin v Wise* [1996] UKHL 15, explains the rationale very neatly:

> There are sound reasons why omissions require different treatment from positive conduct. It is one thing for the law to say that a person who undertakes some activity shall take reasonable care not to cause damage to others. It is another thing for the law to require that a person who is doing nothing in particular shall take steps to prevent another from suffering harm from the acts of third parties … or from natural causes.

example

A little boy, Teddy, has jumped into a lake but can't swim. He is struggling to stay afloat and is taking in a lot of water. Jane, a passer-by, notices this but offers no assistance.

Whilst Jane might have some moral questions to ask herself here about her decision to walk past without offering assistance, on the face of it, she does not owe a legal duty of care in Negligence for her failure to assist (her omission). There is no positive legal duty to act in such a situation. The position might be different, however, if Jane does not do something she *ought* to have done, because of her relationship with Teddy. So, if she is in fact Teddy's mother, or carer, or she was contractually obliged to look after him, perhaps as his nanny, then this might create a positive duty to act.

Exceptions to the general rule in relation to omissions

Lord Goff articulated the general rule and its exceptions in *Smith v Littlewoods Organisation Ltd* [1987] AC 241. He said that 'the common law does not impose liability for what are called pure omissions'.

In this case, the defendants owned a disused cinema which they intended to demolish and replace with a supermarket. Unknown to the defendants, vandals had broken into the site and caused some minor property damage and fire damage over a period of about three weeks, none of which was reported to the defendants (or the police). Shortly after this, the vandals started a fire on the site. This spread and caused damage to neighbouring properties. The claimants sought to bring an action in Negligence against the defendants, arguing that they (the claimants) were owed a duty of care by the defendants to prevent the actions of the third party vandals. The House of Lords stated that the defendants were not liable for their failure to protect the claimants (their omission) given that they had not been aware of the presence of the vandals, nor their previous attempts to start fires.

There are three main exceptions to the general rule that there will be no liability for an omission. They seem to be exceptions because in each case they illustrate a degree of closer proximity between the claimant and defendant, justifying the argument that the defendant ought to be liable for *not* doing something they should have done. Let's look at them one at a time.

Where the defendant has or ought to have a degree of control over the claimant

This might include where there is an established relationship between the parties, such as parent and child. It might also extend to any situation where the defendant is responsible for or has/should have a high degree of control over the claimant's welfare, such as was the case in *Reeves v Commissioner of Police for the Metropolis* [2000] 3 All ER 897. In this case, a man committed suicide while detained in police custody. It was argued (by his partner) that, as a known suicide risk, this was exactly the harm that the police should have prevented, and that they owed the man a duty of care. The police argued that they did not owe a duty of care because he was not mentally ill.

The House of Lords held that a duty was owed, and that the police's duty to prisoners in custody included the positive duty to take reasonable steps to assess the suicide risk of prisoners, and to respond appropriately. The court emphasised the degree of control exercised over prisoners in custody and the known risk of suicide, regardless of the mental state of the prisoner. (However, damages were reduced by 50% on the basis of a partial defence called contributory negligence, as the prisoner deliberately took his own life. We'll look at this defence in **Chapter 6**.)

A later case involving similar facts emphasised the point that the duty on the police did not extend to them being required to treat *all* prisoners as potential suicide risks (*Orange v Chief Constable of West Yorkshire Police* [2002] QB 347).

Where the defendant voluntarily assumes responsibility for the claimant

There is some overlap here with the above exception regarding control. The most obvious example of where a defendant can be said to have voluntarily assumed responsibility for the welfare of the claimant is in a contractual or employment relationship. This isn't necessarily employer/employee but extends to workmates, as it did in *Costello v Chief Constable of Northumbria Police* [1999] 1 All ER 550. In this case, the claimant, a female police officer, was attacked by a prisoner in a cell. A fellow police officer, who had agreed to stand close by and protect the claimant, heard her cries for help but did nothing. The Court of Appeal stated that where a police officer's omission might lead to an avoidable harm to a colleague, a duty is owed.

Similarly, in *Barrett v Ministry of Defence* [1995] 1 WLR 1217, the claimant, Barrett, a naval pilot, got very drunk and was looked after, to begin with, by a fellow officer. Unfortunately, the fellow officer then left Barrett unattended whereupon he choked to death on his own vomit. It was held that, whilst the Ministry of Defence did not owe a duty of care *per se*, it did so from the point at which the fellow officer had assumed responsibility for the claimant. However, the damages were reduced by two-thirds (contributory negligence applied) as more responsibility for the death was held to lie with the deceased than with the officer.

Note that all the examples in this area seem to concern pre-existing relationships between claimant and defendant.

Where the defendant creates or adopts the risk to the claimant

Where it can be said that the defendant creates a dangerous situation, a positive duty to deal with that danger may be imposed. A clear example of this is *Capital & Counties plc v Hampshire County Council* [1997] QB 1004. Here, it was found that the fire service, as a public body (see further **2.6.3** below), will only owe a duty to a property owner when it creates the danger in the first place, or where its positive actions in attempting to respond to an emergency actually make the situation worse. Here, the defendant council was found to be vicariously liable for the fire chief's decision to turn off a sprinkler system in the claimant's property, which allowed the fire to spread more quickly than it would have done had the sprinkler been left on. (So, in actual fact, the duty was imposed here by virtue of a positive act rather than an omission, though the principle as to omissions still holds good.)

As to adopting a risk, in *Goldman v Hargrave* [1967] 1 AC 645, a tree caught fire after being struck by lightning on the defendant landowner's property. The defendant ensured that the tree was cut down, but then omitted to take any further precautions to stop the fire spreading. As a result, the felled tree continued to burn and caused extensive fire damage to a neighbouring property. Although he didn't cause the fire, the defendant was held to have 'adopted the risk' through his omission, ie he allowed the problem to continue. The Privy Council found that a duty of care was owed.

2.6.2 Liability for acts of third parties

As we saw in *Smith v Littlewoods* itself, there is generally no liability to prevent third parties causing damage, and therefore no liability for a *failure* to prevent those third parties from causing damage (the omission-specific part of that rule). Once again, though, as with all general rules, there are exceptions. Many of these overlap with the exceptions we have already discussed, and from that point of view it can be difficult to discern bright lines between the various exceptions within the context of omissions. It was Lord Goff in *Smith v Littlewoods* who articulated the four exceptional situations in which a duty has been imposed on a defendant for the actions of a third party. It's fair to say that some of these exceptions concern omissions, some concern positive acts, but it's right that they're considered in this section and in light of the material on omissions we have already looked at. (They fit better here than anywhere else!)

The four exceptions are as follows:

(1) Where there is a special relationship between the defendant and the claimant.
(2) Where there is a special relationship between the defendant and the third party.
(3) Where someone creates a dangerous situation that may be 'sparked' by a third party.
(4) Where there is a failure to prevent a known danger created by a third party.

Let's look at each of these.

Where there is a special relationship between the defendant and the claimant

This would be where the parties have a special relationship (ie pre-existing/pre-tort) and where, therefore, there is already proximity between them, such that imposing a duty of care on the defendant for the claimant is appropriate.

This kind of special relationship might arise by way of contract or a quasi-contractual relationship, as it did in *Stansbie v Troman* [1948] 2 KB 48. In this case, the claimant employed the defendant, a painter and decorator, to decorate her premises. When she went out, she asked that the defendant ensure he locked up after himself on leaving. He failed to do so (an omission) and the property was burgled. The contractual relationship between the two was enough, said the court, for the imposition of a duty of care, and the defendant owed a duty of care to prevent the burglary by a third party.

The special relationship might spring from an express or implied undertaking to look after the claimant.

Swinney v Chief Constable of Northumbria (No 2) (1999) The Times, 25 May

case example

The claimant, the landlady of a pub, had provided the police with information concerning the suspect involved in the death of a police officer. She gave the information on the condition that she remained anonymous. However, a police file containing her details was left on the backseat of an unlocked police car, and this was stolen. It fell into the hands of the suspect, about whom she had given evidence, and as a result the claimant was harassed, which caused her to suffer psychiatric illness. She also gave up her job as a result. The police argued that they owed no duty of care on the basis of there being insufficient proximity (no special relationship) between them and the claimant. The Court of Appeal disagreed. It said that informers were not to be treated like other members of the public; they had a special relationship with the police (and the policy reasons for protecting claimant informers are also obvious – so as to encourage others to come forward without fear of attack).

This can be contrasted with *Hill v Chief Constable of West Yorkshire* [1989] AC 53, in which the mother of the final victim of Peter Sutcliffe, the 'Yorkshire Ripper', sued the police in Negligence for their failure to apprehend Sutcliffe earlier. He had been questioned by police and released before murdering the woman's daughter. The House of Lords failed to impose a duty for this omission, because there was no special relationship between the defendant police and the claimant (unlike in *Swinney*, above, which followed it).

In *Palmer v Tees Health Authority* [1999] EWCA Civ 1533, the claimant argued unsuccessfully that she should have been owed a duty of care by the local Mental Health Authority, which failed adequately to supervise a psychiatric patient in the community. The patient had previously threatened to kill a child and subsequently attacked and killed the claimant's 4-year-old daughter. The Court of Appeal followed *Hill* in determining that there was no special relationship between the defendant police and the claimant. The claimant would have needed to be someone at risk over and above that of the public at large.

Mitchell v Glasgow City Council [2009] 1 AC 874

case example

Here, the defendant local authority was under no duty to warn a tenant (the claimant) that his neighbour, Drummond, might become violent after being informed, by the council, that he was to be evicted. The claimant was a 72-year-old man, who was beaten and killed by Drummond. Drummond was known to the local authority due to his anti-social behaviour which included threats to Mitchell. The House of Lords said that a duty would only have arisen where the defendant had assumed responsibility for the claimant.

Whilst the rationale here is clear, this still perhaps presents a problematic decision, in that the claimant was known to the defendant council (as was the third-party neighbour, Drummond).

Similarly, in *Michael* (facts discussed above at **2.5.5**), whilst it could be argued that there existed a special relationship between the defendant call operator and the claimant, once the call was accepted (on the basis of an assumption of responsibility), this was explicitly rejected by Lord Toulson in that case. Lord Kerr (dissenting) questioned this approach and makes an interesting point as regards reasonable expectation on the part of the claimant:

> Should someone in a vulnerable state, fearing imminent attack, who believes that the assurance of [timely] assistance has been made when, through negligence on the part of the police, that impression has been wrongly created, be treated differently from another who has in fact received an explicit assurance of immediate help, if both have relied on what they believed to be a clear promise that police would attend and avert the apprehended danger?

Where there is a special relationship between the defendant and the third party

As mentioned, there are overlaps here between this and the previous category. See, for example, *Mitchell* (above) where there was arguably a special relationship between defendant and claimant, *and* between defendant and the third party, and yet a duty was not imposed.

The key case falling within this exceptional category is *Home Office v Dorset Yacht Co Ltd* [1970] AC 1004.

Home Office v Dorset Yacht Co Ltd [1970] AC 1004

case example

Here, the supervisors (for whom the Home Office could be vicariously liable) of a group of young male offenders negligently allowed the offenders to escape and to cause property damage to the claimants' yachts moored in Poole Harbour. The nature of the relationship between the supervisors and the third party (the young offenders) was such that the requisite degree of proximity – the special relationship – was created. The House of Lords found a duty of care, with Lord Reid making the point that the actions of the boys as a result of their negligent supervision were predictable – 'very likely to happen'.

Where someone creates a dangerous situation that may be 'sparked' by a third party

Where a third party's actions exacerbate a dangerous situation created by the defendant, causing loss or harm to the claimant, then a duty may arise between claimant and defendant. An example of this comes from *Haynes v Harwood* [1936] 1 KB 146. The defendant left his horses untethered on a busy street, which then bolted when some children threw stones at them. The claimant was a police officer, who was injured as he tried to control the horses. The defendant owed the officer a duty of care, as he had created a source of danger by omitting to tether his horses in the first place. This danger had been exploited by a third party (the children).

Where there is a failure to prevent a known danger created by a third party

Here, unlike the situation above, the danger is itself created by (not exacerbated by) a third party, and the defendant does nothing to prevent or abate it. Look back at *Smith v Littlewoods* (above at **2.6.1**) where *no* duty was owed because the defendants did not know, and could not reasonably have known, about the fires started on the premises by third party vandals. The *obiter* reasoning in *Smith* was applied in *Clark Fixing Ltd v Dudley Metropolitan Borough Council* [2001] EWCA Civ 1898 and a duty imposed. Here, the defendant council owned property whose roof was shared by the claimant's neighbouring property. Trespassers entered the defendant's property and started a fire, which spread to the claimant's property, causing extensive damage. Unlike in *Smith*, the defendant here was aware of the presence of trespassers starting fires – in fact, the claimant had reported this to the defendant. A duty was therefore imposed for the council's failure to abate a danger caused by a third party.

2.6.3 Public bodies, including the emergency services

A public body is a state-funded body or organisation and includes local councils, educational authorities and the emergency services. This is an area where it is easy to get bogged down, or to stray into other areas of law which we don't have the scope to cover here (for example constitutional and administrative law). There are historical reasons why public bodies have not tended to owe a duty of care, and interesting as they are, it wouldn't assist us here to explore those in depth. Instead, we'll focus on the current position.

The following case is very helpful in that it sets out the law as it currently stands on when and in what circumstances a public body will owe a duty, and it also reviews the law and principles as regards duty that have brought us to this position. In that sense, it acts as a useful consolidation exercise for much that we have looked at so far.

CN & GN v Poole Borough Council [2019] UKSC 25

case example

CN and GN were two boys who, with their mother, were placed by the local authority in accommodation very close to another family who were known to have engaged in anti-social behaviour over a period of time. Following their placement, the family (one of the boys being severely disabled) suffered years of physical and mental abuse at the hands of their neighbours, culminating at one point in the eldest boy running away from home and leaving a suicide note. The claimants argued that the local authority had been under a duty of care to protect them from harm.

This went all the way to the Supreme Court, which decided that no duty was owed here, for reasons we'll look at it a moment. However, they took the time to set out the factors that *would have led to* a duty being imposed, thereby eroding the notion that public bodies would never owe a duty of care in this kind of situation. This was not a good result for the claimants involved but a very useful one for lawyers.

Lord Reed, giving the single judgment of the Court, made the following statements (paraphrased) as regards Negligence liability and public authorities:

(1) *The incremental approach in* Caparo *was approved and reaffirmed.* Lord Reed agreed that the courts should apply established principles of law rather than imposing a so-called three-stage test which in reality was entirely policy-driven.

(2) The principle was reaffirmed as to public authorities being subject to the *same general principles of law as private individuals.* (This is important in that there had previously been a perception, borne out in much case law – as there had with respect also to the police – that public authorities enjoyed something close to blanket immunity.) It was held that a duty of care could arise *when the authority had created the source of danger* (particularly in relation to social welfare cases) *or had assumed responsibility to protect the claimant from harm,* unless the imposition of such a duty would go against or be inconsistent with any statutory framework within which the local authority was operating.

(3) The distinction between *omissions and positive acts* was discussed following *Michael* and *Robinson* (see **2.5.5**). Lord Reed preferred the terminology of making things worse/causing harm rather than 'positive acts', and failing to confer a benefit (or failing to make things better) rather than 'omissions'. Why? He said that the choice of language 'better conveys the rationale of the distinction drawn in the authorities, and … because the distinction between acts and omissions seems to be found difficult to apply'. He also made the point that public authorities, like private individuals, do not generally owe a duty of care to confer benefits on individuals, for example by protecting them from the harm of third parties. (Note: is this another way of saying that there is generally no liability for an omission?)

(4) As to the principle of *assuming responsibility* and how evidence of such can cause a court to impose a duty of care on a defendant where it might not have existed before, the court defined this concept as 'an undertaking that reasonable care will be taken, either express or, more commonly implied,

usually from the reasonable foreseeability of reliance on the exercise of such care'. Here, no such assumption of responsibility arose, said Lord Reed, in that the defendant council's investigating and monitoring of the claimants' situation was not of itself indicative of a provision of service on which they (or their mother) could be expected to rely.

As a side note for our purposes, it was also recognised that, though the carrying out of statutory functions by local authorities did not of itself give rise to a common law duty of care, nevertheless an assumption of responsibility *could* arise within the operation of a statutory scheme where the specific facts revealed that such was the case. This was not the position here.

The Supreme Court found that none of the above were present in this case, and that was the reason why it determined that there was no duty of care. There is more to say here, and in particular if you are interested in the way in which this precedent has influenced subsequent decisions, do explore, for example, *HXA & SXA v Surrey County Council* [2021] EWHC 250 (QB) and the line of cases examining assumption of responsibility in cases concerning children. However, these are outside the scope of this book.

The emergency services – the fire service

We have touched on the fire brigade already, but let's be clear on when and in what circumstances it will owe a duty of care.

case example

Capital & Counties plc v Hampshire County Council [1997] QB 1004

This was actually three cases heard as one, the above citation giving us the case in which a duty of care was owed. The other two cases heard at the same time did not give rise to a duty of care.

Here, the fire brigade responded to an emergency call regarding a building on fire. On arrival, the officer in charge ordered the building's sprinkler service to be turned off. The allowed the fire to spread, causing more damage than it need have done. This was seen as a positive act which made the situation worse. The other two cases involved omissions on the part of the fire brigades – a failure to inspect the property to ensure the fire was out, and a failure to attempt to fight a fire due to the local fire hydrants being inadequate.

There followed much debate in the Court of Appeal as to why and on what basis a duty should be owed, much of it perhaps unsatisfactory and inconsistent. However, we are left with the rather unwieldy principle that the fire service does not owe a duty to attend (the duty attaching to the public at large but not to individuals at this point) but will owe a duty (to the individuals) if, having attended, it makes the situation worse by a positive act.

example

The fire service responds to an emergency call made by Travis whose shop is on fire, but on arrival the firefighters realise they do not have the right length of hose on board to tackle the fire. Another fire engine eventually arrives carrying the right equipment, by which time the fire damage is more extensive than it would have been.

Unfortunately for Travis, it looks unlikely that he will be owed a duty of care (by the first fire service crew at least) because this concerns an omission on the fire brigade's part, which, by its nature, is difficult to argue made the fire worse than it would have been had no fire brigade attended at all. Had the fire brigade made the fire worse by a positive act, it would have owed a duty of care.

Having said this, students sometimes feel surprised (understandably) that the fire brigade can simply side-step liability by not getting involved at all. Whilst it is true that the fire brigade may well escape Negligence liability, there would almost certainly be an investigation into the conduct of the fire service by, for example, its regulatory body (the fire and rescue authority), and so the fire service would not simply avoid the consequences of its omission.

The emergency services – the ambulance service

Unlike the fire service, the ambulance service owes a duty of care from the moment the emergency call is taken – it is a duty to attend within a reasonable time.

Kent v Griffiths [2000] 2 All ER 474

case example

An emergency call was made by a GP requesting an ambulance for a pregnant woman suffering an asthma attack in her home. The GP was told that an ambulance was on its way, but he then called twice more when the ambulance did not arrive. Eventually the ambulance arrived after 38 minutes, by which time the woman had temporarily stopped breathing. This caused her to lose her baby (and later led to her suffering psychiatric harm).

The Court of Appeal rejected the defendant's argument that, on the same basis as the fire service, the ambulance service owed no duty of care. On the contrary, the court found that the ambulance service was distinguishable from the fire service on the basis that it is an extension of the National Health Service (NHS), which owes a duty of care to its patients. As such, the ambulance service owed a duty to individuals as soon as the emergency call was taken. The claimant succeeded.

The emergency services – the police

You'll note that much of our earlier discussion on duty of care has focused on police cases, so do look back at these, but it seems right also to consolidate the law into one section if we can.

When the police do owe a duty

The case of *Robinson* (see **2.5.5** above) has very helpfully confirmed that the police *do* owe a duty of care where, by their positive act, they cause property damage or personal injury. In this case, the Supreme Court imposed a duty on the defendant police in respect of a 76-year-old woman, knocked to the ground and injured in the course of a negligent arrest of a drug dealer on a busy city street. Lord Reed determined that this case was simply an application of established principles of the law of Negligence and did not depend on any 'test' from *Caparo*. The police, it was stated, are afforded no special blanket immunity for positive acts and are to be treated in just the same way as any other private defendant. Note the overlaps here with what was said about public authorities above.

Reassessing Hill

The Supreme Court took the opportunity in *Robinson* to discuss the earlier case of *Hill* (see **2.6.2** above) which many had wrongly construed as bestowing blanket immunity on the police. It was said:

> The case of *Hill* is not, therefore, authority for the proposition that the police enjoy a general immunity from suit in respect of anything done by them in the course of investigating or preventing crime. On the contrary, the liability of the police for negligence or other tortious conduct resulting in personal injury, where liability would arise under ordinary principles of the law of tort, was expressly confirmed. Lord Keith spoke of an 'immunity', meaning the absence of a duty of care, only in relation to the protection of the public from harm through the performance by the police of their function of investigating crime.

It will always be much harder to establish that the police owe a duty in respect of omissions, however, applying the general rule on this principle. Further, as we have seen, there is still a mountain to climb for any claim that seeks to argue that the police owe a duty to protect individual members of the public (see *Michael*, for example) on the basis of assumption of responsibility or other arguments that might ordinarily trump the general rule as to omissions. Having said that, there may be an alternative way forward for claimants by utilising the Human Rights Act 1998 (see below).

The distinction between operational and policy failings

Notwithstanding the law's clarification regarding *Caparo* and its impact on the duty owed by the police, the court will continue, as part of its considerations, to make a distinction, when determining the question of duty owed by the police, between operational and policy failings. Broadly, though it can be difficult always to distinguish between these concepts, examples that have fallen to be categorised as policy matters would include allocation of limited resources, and the way the police conduct and prioritise investigations. The court is less likely to impose a duty in respect of policy failings than it would be in relation to operational failings. You might find it helpful (though it's not a failsafe method) to think of operational failings as *what happened/what went wrong*, and policy failings to cover *why/the reason for the decision made*.

Rigby v Chief Constable of Northamptonshire [1985] 2 All ER 985

In this case, the police negligently fired a canister of gas into the claimant's shop which was under siege, without first taking adequate precautions against the obvious risk of fire. Significant fire damage was caused as a result. The claimant successfully argued that a duty of care was owed by the police for their operational failings.

Although the distinctions didn't arise in *Kent v Griffiths* (see above), the court in this case also suggested that had the delay been caused by policy failings, for example a lack of resources or a decision to deploy resources differently (prioritising), then the defendant ambulance service would be less likely to owe a duty than for obvious operational or procedural failings.

The police and the Human Rights Act 1998

We could spend a great deal of time looking at claims against the police under the Human Rights Act (HRA) 1998, a fascinating area of the law, but for now we will confine our discussion to a summary of the way in which such claims might assist claimants, even where Negligence actions might fail.

A case called *Van Colle v Chief Constable of South Hertfordshire Police* [2008] UKHL 50 (relying on *Osman v UK* (1998) 29 EHRR 245) had already established a duty on the police to investigate and prevent potential breaches of Article 2 of the European Convention on Human Rights (ECHR) (the right to life). Such duties are different from tortious duties and arise irrespective of whether a common law Negligence duty also arises. As was made clear in *Van Colle,* the two 'regimes' have a different basis of liability and a different relationship with policy concerns. (They also, for example, award damages on a different basis.)

The case of *Commissioner of the Police of the Metropolis v DSD and Another* [2018] UKSC 11 went one step further, deciding that Article 3 of the ECHR (prohibiting torture and degrading treatment) *also* imposes an operational duty on the police to conduct appropriate investigations into allegations of ill-treatment.

Between 2003 and 2008, John Worboys, the driver of a black cab in London, committed a series of sexual offences against female passengers. The first and second respondents (DSD and NVB) were two of his victims. They brought proceedings against the Commissioner of the Metropolitan Police Service (MPS) for its alleged failure to conduct adequate or any investigations into Worboys' crimes. The claims against the MPS were brought under ss 7 and 8 of the Human Right Act 1998, arguing that the police failures amounted to a violation of the respondents' rights under Article 3 of the ECHR. This was accepted by the Court of Appeal, which awarded damages to DSD and NVB, finding that Article 3 imposes a general duty on the police to investigate possible violations of this Article by third parties (including private individuals). The police conceded that such a duty was owed, but that it was a duty owed to the public at large, not a private law duty to an individual victim of crime. The Supreme Court dismissed the MPS appeal.

It is likely that this Supreme Court decision, though not wholly relevant for tort law purposes, is likely to have far-reaching consequences for the police, whose investigations of serious crime will surely come under increased scrutiny via human rights litigation.

The armed forces

The case law suggests that a duty of care will only be owed to individuals where an 'assumption of responsibility' arises (see above at **2.6.1** and the discussion of *Barrett v Ministry of Defence*). Subsequent case law has not significantly changed that position.

2.7   Consolidation and reflection

Before we move on to Part II of this chapter, let's pause and reflect on what has been covered so far. There has been a lot of material to get through, much of it fairly complex. As a checklist for yourself, go back and read Part I again and ensure you understand it at a basic level. You can add in the layers once you have the foundation.

Ask yourself:

- Am I clear on what is meant by the term duty of care?
- Where does this fit in the Negligence sequence and why there?
- Why is the type of damage/loss important in determining duty? (This is the area we will move on to in more depth shortly.)
- How does the court determine whether a duty will be imposed on a defendant? Start by working through *Caparo* and its 'modern-day interpretation'. Remember: if there's a precedent, use it!
- Am I clear that there are exceptions to the general rules outlined above? (Much of this Part has focused on those exceptions and on problem situations, but try not to get too bogged down and make sure you understand the basic principles.)

2.8   Further reading

A Linden, 'Toward Tort Liability for Bad Samaritans' (2016) 53 Alberta L Rev 837.
S Tofaris, 'Duty of Care in Negligence: A Return to Orthodoxy?' [2018] CLJ 454.
S Tofaris and S Steel, 'Negligence Liability for Omissions and the Police' [2016] CLJ 128.
N McBride, '*Michael* and the Future of Tort Law' (2016) 32 PN 27.

summary

- Damage and duty are the first two elements in the Negligence sequence and should be looked at in that order.
- The leading case on the question of duty is still *Caparo v Dickman*, though there was confusion for a time as to how it should be interpreted.
- The courts will look to existing precedent first and use that to establish the existence or absence of duty. If there is no existing precedent, they will look to analogous cases and, where these exist, ask whether the loss in the present case was reasonably foreseeable, and whether it would be fair, just and reasonable to develop the law incrementally from the precedent.
- There are general rules surrounding the imposition of a duty of care and exceptions to those. For example, generally there is no duty imposed for an omission, but there are various exceptions to this rule.

test your knowledge

Have a go at these multiple choice questions (MCQs):

Question 1

A cyclist is knocked off his bike as a result of the negligence of a driver. He sustains a broken wrist and has to take a week off work. His bike is damaged beyond repair. The cyclist wants to sue the driver.

Which one of the following options gives the correct answer as to the types of loss for which the cyclist will seek to recover damages?

A   Personal injury, pure economic loss and property damage.
B   Personal injury, psychiatric injury and consequential economic loss.
C   Personal injury, consequential economic loss and property damage.
D   Consequential economic loss, pure economic loss and personal injury.
E   Pure economic loss, personal injury and psychiatric injury.

Answer

The correct answer is option C. The personal injury loss is for his wrist injury. Consequential economic losses are losses flowing from damage to person or property, so these would be applicable here, including as to time off work if the cyclist loses money as a result. Property damage would relate to the bike.

Question 2

You are representing a claimant in a Negligence case and can't yet decide if the claim fits a previous precedent or is analogous to it.

Which one of the following best outlines the likely approach the court will apply when determining the question of duty, based on *Caparo v Dickman*?

A   There is no single test. Instead, the approach will be one based on precedent and on the development of the law incrementally and by analogy with established authorities.
B   The three-stage test from *Caparo* will be used, whereby the court looks at the foreseeability of the loss, how proximate the parties were and whether it would be fair, just and reasonable to impose a duty of care.

C The neighbourhood test from *Donoghue v Stevenson* would be used, whereby the court looks at whether the defendant ought to have had the claimant in contemplation when carrying out the acts or omissions in question.

D There are various tests for duty of care, but essentially the court will only impose a duty where a claim fits an established precedent.

E The court will decide which approach it uses and the way in which it will interpret *Caparo.*

Answer

The correct answer is option A. This is exactly the approach advocated. The others are either no longer used (options B and C) or incorrect (options D and E).

Question 3

A child has fallen into a ditch. A woman passing by hears the child cry out and goes to help. She gently pulls the child out of the ditch but, in doing so, accidentally dislocates the child's shoulder.

Which one of the following is accurate as to whether the woman would owe the child a duty of care in any Negligence action brought against her?

A As the two do not know each other, there would be no duty imposed.

B There is generally no positive duty to assist, and therefore no duty imposed for a failure to assist. Having assumed responsibility for the child, it's possible that the court would impose a duty of care on the woman.

C The woman was under a positive duty to assist and failure to do so would have resulted in a Negligence action brought against her in any event.

D A duty would be imposed as soon as the child suffered personal injury.

E Contributory negligence would likely be successful here and the child's damages would be reduced by up to 100%

Answer

The correct answer is option B. Whilst there is no general duty imposed for an omission, once the woman got involved and assumed responsibility, it's possible that a duty might be imposed.

Question 4

A man calls the emergency services and requests an ambulance. It does not arrive.

Which one of the following is accurate as to whether the ambulance service owed a duty of care?

A The ambulance did not owe a duty to attend but would have owed a duty not to make the situation worse, had it attended.

B The ambulance owed a duty as soon as the call was accepted, and it was a duty to arrive within a reasonable time.

C The ambulance owed a duty to arrive as soon as possible.

D Whether or not the ambulance owed a duty of care is open to interpretation.

E The ambulance owed no duty to respond to the emergency call.

Answer

Option B is the only correct answer from the options given.

PART II PSYCHIATRIC HARM AND ECONOMIC LOSS

2.9 Duty of care where the loss/damage is psychiatric harm

We started to look (at **2.4.2**) at the types of loss for which the court may be reluctant to impose a duty of care. Psychiatric harm is one of those. It's worth spending some time thinking about why that might be, and the rules around when a duty will or won't be imposed for this type of loss.

2.9.1 What is psychiatric harm?

Psychiatric harm is, as the name suggests, a form of personal injury affecting the mind. It used to be that psychiatric harm was only recoverable when it accompanied physical injury, but that has changed now (as medical science has advanced and the fear of fraudulent claims has reduced as a result), so that 'pure' psychiatric harm cases arising out of Negligence can give rise to a duty of care being imposed, in certain carefully controlled circumstances. It also used to be that we adopted the label 'nervous shock' for psychiatric harm (the term was first used in an Australian case called *Victorian Railway Commissioners v James & Mary Coultas* (1888) 13 App Cas 222), but thankfully, especially given that that label is inaccurate and unhelpful, it's now rarely employed, except occasionally as a kind of shorthand for lawyers.

In order to claim, the first step is for the claimant to prove they have suffered a recognised (or 'positive') psychiatric illness. Mere grief, anxiety or distress would not be sufficient to found a claim. In *Reilly v Merseyside HA* [1995] 6 Med LR 246, the court refused to compensate an elderly couple trapped in a lift for over an hour, and who felt frightened and claustrophobic. Well-known psychiatric conditions, such as post-traumatic stress disorder (PTSD), depression and schizophrenia are obviously recognisable as fitting the category of psychiatric harm, and some of these have formed the basis of reported cases, such as *Frost v Chief Constable of South Yorkshire* [1999] 2 AC 455 (PTSD), *Page v Smith* [1996] 1 AC 155 (a recurrence of ME or myalgic encephalomyelitis) and *Vernon v Bosley (No 1)* [1997] 1 All ER 577 (pathological grief syndrome). Other conditions are less easily defined or labelled, and in such cases it falls to be assessed as to whether the severity and duration of the symptoms, in the opinion of medical experts, would be sufficient to found a claim. This is an arena where expert medical evidence is crucial.

2.9.2 Why is the court reluctant to impose a duty?

Why do you suppose the court might be reluctant to impose a duty on the defendant in a Negligence action where the loss sustained is pure psychiatric harm, ie psychiatric harm in the absence of any other type of loss? One word: policy. In particular, the court is wary of floodgates. Why? Let's think through an example.

example

Whilst walking home one evening, Keith witnesses a serious car crash, caused by the negligence of one of the drivers, Bill. Several vehicles are involved, and one of the drivers, Hannah, is killed. Keith recognises one of the cars in the crash as belonging to his mother and is horrified, believing her to have been caught up in the accident. He suffers PTSD as a result of what he witnesses. Others in the street witness the crash too, or hear the noise and come rushing out of their homes to see what has happened. Many of them also suffer psychiatric harm as a result. Over the course of the next few days, Keith tells some friends about what he saw, and some of them feel shocked. The story is reported in the local newspaper and many people read about it.

Let's break this down. Suppose Keith wants to sue Bill in Negligence for his PTSD. Would a duty of care be imposed on Bill? Well, this is part of what we will discuss, but the answer is possibly yes *if* it was in fact his mother in the car. If this was the case, the court is likely to find that his PTSD was reasonably foreseeable. There are other hurdles for Keith here, but he *may* be owed a duty for his pure psychiatric loss.

Can you see that for the other witnesses, the situation is more problematic? For those who saw the crash, as Keith did, but did not have the connection to someone involved in the accident itself, the court is unlikely to find a duty. The court will be concerned that this could lead to a floodgates situation – there are the witnesses at the time, there are people Keith told (and the people they told, and so on), and there are the readers of the newspaper article. This could potentially lead to an infinite pool of claimants, all or most of whom were remote from the incident itself. Not only would this be unwieldy and unworkable for the court system, but it would shift the emphasis and the priorities of the court away from personal injury claims (which is really the kind of Negligence claim the court would always prioritise) and would also trigger another policy concern, namely crushing liability. Suddenly, Bill is potentially crushed disproportionately (financially) in relation to his tort. Is that fair? The law would say it is not, and so, whilst Keith may be able to claim in Negligence, the other witnesses, even if they have suffered recognised psychiatric harm (and many here may not have done) would not be able to claim.

Note: Those people directly involved in the crash, including the estate of the person killed, would probably find it straightforward to bring a Negligence action, and they would almost certainly be owed a duty of care in relation to their physical injuries (and any psychiatric injuries flowing from that).

2.9.3 The process for establishing a duty of care

We already know that a claimant wishing to establish a duty of care against a defendant for Negligence in respect of their psychiatric loss will first need to prove they have suffered a recognised psychiatric injury. But what next? Let's work through the duty part of the claim. (Note: in practice, often, establishing duty is the most difficult part, and for that reason our focus will be on unpicking that. But, of course, even where a claimant *can* establish that they should be owed a duty of care, they would also need to succeed in establishing the other elements of the claim, namely breach, causation, remoteness and so on.)

2.9.4 Categorising the claimant: primary and secondary claimants/victims

The first thing the court will do once satisfied in respect of the loss will be to categorise the claimant. Are they a primary or a secondary victim? The bottom line is that primary victims/claimants (those terms are used interchangeably here) are much more likely to be owed a duty of care than secondary victims. We'll define those terms in a moment, but think of the categories as a hierarchy: if at all possible you would want to be categorised as a primary victim. If that isn't possible, then in the alternative you would have to try your luck as a secondary claimant/victim. ('Best' of all, if that doesn't sound too strange, is to be categorised as a claimant who has sustained *both* personal injury and psychiatric harm at the same time. In terms of establishing a duty, this would put you at the top of the hierarchy, because it is usually easy to establish a duty once personal injury is sustained; therefore other losses flowing from that, for example psychiatric harm, would be deemed foreseeable and would not trigger policy concerns.)

Primary victims

A primary victim is someone who is caught up in the incident itself (the car crash, the stadium disaster, etc), who does *not* suffer personal injury, though this is reasonably foreseeable given their proximity to the incident, but who *does* sustain psychiatric harm. We sometimes say that this type of claimant is present in the physical zone of danger. In *White v Chief Constable of South Yorkshire* [1998] UKHL 45 (which arose out of the facts of the seminal case of *Alcock v Chief Constable of South Yorkshire Police* [1992] 1 AC 310 which we will look at below), the definition given for a primary victim is a neat one: someone 'objectively exposed to danger [ie physical harm] or reasonably [believing] that [they were]'.

Once the claimant has met that threshold test for a primary victim, they will be owed a duty of care. A reasonable belief that physical injury might be suffered is sufficient, though note, as an objective test, the claimant's own belief will not always be accepted as reasonable. In *McFarlane v EE Caledonia* [1994] 2 All ER 1, the claimant was at sea on board a rescue vessel during the Piper Alpha oil rig disaster, during which a huge fire killed over 150 men. He witnessed events and sought to claim as a primary victim due to his belief that he was in the danger zone and might himself be injured. The court disagreed, as the evidence showed he was sufficiently distanced from the event, on a rescue vessel, and therefore was not objectively in the danger zone.

case example

Page v Smith [1996] 1 AC 155

Here, the claimant was a passenger involved in a car crash caused by the defendant's negligence. The claimant escaped physical injury but did experience a recurrence of ME (myalgic ecephalomyelitis), a condition with both physical and psychological manifestations, so seriously as to render him permanently disabled. He was deemed a primary victim because he was clearly in the danger zone, objectively exposed to the danger of physical injury. Therefore, he was owed a duty of care by the defendant.

Rescuers as primary victims

There is often debate as to whether a rescuer who suffers psychiatric harm in the course of their rescue would or should automatically be construed as a primary victim, if for no other reason than on policy grounds (so as to encourage rescuers to get involved). In fact, rescuers do not have any special status in the law, and to recover for their loss they will need to establish their status as a primary victim in the usual way. Having said that, rescuers are clearly in the contemplation of the courts as potentially being primary victims. Look at what was said in *Alcock*: 'The defendant owes a duty of care not only to those who are directly threatened or injured by his careless acts but also to those who, as a result, are induced to go to their rescue.'

As has been mentioned, a primary victim will be involved in the incident itself in some way, or be proximate to it. Whilst there is no formal proximity requirement or test, *Alcock* states that a primary victim will be 'mediately or immediately involved as a participant' (Lord Oliver). In *White*, the claimants, who were police officers on duty during the Hillsborough football stadium disaster (which is what *Alcock* is all about – see below), were unsuccessful in their attempts to claim as primary victims. They were rescuers in the sense that they assisted in removing the dead bodies and carrying the injured to safety, but the court stated that, at the time they were doing this, they were not exposed to danger, as the danger had passed.

In contrast, in *Cullin v London Fire and Civil Defence Authority* [1999] PIQR 314, the claimant, a fireman who went to search of his colleagues caught up in a fire and saw them being unsuccessfully resuscitated, subsequently suffered PTSD and was able to claim as a primary victim. The court found that he was in the danger zone of the still-raging fire (though the defendant tried unsuccessfully to argue that he should have been treated as per the claimants in *White*).

Similarly, a rescuer was allowed to claim as a primary victim in *Chadwick v British Transport Commission* [1967] 2 All ER 945. In this case, the claimant rescuer rushed to the scene of a train crash near to his house in Lewisham. He stayed on board the train throughout the night to try and rescue victims and suffered psychiatric harm as a result. The court found him to be a primary victim, in that he was in physical danger during his rescue attempts (for example because pieces of debris from the wreckage were falling from the train carriage throughout). The court focused here on 'horror of the whole experience which caused his reaction', an approach which was approved in *White*.

Professional rescuers

There is no legal distinction between the treatment of lay and professional rescuers (see *Cullin* and *White* above, both professional rescuers, and *Chadwick*, a lay rescuer). But it is relevant to spend a moment considering the professional rescuer, because their professional status perhaps goes to what is considered reasonably foreseeable, and we can ask whether their training and the expectations of their job mean that in law they are reasonably expected to have a higher tolerance for witnessing objectively shocking incidents. The answer seems to be that whilst that may well be the case, this would not preclude them from claiming for their psychiatric harm if they can meet the threshold tests.

In *Ogwo v Taylor* [1987] 3 All ER 961, the House of Lords looked at the so-called 'fireman's rule' (an American concept) to see whether it should be applicable here. The rule is that professional rescuers cannot recover for anything they experience in the course of their work. The House of Lords held that that rule did not apply in English law, the upshot being that professional rescuers are in the same position as any other claimant seeking to be categorised as a primary victim.

Secondary victims

If primary victims are caught up in the incident itself and therefore objectively in the danger zone, secondary victims are not. Their loss is sustained through them having witnessed the incident. Personal injury for the secondary victim is neither sustained not reasonably foreseeable. Lord Oliver gives us a useful definition (in *Alcock*): the secondary victim/claimant is 'no more than a passive and unwilling witness of injury caused to others'.

For this category (and remember this is the category about which the court is primarily concerned because of the potential for a flood of claims), the House of Lords has put in place a number of hurdles. Claimants wishing to sue as secondary victims must overcome these hurdles to show that they ought to be owed a duty of care, and, as we will see, the hurdles are usually insurmountable. You might think of these hurdles as a strong judicial control mechanism used to 'knock out' as many claims as possible at the duty stage.

Alcock v Chief Constable of South Yorkshire Police [1992] 1 AC 310

case example

This case concerned the Hillsborough football stadium disaster that happened in 1989, during the FA Cup semi-final between Liverpool and Nottingham Forest. As a result of the admitted negligence of the police, 95 spectators were crushed to death and over 400 others physically injured. They had been negligently directed into one part of the stadium by the police who were attempting to control the crowds. Negligence actions were brought against the police, and, as you would expect, there was no difficulty in establishing a duty of care for those claimants who had been physically injured or killed, or who were primary victims. However, there were also huge numbers of secondary victims – mostly friends and relatives of victims who were either present at the ground (but in a different part) or watched on television. The House of Lords considered whether there was a way to limit the number of permissible claims. (The police did not accept they owed a duty to this class of claimant in any event.) The court adopted and approved the criteria, subsequently termed the *Alcock* control mechanisms, that had been used in the earlier case of *McLoughlin v O'Brian* [1983] 1 AC 410 which was essentially based on proximity. None of the secondary victims were owed a duty of care.

Lord Oliver's five criteria can be paraphrased. In order for a duty to be established, the claimant has to prove all of the following:

(1) a 'close tie of love and affection' between the claimant and the primary victim (ie someone caught up in the incident itself);

(2) that the psychiatric harm was caused by the direct perception by the claimant of the 'sudden and unexpected shock', and as a result of witnessing the death

of, extreme danger to, or injury and discomfort suffered by the primary victim; and

(3) that the claimant was present at the scene or witnessed its immediate aftermath.

A 'close tie of love and affection'

This is the court's attempt to ensure that only those secondary victims who are sufficiently emotionally proximate to the victim of the incident itself can claim. In *Alcock*, it was said that a rebuttable presumption in favour of a close tie would arise where the relationship was parent/child or spousal (or of fiancé(e)s). For everyone else and every other type of relationship, there was a rebuttable presumption against such a close tie arising. This has to be proved on a case by case basis.

So, for example, one claimant, Brian Harrison, who was at the stadium on one side and who witnessed the stands collapsing on the other side where both his brothers were, was not allowed to claim because he could not rebut the presumption that he did not have a sufficiently close tie of love and affection with his brothers.

The House of Lords did discuss (*obiter*) the possibility of a mere bystander, with no relationship at all to the primary victims, being able to claim if the circumstances were 'particularly horrific'. Lord Ackner suggested that an example might be witnessing a petrol tanker smashing into a school. This possible exception to the rule has never yet been successfully raised in a reported case.

The means by which the psychiatric harm is caused

Point (2) above is essentially making the point that claimants must show that their psychiatric harm came about suddenly, as a direct result of the sudden and shocking incident, rather than unfolding over a period of time as they process or respond to events or a series of events. (Lord Ackner said there must be 'a sudden appreciation by sight or sound of a horrifying event, which violently agitates the mind'.)

This was construed in favour of the claimant in *North Glamorgan NHS Trust v Walters* [2002] EWCA Civ 1792. The claimant suffered psychiatric harm after negligent medical treatment led to the death of her 10-month-old baby. The Court of Appeal took the view that the 36 hours culminating in the death constituted 'a horrifying event', including witnessing the medical negligence. A duty of care was imposed on the defendant hospital.

However, this case has rarely, if ever, been followed. In an earlier case of *Sion v Hampstead Health Authority* (1994) 5 Med LR 170, the claimant again witnessed medical negligence at the hands of the hospital. His 23-year-old son had been seriously injured in a motorbike accident and brought into hospital. After coming out of a three-day coma, the victim was then in intensive care for over two weeks before dying. The claimant gradually came to the realisation over that period that negligence had contributed to his son's death. It was held that the claimant's damage was not caused by a sudden shock but by 'an accumulation of more gradual assaults on the nervous system over a period of time', and as such he was not owed a duty of care.

Walters, though not overruled, was distinguished in *Wild v Southend University Hospital NHS Foundation Trust* [2014] EWHC 4053 (QB). In this case, the claimant was the father of a foetus who died in utero as a result of negligence on the hospital's part and who was later delivered stillborn. The claimant suffered psychiatric harm as a result of being present at the moment the death was discovered and during the birth. The claim was dismissed, as the judge did not consider that the claimant's witnessing of the defendant's negligence and its consequences was the same as witnessing an horrific event. Critics have suggested there is not much factual difference between *Walters* and *Wild*.

There followed a series of unsuccessful claims, suggesting that secondary victims would rarely, if ever, be able to get over the hurdle of the seemingly arbitrary 'sudden shock' requirement. However, an exception is *RE (A minor by her mother and Litigation Friend LE) and Others v Calderdale & Huddersfield NHS Foundation Trust* [2017] EWHC 824 (QB). The claimant grandmother was able to recover damages for psychiatric harm (PTSD) as a secondary victim. She was present during her daughter's distressing labour and the delivery of RE. The midwife negligently failed to diagnose shoulder dystocia and failed to summon help. The evidence showed that, had she done so, the baby would have avoided all harm. At one point, the claimant believed that RE was dead. The 'close tie of love and affection' between grandmother and daughter was accepted. The question was as to whether the event was sufficiently sudden and shocking to form the basis of a claim. Goss J held that it was, saying: 'I am satisfied that her first-hand observation of the first 15 minutes of life ... was the triggering event for PTSD ... I find that the event was sufficiently sudden, shocking and objectively horrifying to reach the conclusion that her claim for damages ... is established.'

Present at the scene or witnessed its immediate aftermath

There is a requirement that the claimant must be proximate in time and space to the event. The more removed from the event, the less likely a duty will be imposed. Generally speaking, a claimant must witness the event with their 'own unaided senses' rather than, for example, hearing about it from someone else or watching an edited report on the television.

Robert Alcock searched the Hillsborough ground for his brother-in-law and found him in the temporary mortuary around eight hours later, his body blue with bruising and his chest red with dried blood. This time lapse was held to be too long – the claimant had not witnessed the event nor its immediate aftermath. This can be contrasted with *McLoughlin v O'Brian* [1983] 1 AC 410, in which Mrs McLoughlin was allowed to claim, because although she had not witnessed the crash which had caused serious injury to her husband and child, she had been present at the hospital very soon afterwards, before the staff had had the opportunity to 'clean up' the victims. It was as if, in witnessing the 'immediate aftermath', she had witnessed the event itself. Lord Wilberforce in *Alcock* said that

Mrs McLoughlin was 'part of the catastrophe itself for none of the victims had been cleaned up or were attended to'.

The claim, based on 'immediate aftermath', was successful in *Galli-Atkinson v Seghal* [2013] EWCA Civ 679. The claimant's 16-year-old daughter, Livia, died at 7.05pm when the defendant's car mounted the pavement and killed her instantly. The claimant saw the accident site but was unaware that anything was wrong, though she did attempt to cross the police cordon as she knew that her daughter was in the vicinity. She was told that her daughter had been killed about one hour later, but she did not believe this at first. The claimant and her husband viewed Livia's body in the mortuary at 9.15pm. The claimant then sustained psychiatric injury as a result. Having been unsuccessful at first instance, the Court of Appeal held that the claimant *could* recover, as the visit to the mortuary was the equivalent of witnessing the immediate aftermath. It was an 'uninterrupted sequence of events' from the moment of the accident until the viewing in the mortuary.

However, in the same year, the claimant was unsuccessful in *Taylor v A Novo (UK) Ltd* [2013] EWCA Civ 194. Here it was held that the claimant (the victim's daughter) was not close enough in time and space to the shocking event in question. Much turned here on what was the relevant event from which point time started ticking. The court decided that the original incident at the victim's place of work (negligence not witnessed by the claimant) was the relevant event for the purposes of establishing proximity, rather than the death of the victim, some three weeks later, which the claimant did witness.

2.9.5 Conclusion

Remember that we are looking at a type of loss – psychiatric harm (in particular pure psychiatric harm) – for which it can be difficult for claimants to establish a duty of care due to policy reasons. We have focused on the issue of duty of care, though as mentioned a claimant would also need to satisfy the rest of any Negligence claim even where duty is proven.

To conclude, any claimant will need to show that they have suffered recognised psychiatric harm. After that, it is about categorising that claimant so as to determine the question of duty. Is that claimant a primary victim (duty of care likely to be owed) or a secondary victim (duty of care unlikely to be owed). Where it is not clear on the facts, the correct approach would be to examine your claimant first as a primary victim and then, in the alternative, as a secondary victim, in the event that the primary claim argument fails.

It's fair to say that it is very difficult to establish a duty where the claimant is a secondary victim, and such claims very rarely succeed.

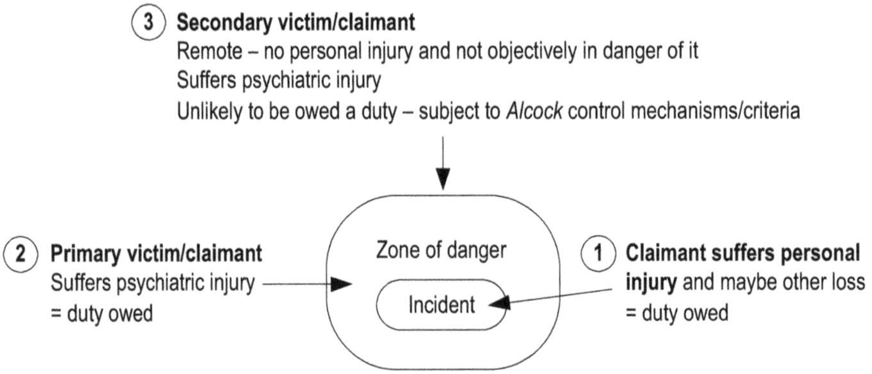

(3) Secondary victim/claimant
Remote – no personal injury and not objectively in danger of it
Suffers psychiatric injury
Unlikely to be owed a duty – subject to *Alcock* control mechanisms/criteria

(2) Primary victim/claimant
Suffers psychiatric injury
= duty owed

Zone of danger
Incident

(1) Claimant suffers personal injury and maybe other loss
= duty owed

Figure 2.3 Different categories of victim

2.10 Pure economic loss and duty of care

We have already touched on the definition of pure economic loss (financial loss not flowing from damage to person or property) and on the general rule that no duty will be owed in respect of this type of loss. For a reminder, see **2.4.2** above and remind yourself about the key case of *Spartan Steel v Martin*.

In this section we will concentrate on the key exception to the general rule: that is, the circumstances in which a claimant may be owed a duty of care in respect of pure economic loss. The exception concerns negligent misstatement, which translates as careless or negligent advice provided by the defendant. Where this is relied on by the claimant to their detriment, and they suffer pure economic loss, the court may impose a duty of care, where the circumstances fit those first expounded in the seminal case of *Hedley Byrne & Co Ltd v Heller & Partners Ltd* [1964] AC 465.

case example

Hedley Byrne & Co Ltd v Heller & Partners Ltd [1964] AC 465

The claimant, Hedley Byrne, was an advertising agency which was asked to do some work for a company called Easipower Ltd. In anticipation, Hedley Byrne decided to credit-check the company to ensure that it was creditworthy, and so it contacted Easipower's bank, Heller, twice. On each occasion, the bank confirmed that Easipower was creditworthy, and so the claimant carried out work for it costing £17,000. Easipower then collapsed, and so Hedley Byrne, unable to sue Easipower, sought to claim back the lost money (pure economic loss) from Heller, having relied on Heller's negligent advice.

When providing the advice, Heller had attached a disclaimer saying that it was provided 'without responsibility on the part of this bank …'. The House of Lords found that, by virtue of this disclaimer, the defendant Heller did not owe a duty of care, but that it would have done so had that disclaimer not been attached. (Note: attempts to exclude or limit liability would now be considered in light of the Unfair Contract Terms Act 1977 or the Consumer Rights Act 2015. We will look at this area in more detail when we get to Occupiers' Liability (**Chapter 10**).)

The court then went on to discuss, *obiter*, the way in which a duty of care might arise in a situation like this. It said that a duty could arise in some situations where advice was given, causing only pure economic loss, provided that:

(1) a special, or fiduciary, relationship of trust and confidence exists between the parties;

(2) the party preparing the advice or information has voluntarily assumed responsibility for that advice or information;

(3) the claimant actually relied on the advice given, to their detriment; and

(4) it was reasonable for the claimant to have relied on that advice.

This principle continues to form the basis of the law in this area regarding duty of care. It perhaps makes sense to jump now to the current position, and to analyse how we have arrived here by reference to other cases that were decided along the way.

2.10.1 The current position

Some recent Supreme Court cases have not only underlined the correct law to be applied in this area but also used the opportunity to review the case law thus far. We will consider the two most significant of these and look backwards where appropriate to see where we've come from.

Steel and Another v NRAM Ltd (Scotland) [2018] UKSC 13

case example

This case looked at the circumstances in which a solicitor for one party may owe a duty of care in respect of a negligent misstatement to the other party. (Although a Scottish case, the principles considered were the same as in England and Wales.) In this case, it was found that a duty of care was not owed.

Ms Steel was a solicitor who acted for a company called Headway Caledonian Ltd. Headway owned a business park made up of four units, the purchase of which it had funded in part via a loan from NRAM. Headway granted NRAM a standard security over the business park. It sold unit 3 and NRAM agreed to restrict its security in return for a payment in partial redemption of the loan. The following year, Headway contracted to sell unit 1, and NRAM agreed to accept £495,000 from the sale of unit 1 in reduction of Headway's loan. Just before the sale, Ms Steel emailed NRAM, which had no legal representation, stating (incorrectly) that the whole loan was being paid off for the business park, and requesting that NRAM sign a discharge of the security it still held over the business park. In fact, Headway's loan from NRAM was only being paid off and she did not have a settlement figure for full redemption of the loan, nor any instructions in this regard. She should have attached a deed to restrict but not to discharge the security.

NRAM signed the discharge without questioning or seeking to verify the accuracy of Ms Steel's assertions. The fact that the security had been discharged was only discovered by NRAM around three years later when Headway went into liquidation. NRAM brought a claim in Negligence against Ms Steel, claiming that she owed it a duty of care in respect of her inaccurate statements, which it had relied on to its financial detriment.

The Supreme Court unanimously held that Ms Steel did not owe a duty of care to NRAM. Lord Wilson gave the leading judgment, taking the opportunity to look again at the principles which apply when determining whether a duty of care is owed in relation to negligent misstatements (and also to consider when a solicitor for one party may owe a duty of care to the other party).

Lord Wilson said that *Hedley Byrne* was the starting point, and that at the heart of that decision was the need for the claimant to have relied, reasonably, on the representation made by the defendant, and for the defendant reasonably to have foreseen that the claimant would do so. He said whilst often linked, these were two separate enquiries, and together they amounted to an assumption of responsibility.

However, not all cases, he said, could be dealt with purely by reference to whether the defendant had assumed responsibility for the statement/advice given. The case of *Smith v Eric S Bush* [1990] 1 AC 831 was one of those where more consideration was needed, and it had led the House of Lords in that case to put forward a threefold test (comprising consideration of foreseeability of damage, proximity between the parties and whether it was fair, just and reasonable to impose a duty – do you recognise that from anywhere?). This test was then considered by the House of Lords in *Caparo v Dickman* (there it is!). The Lordships in that case had actually *queried* the utility of it and not, as had been supposed by many, *endorsed* it. A number of recent Supreme Court cases on duty have now confirmed this. Lord Wilson in *Steel* said that what *Caparo* did was to reassert the need for a claimant to establish that it was reasonable for them to have relied on the representation and that their doing so was or ought to have been foreseeable to the defendant. A duty was more likely to be imposed, according to *Caparo*, where the defendant knew that it was likely that the claimant would rely on the statement given without independent verification. In practice, Lord Wilson noted, the concept of assumption of responsibility remains the foundation of liability in negligent misstatement cases, though it may require cautious incremental development to fit certain cases and situations. The instant case, he said, fitted the concept of assumption of responsibility very well, and there was no need to consider incremental development.

Banca Nazionale del Lavaro SPA v Playboy Club London Ltd [2018] UKSC 43

case example

In October 2010, Mr Barakat, a resident of Lebanon, wished to gamble at the London Playboy Club ('the club'). He applied for a cheque cashing facility of £800,000 and named his bank as Banca Nazionale del Lavaro ('BNL'). The club's policy was to obtain a credit reference from the gambler's bank for twice the amount being sought. In order to avoid disclosing the purpose of the credit facility, the club arranged for an associated company to obtain the reference: the company was called Burlington Street Service Ltd ('BSS').

A few days later, BSS made a credit request to BNL to check that Mr Barakat would be able to meet a financial commitment of £1,600,000, and this was sent with a consent form signed by Mr Barakat. BNL responded, in strictest confidence, to say that Mr Barakat was creditworthy to the amount sought. In reliance on that reference, the club granted the credit facility to Mr Bakarat and even extended it over the four days during which Mr Bakarat was gambling. He then returned to Lebanon, but his cheques went unpaid. The club suffered a loss of over £800,000.

It was accepted by BNL that it had no basis for its reference. Mr Bakarat did not hold an open account with BNL until two days after the reference was sent. The club brought an action against BNL on the basis of negligent misstatement, and at first instance the court found that no duty was owed in relation to the reference. The Court of Appeal disagreed and the matter progressed to the Supreme Court.

The Supreme Court noted that it is fundamental that the party to whom the defendant assumes responsibility must be identifiable (although not necessarily identified), and that duty cannot be to the world at large or to a wholly indeterminate group. Lord Sumption held that BNL had no reason to suppose that BSS was acting for someone else, and that it knew nothing of the club. It could not be treated as though it had assumed responsibility to the club. As such, the club's appeal was unanimously dismissed (although Lord Mance stated that BNL was 'very lucky' to avoid liability). No duty was imposed.

The case clarifies rather than changes the law from *Hedley Byrne*. A duty can only be owed to a 'specific person or group of people to whom a defendant can be said to assume responsibility', and not to the world at large.

2.10.2 Summary so far

What we can glean from the above is that *Hedley Byrne* remains good law, and that the most important aspect, in determining whether a duty is owed, is as to *whether the defendant assumed responsibility to the particular claimant*. Where that has happened, a duty of care may be imposed. (This was lacking in the above cases.)

This was considered in *Caparo* itself, as was the question of whether the reliance by the claimant was reasonable. It was held not to be so.

example

Simon relies on the information contained within a surveyors' report as to a house he wishes to purchase. The report states that the house's roof is sound. He buys the house. In fact, the roof is defective (a fact about which the surveyor ought to have been aware) and, as a result, soon after Simon moves in, it caves in. The house is now worth significantly less than it was when Simon purchased it. Simon wants to sue the surveyors in respect of their negligent misstatement.

Simon is likely to succeed in a claim such as this. That is, the surveyors are likely to owe a duty of care, in that, applying *Hedley Byrne*, they have assumed responsibility for the advice given, the advice was intended for Simon to inform him on whether to purchase the house, and it was reasonable for Simon to rely on that advice. Even if the surveyors had attached a disclaimer to their advice (which they probably would have done), this would be unlikely to affect the outcome in light of the Unfair Contract Terms Act 1977 applied in the case of *Smith v Eric S Bush* [1990] 1 AC 831.

Note the loss sustained. It is pure economic loss – the diminution in house value – in that it is financial loss flowing not from any damage to person or property.

***Caparo Industries plc v Dickman* [1990] 2 AC 605**

case example

Caparo, a company, was considering a takeover bid of another company called Fidelity. With this in mind, Caparo looked at financial information regarding Fidelity provided by Fidelity's auditors, Dickman. Caparo was able to access this information because it already had shares in Fidelity. The information suggested that Fidelity was financially sound, and, in reliance on this, Caparo launched a takeover bid. It then transpired that Fidelity was actually almost worthless. Caparo sued Dickman, on the basis of negligent misstatement, for its pure economic loss.

The House of Lords found that no duty was owed by Dickman. The main reason was that it was not reasonable for Caparo to have relied on the financial audit information they had accessed. This information was provided as part of a statutory requirement and was intended for shareholders, not potential investors (because the latter would include a class of persons of indeterminate size).

In light of *Banca Nazionale* above, another way of interpreting this would be to say that no duty was owed because the defendant had not assumed responsibility to the particular claimant for the purpose for which the claimant chose to use the information. In Caparo's capacity as shareholder of Fidelity, the information could be reasonably relied upon, but in its capacity as potential investor, it could not.

2.10.3 Extension of the principle to incorporate not just negligent advice but the negligent provision of services

For discussion as to how this principle, in relation to negligent advice, has been extended to negligent provision of services, for example as to the drafting of wills and references, see the House of Lords cases of *White v Jones* [1995] UKHL 5 on wills, and *Spring v Guardian Assurance Plc* [1995] 2 AC 296 on references. In *White*, a claim was brought in Negligence by would-be beneficiaries against a solicitor, the issue being that the solicitor had failed correctly to amend the will before the testator's death, and as a consequence the claimants had not benefitted under the will as they should have done. (This was pure economic loss.) The claim succeeded and a duty imposed in respect of the negligent misstatement.

In *Spring*, the House of Lords found that the employer had been negligent in providing a reference which relied upon unproven allegations, not properly investigated. An employer owes a duty to provide a fair and accurate reference so far as is reasonable. This principle was applied in *McKie v Swindon College* [2011] EWHC 469 (QB), though this concerned not a reference as such, but an inflammatory and inaccurate email.

2.11 Further reading

Psychiatric harm

R Mulheron, 'The "Primary Victim" in Psychiatric Illness Claims: Reworking the "Patchwork Quilt"' (2008) 19 Kings LJ 81.

S Bailey and D Nolan, 'The *Page v Smith* Saga: A Tale of Inauspicious Origins and Unintended Consequences' [2010] CLJ 495.

Pure economic loss

T Foxton, 'Second Degree *Byrne*' [2019] 78(1) CLJ 18–21.

A Duncan, 'Discharge of standard security – unrepresented creditor – duty of care owed by borrower's solicitor' (2018) 156 Prop LB 8.

- Psychiatric harm is a type of loss in Negligence claims giving rise to particular policy concerns for the court relating to duty.
- The court will categorise claimants as primary or secondary victims, and a duty is rarely imposed in relation to secondary victims, unless all the criteria in *Alcock* are satisfied.
- Pure economic loss is a type of loss in Negligence claims for which a duty of care will not normally be imposed.
- The main exception to this rule concerns pure economic loss caused via negligent misstatements and the key case is *Hedley Byrne v Heller*. Where the claimant can show that its circumstances fit those described in *Hedley*, a duty may be imposed.

Have a go at these multiple choice questions (MCQs):

Question 1

A girl is at the fairground with her friend. The girl has a go on a ride while her friend watches. During the ride, something goes wrong and the girl is stuck on it for almost an hour. A piece of machinery comes loose, falls to the ground and just misses the girl's face. The girl is unharmed but afterwards suffers from a form of post-traumatic stress.

Which one of the following options best outlines the category of claimant that the girl will fit for the purpose of a claim in Negligence for her psychiatric harm?

A   She will probably be categorised as a primary victim and therefore will be owed a duty of care.

B   She will probably be categorised as a primary victim and therefore will not be owed a duty of care.

C   She could be categorised as either a primary or secondary victim.

D   She will probably be categorised as a secondary victim and therefore will be owed a duty of care.

E   She will probably be categorised as a secondary victim and therefore will not be owed a duty of care.

Answer

The correct answer is option A. The girl was in the zone of danger though she escaped physical harm. On the face it if she would be owed a duty of care on this basis.

Question 2

A man is in a stadium at a music gig. His sister is on the other side of the stadium when a piece of the stadium rigging falls. It kills some spectators and injures others. The man believes his sister may have been killed or seriously injured and suffers clinical depression as a result

Which one of the following best outlines the likely approach the court will apply when determining the question of duty, based on *Alcock v Chief Constable of South Yorkshire?*

A   The man would be a primary victim and so would not be owed a duty of care.

B   The man would be a secondary victim and would not be owed a duty because he was on a different side of the stadium from his sister.

C   The man would be a secondary victim and would need to rebut the presumption that he does not have a close tie of love and affection with his sister.

D   The man would be a secondary victim and the presumption would be that he has a close tie of love and affection with his sister.

E   The man would be a primary victim and so would be owed a duty of care.

Answer

Option C is correct as for siblings there is a rebuttable presumption against the requisite 'close tie' arising.

Question 3

A man finds a document in the street that seems to be an extract from a report on the financial standing of a company called Invest Ltd. On the basis of that extract, the man decides to buy shares in the company. Shortly afterwards, Invest Ltd loses all its money and folds. The man loses money as a result.

Which one of the following best describes whether and why the man would be owed a duty of care in respect of his pure economic loss?

A   No duty would be imposed applying *Hedley Byrne v Heller* because there is generally no duty imposed for pure economic loss.

B   A duty would be imposed applying *Hedley Byrne v Heller* because there is generally always a duty imposed for pure economic loss.

C   No duty would be imposed applying *Hedley Byrne v Heller* because there is no assumption of responsibility on the part of the defendant towards the claimant, and this is analogous in some ways with *Caparo v Dickman*.

D   A duty would be imposed applying *Hedley Byrne v Heller* because there is no assumption of responsibility on the part of the defendant towards the claimant, and this is analogous in some ways with *Caparo v Dickman*.

E   A duty would be imposed applying *Hedley Byrne v Heller* because there is an assumption of responsibility on the part of the defendant towards the claimant.

Answer

The correct answer is option C. This is in some ways analogous to *Caparo v Dickman* in which no duty was owed. The report was not intended for the man, nor is there evidence that it was intended for the purpose for which the man uses it. No responsibility is assumed by the writer of the report to the man.

Question 4

A woman has applied for a job and asks her current employer for a reference. The employer provides this, stating in it that the woman would not be suitable for the job because she was once subject to an investigation and cannot be trusted. In fact, the investigation was concluded many years ago, and the woman completely exonerated. The woman is not offered the job and struggles to find work at all as a result of the reference.

Which one of the following is accurate as to whether the employer owes the woman a duty of care in relation to her pure economic loss?

A   No, the employer does not owe a duty of care because the woman's only loss is pure economic loss.

B   Yes, the employer owes a duty of care to write a fair and accurate reference so far as is reasonable.

C   Yes, the employer owes a duty of care to write a positive reference.

D   No, the employer does not owe a duty of care because it is correct that the woman was once the subject of an investigation.

E   Yes, the employer owes a duty of care but that duty extends to the potential new employer, not to the woman.

Answer

Option B is the correct answer applying *Spring v Guardian Assurance*.

3   General Negligence – Breach

After reading this chapter, you will be able to understand:
- what is meant by the term 'breach of duty'
- where in the Negligence sequence breach fits
- that there are two stages to breach: (1) setting the standard, and (2) assessing whether that standard has been breached
- how the law is used to determine whether there has been a breach of duty.

3.1   Introduction

So far, we have analysed the first two elements in the Negligence sequence, namely loss or damage and duty. The next element to consider is breach, which is the point where the court looks to see whether the defendant has fallen below the standard expected of them, in other words whether they have breached that standard. This element is very important – many cases turn on it. You might think of breach as meaning 'what went wrong and why'.

As we'll see, this is in fact a two-stage test. First, we set the standard expected of the defendant, and we do that by reference to the law. This is the part where we are effectively suggesting how the defendant ought to have conducted themselves. Next, we try to decide whether the defendant has fallen below that standard, and we say that that is a question of fact rather than law, because the court will look at the factual circumstances of the case to help it determine whether there has actually been a breach or not. This is the part where we ask what actually happened.

In this chapter, we'll work through both stages and look at plenty of examples.

3.2   The Negligence sequence – breach

A reminder that we have reached this stage:

> **Loss/Damage – Duty – Breach** – Causation – Remoteness – Defences – Remedies

Figure 3.1   The Negligence sequence

If the claimant can prove that the defendant has breached the duty of care, we then move on to causation, which we'll look at in **Chapter 4**.

3.3 Setting the standard – the so-called 'reasonable person'

When we are setting the standard expected of the defendant, it's important to note that the law does not expect perfection from an individual, but reasonable competency. Remember that the most overused word in tort is 'reasonable'. It's everywhere. Think about *Donoghue v Stevenson* by way of example. Lord Atkin said: 'You must take *reasonable* care to avoid acts or omissions which you can *reasonably foresee* would be likely to injure your neighbour.' So how do we measure what is reasonable?

This is done by asking what the hypothetical reasonable person would have done in the circumstances or, for omissions, would *not* have done.

So who is the hypothetical reasonable person? Case law tells us that the reasonable person is:

*   'the man on the Clapham Omnibus' (Greer LJ, *Hall v Brooklands Auto-Racing Club* [1933] 1 KB 205);
*   the 'anthropomorphic conception of justice' (Lord Radcliffe, *Davis Contractors v Fareham Urban District Council* [1956] AC 696);
*   a 'traveller on the London Underground' (Lord Steyn, *McFarlane v Tayside Health Board* [2000] 2 AC 59); but
*   not a 'paragon of circumspection' (Lord Reid, *AC Billings & Sons Ltd v Riden* [1958] AC 240).

The above tells us very little about the so-called reasonable person, beyond their fondness for public transport and the idea that they might not be a bundle of laughs on a date. And that's because, obviously, we're not talking about a real person here but a legal construct – the personification of reasonableness, and a marker against whom to measure the acts or omissions of our defendant.

3.3.1 An objective standard

It's important to note that the standard of care to be imposed on a defendant is (almost always) objective. The question is: 'Did the defendant meet the standard of the reasonably competent ... [and then we insert the task or activity or role being attempted by the defendant]?' So, for example, 'Did the defendant meet the standard of the reasonably competent driver/surgeon/DIY enthusiast/employer on a construction site?'

Ordinarily, there is no room for subjectivity. The standard attaches to the task and not the individual, or to 'the act and not the actor', to use the wording from *Wilsher v Essex Area Health Authority* [1988] 1 AC 1074, a case we'll return to in our chapter on Clinical Negligence (**Chapter 7**). It is not who the defendant is that determines the standard; it is what they are doing. Similarly, the standard doesn't change according to the defendant's experience or inexperience: it is all about meeting the standard required of the task.

example

Grayson is a learner driver having a driving lesson. During this lesson, he brakes too late whilst pulling up to a junction and shunts the car in front, being driven by Freya. Freya wants to sue Grayson in Negligence for the property damage to her car, but he claims that, as a learner driver, he is not expected to meet the standard of a more experienced driver and so hasn't breached his duty of care to her.

This is reminiscent of a well-known case called *Nettleship v Weston* [1971] 2 QB 691, in which a learner driver had a minor crash during a lesson being given by her friend, Nettleship, causing him to fracture his knee. In that case, the Court of Appeal made the point that the standard of care was objective and attached to the task of driving, regardless of whether the defendant had been driving for 10 minutes or 10 years. In that case it was said, 'The standard of care ... is measured objectively by the care to be expected of a ... careful driver.' Applying that here, Grayson will judged by the standard of the reasonably competent driver (not the reasonably competent learner driver), and he will almost certainly be held to have breached that standard.

This works the other way round, too. Had Grayson been a very experienced driver, for example, he would not have been judged by a higher standard than that of the reasonably competent driver.

Note also that Freya has suffered recognisable loss (property damage) and was owed a duty of care by Grayson (applying *Nettleship* or *Fitzgerald v Lane & Patel* [1989] 1 AC 328). These are of course the first two elements of a Negligence action. Note also that, in *Nettleship* itself, the claimant's damages were reduced by 50% to take into account his own contributory negligence. We explore the defence of contributory negligence in **Chapter 6**.

The outcome in *Nettleship* may feel harsh, but the rationale is sound. There are policy and other reasons why there shouldn't be a sliding scale of competence as regards setting the standard. Drivers must have insurance to drive, so it makes sense that they should be financially liable when they have insurance in place to deal with the very situation that has arisen. Also, who would police a sliding scale, and what would it look like? Would there be a different standard expected of someone who had been driving for three weeks, three months or three years?

Another example of this objective standard being applied comes from *Wilsher v Essex Area Health Authority* (see above). The junior defendant doctor was held not to the standard of a junior doctor, but to the standard of the task they were carrying out at the time. The law took no account of their inexperience.

3.3.2 Is the objective standard ever lowered, ie subjective?

There *are* occasions where the standard imposed on the defendant is altered, though this doesn't happen often.

Mansfield v Weetabix Ltd [1998] EWCA Civ 1352

case
example

In this case, the Court of Appeal found that the defendant lorry driver was not liable in Negligence when he accidentally crashed his lorry into the claimant's shop whilst driving. Unknown to the defendant, he was suffering from a medical condition called malignant insulinoma, which gradually starved his brain of glucose. As the defendant drove a distance of about 40 miles, he had three episodes, the last of which culminated in his crashing into the defendant's property. Importantly, he had not been aware of his condition at all during this period. For that reason, the court said he had not breached the duty of care he owed to the shopkeeper. The interesting part for our purposes is that the standard applied here was modified a little, to the standard of the pithily titled 'reasonably competent driver, unaware that he is, or may be, suffering from a condition that impairs his ability to drive'.

We can contrast this with a situation where the defendant driver is, or ought to be, aware of their condition. Where this is the position, the court is less likely to be sympathetic, and more likely to impose the usual standard on the driver, and to find that they have breached that standard.

Roberts v Ramsbottom [1980] 1 WLR 823

case
example

The defendant knowingly suffered a stroke before starting to drive but felt that he was able to drive. As he did so, he began to feel much worse, and he collided with a stationary van, knocked a cyclist from his bike, and ran into the claimant's car, causing injury to the claimant and property damage.

It was held that the defendant, knowing that his ability to drive was impaired, should not have done so. This was different from the position in *Mansfield* where the driver was genuinely unaware of his condition. As such, the court imposed on the defendant the standard of the reasonably competent driver and found that he had breached that.

So, where the defendant suffers from an illness about which they are unaware, the court may modify the standard of care. The other situation where this might happen is when the defendant is a child.

Orchard v Lee [2009] EWCA Civ 295

case
example

Two 13-year-old boys were playing a game of tag in their play area at school. One of them, the defendant, was running backwards, but accidentally ran into the claimant, a lunchtime supervisor at the school, with his head hitting her cheek. The claimant supervisor claimed in Negligence, arguing that the boy had breached his duty of care towards her. However, the trial judge dismissed her claim (and the Court of Appeal agreed), finding the incident to be just horseplay between boys who didn't know any better.

The Court of Appeal, in agreeing, said that that a child would only be liable in Negligence if their conduct was careless to a very high degree or fell significantly outside the norm for a child of their age. The standard imposed was therefore that of a reasonably competent 13-year-old, the standard 'objectively expected of a child of that age'. There was no breach of that standard.

3.3.3 The standard for professionals acting in their professional capacity

Remember that a standard is not imposed on a defendant by virtue of who they are, but of what they do. So, for example, a professional chef, if she causes an accident through her Negligence on the way home from work, would be judged by the standard of the reasonably competent driver, not that of the reasonably competent chef.

example

A surgeon, Stella, is at home with her family. She does some sewing for a friend, Carmen, but accidentally leaves the needle in the garment which injures the friend. Carmen wishes to sue Stella in Negligence and tells her, 'You're a surgeon. I would have expected your sewing to be done very carefully!'

Aside from the question mark over whether a court would impose a duty of care on Stella in this situation, even if it did, the standard imposed would not be that of a reasonably competent surgeon, because, even though she was sewing, Stella was not working in her professional capacity as a surgeon at the time. The appropriate standard would be that of a 'home-sewer' (for example, there's no evidence that she is a professional tailor or seamstress).

Where professionals are acting in their professional capacity, they will be judged by the standard of the reasonably competent professional carrying out that particular task. This standard is simply the objective standard in a professional context and comes from an important case we'll look at next.

Bolam v Friern Hospital Management Committee [1957] 1 WLR 583

case example

The claimant was a patient who was given electro-convulsive therapy without a relaxant drug and without the appropriate physical restraints. During his treatment, he fractured his hip, and this may have been caused by the lack of restraint. He had not been warned of this as a possibility. At the time, there were two schools of thought in the medical profession regarding the need to offer relaxant drugs and to restrain, and about the requirement to warn patients about the risk of injury.

We will consider this case again when we look at whether there has, in fact, been a breach (see below at **3.4**) and also again in the context of Clinical Negligence in **Chapter 7**. For now, it assists us in that it gives us the wording that should be used as we set the standard for professionals acting in their professional capacity. The professional defendant should reach the standard of the reasonably competent professional: 'the ordinary skill of an ordinary competent man exercising that particular art' (McNair J). This standard applies to all professionals, not just clinicians.

3.4 Establishing breach – question of fact

Once we are clear on the standard expected of the defendant, we then move on to discuss whether that standard has been breached. As mentioned, that is usually a question of asking what went wrong and why. The court will look at the facts of the case. For example, a driver held to the standard of a reasonably competent driver, and who then skids on the road and crashes, may or may not have breached their duty of care. Why did they skid? If it was because they were careless, or going too fast, or because they conducted themselves in some other way that the reasonable driver would not have done, then fairly obviously that would be a breach. But if they skidded because there was a patch of black ice on the road, in circumstances where the driver didn't know and wouldn't have been expected to know that the black ice was there, then it may be that the court will decide that there was *no* breach, on the basis that no reasonably competent driver could have avoided the ice.

The court may take into account any relevant factors that arise from the facts. Having said that, there are some recurring factors that often arise, and it's worth having these in our minds as we work through this section.

3.5 Factors the court may take into account in determining whether there has been a breach

3.5.1 Likelihood of harm

It stands to reason that the more likely someone is to be injured, the more likely that there will be a breach. The thinking here is: the defendant knew or ought to have known that the likelihood of harm was high – so why did they not prevent against it? The reasonable defendant carrying out X activity would have been expected to. On the flip side, a defendant does not have to guard against harm where it is highly unlikely to occur.

case example

Bolton v Stone [1951] AC 850
The claimant, Miss Stone, suffered a head injury outside her house when a cricket ball was hit out of the cricket ground. The defendant club argued that it hadn't breached its duty of care (as a reasonably competent cricket club) because the likelihood of harm was so small. Evidence showed that a ball had left the ground only six times in the last 30 years, and that the club had already erected a 17-foot-high fence around it.

The House of Lords agreed – there was no breach here. (It probably helped the defendant that Lord Denning was one of the judges, a passionate cricket enthusiast!)

3.5.2 Potential seriousness of injury

This factor is less to do with how likely the harm is to happen, and more to do with the potential seriousness of any harm if it does. Where an activity brings with it the potential for serious harm, the defendant will be in breach if they do not reasonably protect against that harm occurring.

Paris v Stepney Borough Council [1951] AC 367

In this case, the claimant employee, a welder, was already blind in one eye before beginning work for the defendant, a fact about which the defendant knew. Despite this, the claimant was not provided with protective goggles and he became completely blind when a piece of metal flew into his sighted eye. The House of Lords found that the defendant Borough Council had breached its duty to the claimant (to act as a reasonably competent employer) because the potential for serious injury here was so great.

Watson v British Boxing Board of Control Ltd [2001] QB 1134

The boxer, Michael Watson, was seriously injured in a boxing match against Chris Eubank governed by the rules of the defendant Boxing Board (the sole controlling body regulating professional boxing). Although ringside medical facilities were available, they did not provide immediate resuscitation, and by the time Watson was resuscitated in hospital he had sustained permanent brain damage.

The Court of Appeal concluded that the defendant had breached its duty, especially given that 'serious brain damage … represented the most serious risk posed by the sport and one that required to be addressed'.

Perry v Harris [2008] EWCA Civ 907

Here, the defendant was a parent who had hired a bouncy castle for her child's birthday party. Another child using it sustained severe and permanent injuries. The Court of Appeal held that there was no breach, stating:

> A reasonable parent could foresee that if children indulged in boisterous behaviour on a bouncy castle, there would be a risk that, sooner or later, one child might collide with another and cause that child some physical injury of a type that can be an incident in some contact sports. We do not consider that it was reasonably foreseeable that such injury would be likely to be serious, let alone as severe as the injury sustained by the claimant. (Lord Phillips CJ)

3.5.3   Common practice

If a defendant can show they have acted in accordance with a practice followed by others in the field then they may escape liability, in that the claimant may not be able to prove a breach. This is most often deployed as an argument by defendants in a clinical context (part of the *Bolam* argument (see **3.3.3**), and we'll return to this in **Chapter 7** as there are many examples) but is also used in non-clinical contexts.

However, it is open to the court to find the usual or common practice being relied upon to be unsafe. In a clinical context, this is provided for by *Bolitho v City and Hackney Health Authority* [1998] AC 232, although as we'll see in **Chapter 7**, in this case the court did not in the end find a breach. For a non-clinical example, *Re Herald of Free Enterprise* (1987) *The Independent*, 18 December concerned a roll-on, roll-off ferry disaster. It was standard practice at the time for car ferries to sail with their bow doors open and that is what the Herald of Free Enterprise did. The ferry filled with water and started to sink, and many people were killed and injured. The defendant ferry company tried to argue that it had not breached its duty of care because it was simply following the practice of others in the field, but the court found this practice to be illogical and unsafe. The defendant had breached its duty.

3.5.4 The practicality of taking precautions

The court will take into account how easy it would have been for the defendant to protect against the harm. Would it have been prohibitively expensive to do so? Would it have taken resources the defendant did not have? The defendant need only act reasonably to prevent harm to the claimant – the court is not looking for unattainable perfection.

case example

Latimer v AEC Ltd [1953] AC 643

The defendant owned a factory and the floor became slippery after a flood. To prevent against injury to employees, the defendant had already put down three tonnes of sawdust, and yet the claimant slipped and fell, and then sought to claim against the defendant for its breach.

   The Court found that there was no breach here. The defendant could reasonably have done no more, short of ceasing factory operations altogether, or employing more people to mop up the water. Neither of these options was feasible given the resources of the defendant (and the likelihood of harm being low). There was no breach.

Bottomley v Secretary and Members of Todmorden Cricket Club (2003) The Times, 13 November

In this case, the defendant cricket club held a fireworks display on its ground. Unfortunately, the claimant was injured by a firework and sued the defendant club. The club was found to be in breach because, having engaged an independent contractor to present the fireworks display, it had not taken reasonable precautions in ensuring that the independent contractor had public liability insurance and safety plans. This, the court said, would have been an easy step for the defendant to take.

3.5.5 Foresight not hindsight

It should be noted that the defendant's conduct is assessed by the standards that existed at the time of the alleged breach (and not by present day standards, if these have moved on by the time of trial).

case example

Roe v Minister of Health [1954] 2 All ER 131

In this case, the claimants were paralysed after being injected with contaminated spinal anaesthetic during a routine operation. The anaesthetic (nupercaine) had been stored in sealed glass ampoules placed in a solution of phenol ready for use. Unknown to the hospital, the phenol had seeped into the ampoules through minuscule cracks, causing the paralysis.

   It was held by the Court of Appeal that there was no breach here. Whilst it was clear in hindsight that the hospital was at fault, at the time of the operation, it was not known that it could be dangerous to store glass ampules in phenol solution. Evidence suggested that neither the anaesthetist nor any of the hospital staff were aware of the potential harm. Lord Denning made the point, 'We must not look at the 1947 accident with 1954 spectacles.' This is because the accident occurred in 1947, and more was known about the dangers by the time of the trial in 1954.

3.5.6 Social utility/value of the activity

Where the defendant's activity has some utility or value, for example an act carried out by the emergency services, then that may be less likely to result in a breach. For example, the driver of a speeding ambulance that injures a pedestrian may not have breached their duty, whereas a motorist driving over the speed limit in a non-emergency situation definitely will have done. (Much is fact specific here, and there is no special exemption for the emergency services *per se*.)

Watt v Hertfordshire County Council [1954] 1 WLR 835

In this case, a claimant fireman was injured in a lorry on his way to an emergency call. The equipment needed to tackle the incident was on board the lorry but had not been properly secured in transit (the lorry was not designed to carry such gear in an emergency). As a result, the fireman was injured when the equipment fell on him.

The Court of Appeal rejected the claimant's claim and held that there had been no breach of duty, because the public benefit/social utility argument outweighed the risk to an individual travelling in the vehicle. Lord Denning said: 'You must balance the risk against the end to be achieved ... The saving of life or limb justifies taking considerable risk.'

Ward v London County Council [1938] 2 All ER 341

By way of contrast, here, the defendant fire brigade was held to have breached its duty when a fire engine jumped a red light on its way to an incident. It was decided that, despite the emergency context, this did not allow emergency services carte blanche to drive recklessly: the risk of injury to claimants was too high and outweighed the utility argument.

Scout Association v Barnes [2010] EWCA Civ 1476

In this case, the social utility argument was again considered, though not in an emergency context. The claimant scout, aged 13, was injured while playing a game called 'objects in the dark'. This was a little like musical chairs to the extent that a number of wooden blocks were piled in the middle of the scout hall (one less than the number of boys), and once the lights went out, the boys had to dash to the middle and try to grab a block. The boy who failed to find a block would be eliminated, and this would continue until there was one winner. The claimant accidentally ran into a wooden bench whilst playing and badly injured his shoulder. He also sustained concussion.

The Court of Appeal, by a majority, upheld the trial judge's decision that the defendant scout association had breached its duty to the claimant. As Smith LJ said: 'The darkness did not add any other social or educative value but it did significantly increase the risk of injury.'

3.5.7 Balancing the factors

The above are just some of the factors that might arise in any given case. It's not an exhaustive list. What we do know, as summed up neatly by Lord Hoffman in *Tomlinson v Congleton Borough Council* [2004] 1 AC 46 (and we look at this case also in the context of Occupiers' Liability in **Chapter 10**), is that the courts are engaged in a balancing act at this stage in the Negligence sequence. What must be assessed, he said, is '... the likelihood that someone may be injured and the seriousness of the injury which may occur, but also the social value of the activity which gives rise to the risk and the cost of preventative measures. These factors have to be balanced against each other.'

Figure 3.2   The two stages of breach

3.6   *Res ipsa loquitur*

This is a doctrine or maxim, meaning 'the thing speaks for itself', that can be invoked by the claimant at the breach stage of a Negligence claim. Legal academics disagree on its precise status and even impact, but essentially it is raised where the only plausible explanation for the claimant's damage is that the defendant must have been negligent. The doctrine, which is rarely invoked, allows claimants to short-circuit the need to adduce evidence of breach. It's been applied, in a personal injury setting, to a range of Monty Python-esque sounding scenarios, from objects falling from the sky, to collapsing cranes, to stones in buns.

This doctrine first arose in *Scott v London and St Katherine Docks & Co* (1865) 3 H & C 596, in which the claimant was injured when a large sack of sugar fell onto her. She could not explain how this had occurred. But clearly the sacks of sugar were, or should have been, in the defendant's control, and the court was prepared to infer, from what little information it had, that the defendant must have been negligent, because sacks of sugar don't simply fall from the sky by themselves.

The accident must be of a kind that would not have happened without negligence. Another example of this doctrine being applied successfully was *Mahon v Osborne* [1939] 1 All ER 535 in which the claimant was successful in Negligence in a case where surgical swabs had been left inside her after surgery. The procedure was or should have been in the control of the defendant and the swabs couldn't have got there by themselves.

The doctrine was brought to life by Denning LJ's explanation of it in *Cassidy v Ministry of Health* [1951] 2 KB 343 and its application to clinical negligence: 'I went into hospital to be cured of two stiff fingers. I have come out with four stiff fingers and my hand is useless. That should not happen if due care had been used. Explain if you can.'

The question for the court to consider is whether the evidence taken as a whole points towards the defendant's negligence. This means that even where a defendant is unable to explain how an accident occurred but can show that they exercised all reasonable care in the circumstances, then the claim against them will fail (see *J v North Lincolnshire County Council* [2000] LGR 269).

It should be said that, post-*Bolam*, the use of *res ipsa loquitur*, certainly in a clinical setting, has faded. Stuart-Smith LJ stated that he was doubtful whether *res ipsa loquitur* would be of assistance in medical negligence cases, where unexpected results often occur in the absence of negligence.

However, every so often, it would seem, it is successfully pleaded. For example, in *Glass v Cambridge Health Authority* [1995] 6 Med LR 91, a fit and healthy 35-year-old patient underwent an exploratory laparotomy, during which the oximeter alarm went off. It was taken to be a false alarm and turned off. However, later the patient went into cardiac arrest during surgery and suffered brain damage as a result. The Court of Appeal held that the maxim applied, and that the defendant had not discharged the reversed burden.

3.7 Further reading

D Nolan, 'Varying the Standard of Care in Negligence' [2013] CLJ 651.
A Beever, 'Negligence and Utility' (2017) 17 Oxford University Commonwealth LJ 85.

* Breach is made up of two stages.
* We first of all set the standard expected of the defendant objectively and by reference to the task or activity the defendant is undertaking.
* The second stage is to look at the facts to establish breach. This is where we ask the question what went wrong and, importantly, why.
* Occasionally claimants may be able to use the doctrine of *res ipsa loquitur*, which means the thing speaks for itself, rather than having to prove breach, but only where there has been negligence on the defendant's part but the facts are unascertainable.

Have a go at these multiple choice questions (MCQs):

Question 1

A man is hit by a golf ball that has been hit out of the golf course. Golf balls frequently escape the golf course and passers-by are often injured. The golf club is aware of this but has taken no precautions to guard against the risk, even though it would be relatively easy for it to do so.

Which one of the following options best describes whether the golf club will have breached its duty of care to the man?

A   No, the club won't have breached its duty because of the social benefit of golf for many people.

B   Yes, the club is likely to have breached its duty, because the likelihood of harm was high and it would have been easy for it to take appropriate measures.

C   No, the club is not likely to have breached its duty, because the likelihood of harm was high and it would have been easy for it to take appropriate measures.

D   Yes, the club is likely to have breached its duty because it should have taken every measure possible to prevent golf balls escaping.
E   No, the club is not likely to have breached its duty because the man should not have walked close to a golf course.

Answer

The correct answer is option B. The club did not do what a reasonable golf club would have done, given that likelihood of harm was high and it was easy to take precautions.

Question 2

On his way home from work, a vet comes across a woman who is unconscious in the street. He attempts to move her to safety and do some basic first aid but in doing so dislocates her wrist.

Which one of the following is most likely to be correct as to the standard of care that would be imposed on the vet if a Negligence action were brought against him?

A   The standard of the reasonably competent first-aider.
B   The standard of the reasonably competent vet.
C   The standard of the reasonably competent professional carrying out that particular art.
D   The standard of the reasonably competent doctor.
E   The standard of the reasonably competent surgeon.

Answer

The correct answer is option A. The standard attaches to the task, not the person carrying it out, and as the vet attempted what appears to be first-aid, he would be held to this standard.

Question 3

A boy of 11 is having a play fight with another child of the same age. The boy accidently throws a pen towards the other child's eye and causes an eye injury.

Which one of the following is most likely to be correct as to the standard of care that would be imposed on the boy if a Negligence action were brought against him?

A   The standard of the reasonably competent friend.
B   The standard of the reasonably competent child.
C   The standard of the reasonably competent play fighter.
D   The standard of the reasonably competent man.
E   The standard of the reasonably competent 11-year-old child.

Answer

The correct answer is option E. This is an occasion where the court is likely to modify the objective standard of care to take into account the boy's age.

Question 4

A cafe owner spills a small vat of oil on the floor of his café. He only has one other member of staff, and so asks her to mop up the oil as best she can. Meanwhile, he tries to cordon off the area and makes a sign to warn customers of the slippery floor. Despite all this, a customer slips in the oil and breaks her ankle.

Which one of the following options best describes whether the café owner will have breached his duty of care to the customer?

A   Probably not, as she should not have been in the café if there was oil on the floor.

B   Probably not, as there is a benefit to the public in keeping the café open.

C   Probably not, as he did all that he reasonably could with the resources he had.

D   Probably, as he should have closed the café.

E   Probably, as he should have employed more staff to clear up the oil.

Answer

The correct answer is option C. This feels analogous to *Latimer v AEC* in which there was no breach as the factory had done all it reasonably could to keep staff safe – it goes to the practicality of taking precautions.

General Negligence – Causation

 study points

After reading this chapter, you will be able to understand:

- what is meant by the term causation and where it fits within the Negligence sequence
- the difference between factual and legal causation
- the general rule for establishing factual causation and the alternatives to that rule
- the three types of act that can break the chain of causation at the legal causation stage.

4.1 Introduction

The claimant has established that they have suffered recognisable loss, that they are owed a duty of care by the defendant in respect of that loss, and that the defendant has breached that duty. But there's still more work to do. The next step is for the claimant to prove that the breach *caused* their loss (factual causation). In addition, even where factual causation is established, the courts will look to see whether an intervening act, which happened after the initial breach, has broken or affected the 'chain of causation' in some way. Should the defendant be liable for all of the claimant's loss, some of it or none of it? These are the questions we will consider in this chapter.

It should be noted that causation (especially factual causation) can appear complicated and inconsistent sometimes. Even the judges agree that it is probably the most complicated element of Negligence, and it can be problematic, especially in the context of Clinical Negligence (as we'll see in **Chapter 7**) where often it is very difficult to prove, even on the balance of probabilities, that the defendant's breach caused the claimant's loss. A sensible way through is to bear in mind that the rules relating to causation are really more like tools than rules. This is a highly pragmatic area, and one where, as lawyers, it's about picking up a causation tool, seeing whether it works, and if not, asking why not and trying another. You might find it helpful to re-read this paragraph after you've worked through this chapter. See whether this suggested approach reflects what you see has happened within the law.

Role of policy within causation

Policy considerations undoubtedly steer much of the reasoning that underpins causation. The other area where you perhaps see this as blatantly is at the remoteness stage (see **Chapter 5**). For example, as you'll see when we consider legal causation, only those acts which are considered unreasonable will break the chain of causation. Questions as to what constitutes reasonable and unreasonable are always going to be policy-infused. See if you spot any evidence of that when you reach the discussion in this chapter at **4.5.1** and **4.5.2**.

4.2 The Negligence sequence – causation

Let's check where we have got to in the Negligence sequence:

Loss/Damage – Duty – Breach – Causation – Remoteness – Defences – Remedies

Figure 4.1   The Negligence sequence

Hopefully you can see that by building in a new element each time, you are able to consolidate everything up to and including the new element each time. So, we don't look at, say, causation in isolation; we look at damage, then duty, then breach, then causation, and you are able to revise each part again before arriving at the next element.

Causation is looked at in two parts: factual and legal, and in that order. So let's begin with factual causation.

4.3 Factual causation – the 'but for' test

The place to start with factual causation is always the 'but for' test. The claimant must prove that but for (had it not been for) the defendant's breach, the loss to the claimant would not have happened at that time and in that way.

A note on this: we don't know whether a defendant has been negligent or not until we have been through the entire Negligence sequence. Yet, often, the but for test is wrongly stated as 'but for the defendant's *negligence*', when it should be 'but for the defendant's *breach*'. The latter is surely the correct approach. (If the former were correct, then we have already established Negligence, so why are we seeking to go behind it?) Do look out for this error in cases and commentaries, as it arises frequently.

Let's give you an example of the but for test here.

Barnett v Chelsea and Kensington Hospital **[1969] 1 QB 428**

The claimant presented himself at the defendant hospital's accident and emergency department complaining of stomach pains. The triage nurse saw the claimant and telephoned through to the doctor on duty, who was in a different room at the time (feeling unwell). The doctor did not examine the claimant but advised the nurse to tell the claimant to go home and rest, and to return in the morning if he still felt unwell. A few hours later, the claimant died, and the evidence showed that he had died from arsenic poisoning. This was so far advanced that, even if the doctor had examined the claimant, there would have been nothing that could have been done to prevent the death.

The claim failed at the factual causation stage, because, whilst the doctor owed a duty of care to the claimant, and had breached that duty by failing to examine, that breach did not cause the damage. The death would have happened anyway. The questions was: *but for the doctor's breach, would the claimant have suffered their loss, at that time and in that way?* The answer was yes (on the balance of probabilities) and so the claim failed.

This is by no means a failsafe test, and one could write a whole book looking at what causation really means, and whether it can and should be attributed to a breach by the defendant, but we don't have the space for that kind of discussion, so let's work with what we have. The but for test works well where there is a single cause of the damage, and/or one breach. There are more examples of it in case law than would be possible to show here, and of claims failing and succeeding at this stage. A more recent example of the but for test being applied, as it was in *Barnett*, its effect being to end the claim, can be seen in *Nyang v G4S Care & Justice Services Ltd and Others* [2013] EWHC 3946 (QB). Here, the clamant, Mr Nyang, who was detained at an immigration removal centre pending deportation to Gambia, tried to commit suicide by running into a concrete wall. He broke his back and was rendered tetraplegic. The staff at the centre were found to have breached their duty to him, by their various acts and omissions, especially insofar as they had failed to identify his psychological condition. However, the judge, Lewis J, decided that but for the breaches of duty, the claimant would still have suffered the same harm, and so the claim failed.

example

Leonard is riding his motorbike but becomes distracted by thoughts about what he might have for dinner later. He carelessly runs over a pedestrian, Trudy, severely injuring her. She wishes to bring an action in Negligence.

This looks on the face of it looks like a straightforward claim. Trudy has suffered personal injury. Leonard owes her a duty of care. He looks to have breached that through his careless driving (and he has not met the standard of the reasonably competent motorcyclist). But for his breach, Trudy would not have been injured at that time and in that way, and so her claim so far looks strong.

4.3.1 Problems with the but for test

Whilst it should always be the starting point at the factual causation stage of a claim, the but for test sometimes runs into problems. The main problem is where there are *multiple potential causes of harm* (rather than just one), and a lack of scientific knowledge renders it impossible to determine whether the breach caused the loss or whether it would have happened anyway. This arises most often in complex medical situations and in, for example, road traffic accidents involving multiple vehicles.

There are exceptional approaches to factual causation which the courts will sometimes entertain, where the above circumstances arise, and we'll look at those now.

Multiple potential causes

Where there is more than one potential cause of the damage, it can be difficult to prove that any of the potential causes are more likely than not to be *the* cause. This could lead to an absurd situation where you potentially have two defendants, both of whom caused the death of the claimant (say, by shooting at the claimant at the same time) but neither of whom are held liable through application of the but for test.

In *Wilsher v Essex Area Health Authority* [1988] 1 AC 1074, there were multiple potential causes of the claimant baby's blindness. The baby, Martin Wilsher, was born prematurely and subsequently developed an incurable retinal condition called RLF, which left him permanently blind in one eye and almost blind in the other. This may have been caused by a breach on the part of the junior doctor who twice incorrectly administered oxygen. Or it could have been caused by any of the non-tortious factors that can come into play when a baby is born prematurely. In total, there were five possible causes of the claimant's damage here. The House of Lords, applying the but for test, found against the claimant. It was not persuaded that, but for the doctor's (obvious) breach, the loss would not have happened. The court did not seek to go behind the but for test, or to choose another test. The claim simply failed at the factual causation stage.

This does not always mean, however, that where there are multiple potential causes, the claim will always fail. Two cases that pre-date *Wilsher* each used a different approach to factual causation.

Material contribution to the harm

case example

Bonnington Castings Ltd v Wardlaw [1956] AC 613

In this case, a claimant employee working in a factory contracted a lung condition, called pneumoconiosis, from inhaling silica dust. He sued his employer in Negligence and the claim turned on the causation issue. Evidence showed that *some* dust existing in the air, and therefore some inhalation, was inevitable (this was termed the 'innocent' dust). However, the House of Lords found that there were higher levels of the dust in the air than there should have been, and this was caused by the defendant's breach in not providing adequate ventilation (the so-called 'guilty' dust). The difficult causation question was whether the guilty dust caused the claimant's damage.

The but for test didn't really fit here because, importantly, the medical evidence established that the lung disease was progressive, or cumulative. It was caused by the build-up of silica dust in the lungs. Put simply, the higher the levels of dust, the worse the disease. So it could not be established that but for the defendant's breach in failing to provide adequate ventilation, the defendant would not have suffered their harm. The House of Lords determined that in this specific case, due to the cumulative nature of the disease, they could bypass the standard but for test and use an exception. They said that provided the claimant could show that the defendant's breach made a *material contribution to the harm*, that would satisfy factual causation.

There have been many questions raised about why the House of Lords would seek to find and apply an exceptional test. Certainly, at the time, it was supposed that, for policy reasons, the courts wanted to protect employees at work and that, perhaps, this kind of exception to the but for test would not be used outside of an employer/employee context, but it has been.

Material contribution to the harm approach applied in other cases

This approach has been applied many times, most notably in medical contexts. In *Bailey v Ministry of Defence* [2008] EWCA Civ 883, the claimant suffered brain damage, caused by cardiac arrest. There were two potential causes of the cardiac arrest, however: (1) the natural progression of the claimant's condition (a non-tortious potential cause); and (2) the breach by the defendant hospital as regards its lack of care (tortious). The medical evidence was inconclusive as to whether, on the balance of probabilities, the breach by the hospital caused the cardiac arrest and subsequent brain damage (meaning the claim would ordinarily have failed at the but for stage). However, the evidence *did* conclude that the brain damage was caused by the cumulative effect of the breach *and* the natural progression of the claimant's condition. The Court of Appeal therefore applied the *Bonnington* exceptional approach to factual causation, with Waller LJ stating:

> In a case where medical science cannot establish the probability that 'but for' an act of negligence the injury would not have happened but can establish the contribution of the negligent cause was more than negligible, the 'but for' test is modified and the [claim] will succeed.

This has been applied in other medical negligence cases, for example the Privy Council case of *Williams v The Bermuda Hospitals Board* [2016] UKPC 4 (where the negligent diagnosis and subsequent delay in treatment were found to have materially contributed to the claimant's harm). See also the case of *John v Central Manchester and Manchester Children's University Hospitals NHS Trust Foundation Trust* [2016] EWHC 407 (QB) in which the claimant was able to prove that delay in treatment following his fall (and attributable to the breach by the defendant) materially contributed to his brain injury.

Material increase in risk of harm

McGhee v National Coal Board [1973] 1 WLR 1

Almost 20 years after *Bonnington* came another case, *McGhee v National Coal Board*. On the face of it, this looked similar to *Bonnington*, in that it concerned an employer/ employee situation and a claimant bringing a Negligence action against his employer in relation to working conditions. Once again, scientific evidence was unable to determine whether the so-called innocent or guilty dust was the cause of the claimant's condition. However, here the claimant sustained a serious form of dermatitis, caused by exposure to brick dust. The innocent brick dust was that which was occurring in the air at the brick kiln where the claimant worked. The guilty dust was that which was attributable to the defendant's breach in not providing adequate washing facilities. The effect of this was that the claimant had to cycle home and have a shower each day after work, and so he was exposed for longer than he ought to have been to the brick dust particles.

Unlike in *Bonnington*, the nature of this condition was different. It was recognised that dermatitis was not necessarily a cumulative condition, ie one that could be made worse by prolonged exposure, but could in fact be triggered by one single exposure. It was all or nothing – you had the condition or you didn't. Therefore, the guilty dust did not so much *contribute* to the harm itself but rather *increased the risk of the harm occurring*.

The House of Lords held that, as in *Bonnington*, a different exceptional approach should be used to determine factual causation. The claimant successfully satisfied factual causation by proving, on the balance of probabilities, that the defendant's breach had materially increased the risk of harm. Once again, the House of Lords, you might argue, worked backwards from the result they wished to achieve and manufactured a new exceptional test for factual causation to reach that end point. (It should be noted that the but for test was still in play here, to the extent that the claimant needed to prove that but for the defendant's breach, the material increase to the risk would not have occurred.)

Material increase in risk of harm applied in other cases

Again, for some time it was thought that perhaps this approach, too, would be confined to employers' liability claims, but it has been applied in other contexts. Most notably, it was applied in the following case concerning mesothelioma. One way to look at this and subsequent mesothelioma cases would be to consider them almost as a separate category in their own right. But as they also fit here, being an application of *McGhee*, let's analyse the key case now.

Fairchild v Glenhaven Funeral Services Ltd [2003] 1 AC 32

This case involved a group of claims made against multiple defendant employers by three employees, all of whom had developed mesothelioma (a fatal lung cancer) caused by exposure to asbestos. Only one claim ultimately got beyond a first instance trial and that was *Fairchild*.

In this case, it was clear (and not in dispute) that the employer had breached its duty of care in allowing the claimant to be exposed to asbestos. The problem was in determining which employer or employers should be liable, because the claimant had been exposed by a series of negligent employers. As in *McGhee*, the medical evidence showed that mesothelioma was an all-or-nothing case: it could be caused by a single strand of asbestos and in a single moment. The claimant could not show when the 'relevant' exposure occurred and so could not prove, on the balance of probabilities, which of the employers was the factual cause of the harm.

The Court of Appeal dismissed the claim on this basis – that the but for test failed and therefore the claim failed. However, the House of Lords held that the but for test produced an unjust result, in that potentially the claimant would be left without a remedy where it was clear that the employers had been negligent. To circumvent this, they applied *McGhee*, approving material increase in risk as an exception to the but for test for factual causation.

What about Wilsher?

Remember that *Wilsher* was reported in 1988, after both *Bonnington* and *McGhee*, and before *Fairchild*. The *McGhee* approach was actually raised but rejected in *Wilsher*. The precise reasons why are perhaps unclear, but an argument that policy played its part in *Wilsher* – this time to protect the profession (as opposed to it protecting the employee in *McGhee*) – is as good a reason as any.

And then in *Fairchild*, we have seen that the Court of Appeal applied the but for test from *Wilsher*, but the House of Lords rejected that, preferring *McGhee*! They chose not to overrule *Wilsher*, but distinguished it on its facts, stressing that *Fairchild* was an exception to the norm (and that, by implication, *Wilsher* represented the norm). The approach in *Fairchild*, which has since been applied in other mesothelioma cases, has become known as the '*Fairchild* exception', though it is in fact an application of *McGhee* in a specific context.

Interestingly, in terms of procedure – and perhaps what takes *Fairchild* away from the line of cases we have looked at and into a new mesothelioma category of its own – the court decided that each of the negligent employers was jointly and severally liable, meaning that it would fall to each employer who had been brought to court to seek financial contributions from those who had not, under statute (Civil Liability (Contribution) Act 1978, s 1(1)). This approach was departed from in *Barker v Corus Ltd* [2006] UKHL 20 for reasons we don't need to explore further here.

It should also be noted, in terms of evidence, that whilst no one has suggested that *Fairchild* was wrongly decided, the 'single fibre' theory has since been discredited by medical experts (see *Sienkiewicz v Greif (UK) Ltd* [2011] UKSC 10). The right approach here is to conclude that the harm is 'indivisible' and that the state of scientific knowledge renders further proof of causation impossible. So: right law and right approach in *Fairchild* but, in retrospect, wrong gloss in respect of the scientific reasons?

Other exceptions to the but for test – Chester v Afshar

Though not without its critics, there is another exceptional approach that was used in a case concerning failure to warn a claimant about risks associated with surgery. Our focus here is not so much on breach (whether the failure to warn was a breach – which it was) but on proving that a failure to warn was a cause of the harm sustained – a difficult mental leap to make.

Chester v Afshar [2005] 1 AC 134

The claimant developed a serious spinal condition following an operation on her spine that the defendant surgeon had advised her to have. (She had been reluctant.) The defendant had failed to warn her of the small risk of developing the spinal condition, and the claimant sued in Negligence, stating that, had she been aware of the risk, she would have sought advice on alternatives to surgery and the operation would not have taken place there and then, though it might have happened at some point in the future.

The majority in the House of Lords found that the claimant's claim failed at the but for stage. Due to the fact she may have had the operation at a later date, the defendant's failure to warn of the risks associated with it neither affected the risk nor was the cause of her injury. However, the Lords then went on to apply an exception to the factual causation rules. The defendant surgeon owed the claimant a duty to advise her of the disadvantages of the surgery, and this, they said, was closely connected with her ability to make an informed decision about whether to have the operation. Since the injury she sustained was within the scope of the defendant's duty to warn, then the failure to warn was both a breach of his duty and the cause of the claimant's loss. Lord Steyn said: 'Her right of autonomy and dignity can and ought to be vindicated by a narrow and modest departure from traditional causation principles.'

Some commentators regard this as simply a departure from the but for principles – an answer to the causation questions shoehorned into place, which doesn't really fit, to achieve a fair outcome on policy grounds. It *could* also be viewed as a slightly convoluted application of the but for test: but for the defendant's breach in failing to warn, the claimant would not have suffered her loss at that time and in that way because she would have chosen either not to have the operation at all, or to have had it on another day in the future, creating only a 1–2% chance of the risk materialising.

Chester has been applied in, for example, *Hassell v Hillingdon Hospitals NHS Foundation Trust* [2018] EWHC 164 (QB), though in *Duce v Worcestershire Acute Hospitals NHS Trust* [2018] EWCA Civ 1307 it was found that the claimant (who was left with nerve damage) could not establish that she would not have gone ahead with the operation, had she been warned of the risks. Her claim failed and the Court of Appeal did not accept her argument that *Chester* created a separate pathway for establishing causation in cases concerning consent.

There are other exceptions, but we have analysed the most important ones. The so-called 'loss of a chance' cases (where the claimant argued that the defendant's breach, if it had not caused the loss, had caused the claimant to lose the chance of recovery) seemed to provide an exception at one stage, with *Hotson v East Berkshire Health Authority* [1987] AC 750 and *Gregg v Scott* [2005] UKHL 2 both discussing but ultimately dismissing this way of circumventing or adapting the but for test. It seems that, for now at least, the loss of a chance argument is not one that holds up where the loss is personal injury, though the courts have allowed the principle to be argued in cases involving potential pure economic loss, such as *Allied Maples Group v Simmons & Simmons* [1995] 1 WLR 1602, and references (see *Spring v Guardian Assurance Plc* [1995] 2 AC 296 (discussed in the context of duty in **Chapter 2**)).

4.3.2 So how do we determine factual causation?

Go right back to the beginning of this chapter, and you'll see that we said that factual causation can be a complex, sometimes seemingly inconsistently applied element in the Negligence sequence. It's often more about tools than rules. Take a look at the flowchart overleaf, which represents a summary of what we have so far discussed. Is it helpful for you to have the law as it currently stands set out in this way? How would your own flowchart differ from this one?

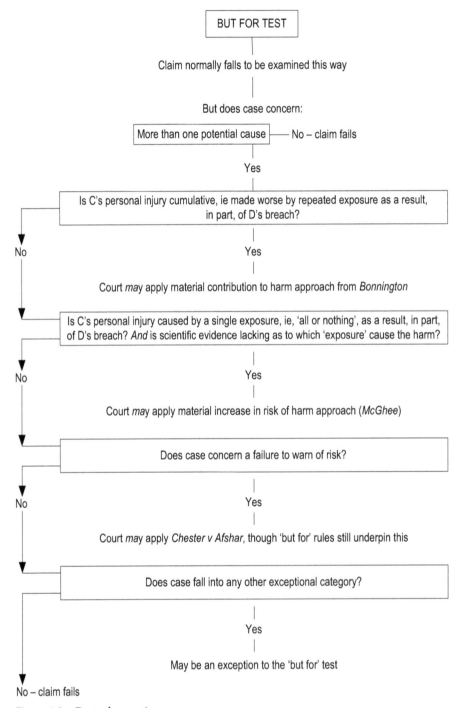

BUT FOR TEST

Claim normally falls to be examined this way

But does case concern:

More than one potential cause —— No – claim fails

Yes

Is C's personal injury cumulative, ie made worse by repeated exposure as a result, in part, of D's breach?

No   Yes

Court *may* apply material contribution to harm approach from *Bonnington*

Is C's personal injury caused by a single exposure, ie, 'all or nothing', as a result, in part, of D's breach? *And* is scientific evidence lacking as to which 'exposure' cause the harm?

No   Yes

Court *may* apply material increase in risk of harm approach (*McGhee*)

Does case concern a failure to warn of risk?

No   Yes

Court *may* apply *Chester v Afshar*, though 'but for' rules still underpin this

Does case fall into any other exceptional category?

Yes

May be an exception to the 'but for' test

No – claim fails

Figure 4.2   Factual causation

4.4 Legal causation

Having established factual causation – and we sometimes think of factual causation as the chain that links the breach with the damage to the claimant – we now look to see whether that chain has been broken or affected by a subsequent intervening act. This is called legal causation and is really a consideration of whether, in law, the defendant ought to be responsible for all that follows their breach. Certain subsequent events may break the chain of causation in certain circumstances, rendering the first defendant no longer liable, or only partially liable.

Here's what we mean in handy diagram form!

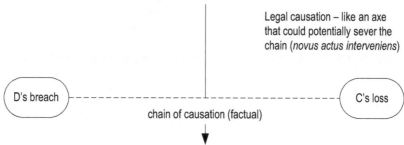

Figure 4.3   Legal causation

Legal causation versus remoteness

There are different ways to consider legal causation. Some academics consider it as an aspect of remoteness, because they are related topics, and both look to determine the extent of the defendant's liability. Here, we will look at these concepts separately, as this helps to simplify what is already a complex process. (Remoteness is considered in **Chapter 5**.)

4.5 Intervening events – *novus actus interveniens*

There are three types of intervening act (or *novus actus interveniens* – meaning 'new act intervening') that we need to consider. They are:

- acts of the claimant
- acts of third parties
- acts of God/natural events.

Let's take each of these in turn.

4.5.1 Acts of the claimant

Sometimes, the claimant's own actions will potentially break the chain of causation. Remember that, chronologically, with legal causation, we are looking for something that happens after the initial breach, not before or at the same time.

example

Carrie is the passenger in a car being driven by her boyfriend, Derek. Derek drives too quickly and causes an accident, in which Carrie suffers personal injury (a broken leg). She sues him for his Negligence. Later, at the hospital, she is advised not to put weight on her leg for three weeks but decides to ignore that advice. Shortly afterwards, when putting weight on the leg, she damages it further. The driver of the car that Derek hit, Ash, sustains head injuries in the accident. He wasn't wearing a seatbelt at the time of the crash.

There is a fair amount going on here, but for our purposes we are going to focus on legal causation. (However – top tip: you can use this mini scenario as an opportunity to revise your knowledge of Negligence. Set out the parties and then discuss and advise on each element of each claim in order.) In relation to Carrie, Derek was certainly the factual cause of her broken leg. However, when she then ignores advice and damages the leg further, this could be seen as a *novus actus interveniens* – an act of the claimant that breaks the chain. We'll see below how the court would deal with this in terms of liability.

For Ash, again we can assume that his Negligence claim against Derek is strong. However, his failure to wear a seatbelt is a problem for him. Strictly speaking, this is likely to be considered at the defence stage – it will probably provide Derek with a partial defence of contributory negligence (see **Chapter 6**), rather than representing a *novus actus interveniens*. This is because the failure to wear a seatbelt didn't happen after Derek's breach and so can't really be said to 'break the chain'.

Acts of the claimant are likely to break the chain where they are considered unreasonable and/or unforeseeable. This is an attempt by the courts to decide matters fairly. As Sedley LJ states:

> In relation to tortious liability for personal injury, this point is reached [namely the point at which it becomes unfair not to 'halt liability'] when (though not only when) the claimant suffers a further injury which, while it would not have happened without the initial injury, has been in substance brought about by the claimant and not the tortfeasor. (*Spencer v Wincanton Holdings Ltd* [2009] EWCA Civ 1404)

McKew v Holland and Hannen and Cubitts (Scotland) Ltd [1969] 3 All ER 1621

case example

Here, the claimant suffered a leg injury at work caused by the negligence of the first defendant. This resulted in impaired mobility and stiffness in that leg. Shortly afterwards, and in the course of his work, the claimant went to inspect a flat which could only be accessed by descending a steep flight of stairs that had no handrail. As he was about to walk down the stairs, his leg buckled and so he threw himself forwards in an attempt not to fall. He broke his ankle. The claimant tried to argue that the defendant should be liable as this was an extension of his first injury and effectively caused by the defendant. The House of Lords disagreed, stating that he had thrown himself down the stairs for no good reason. This was unreasonable and his action broke the chain of causation. Therefore the defendant was not liable for the broken ankle.

We can contrast that with our next case:

Wieland v Cyril Lord Carpets Ltd [1969] 3 All ER 1006

case example

Here the claimant's actions did not break the chain of causation because they were considered reasonable and foreseeable in the circumstances. As a result of the defendant's negligence, the claimant had to wear a neck brace. This restricted her movement and vision and made it hard for her to see properly when using her bifocal glasses. As a result, she fell down some stairs and injured her ankle.

It was held that her actions did not break the chain and that therefore the defendant should be liable for the second injury as well.

What about where a claimant commits suicide after an initial breach by the defendant? This was considered in *Corr v IBC Vehicles Ltd* [2008] 2 WLR 499. The claimant was almost killed in an accident at work caused by the negligence of his employer. He developed clinical depression as a result and later committed suicide. The question for the court was whether his own act of suicide broke the chain of causation in relation to his estate's claim against his employer.

The House of Lords found that the chain was not broken, with Lord Bingham stressing that the suicide was not a free and voluntary choice, and it was not unforeseeable, because of the effect of the initial negligence of the employer, which remained on the claimant's mind.

Note in *Gray v Thames Trains Ltd* [2009] UKHL 33 that a later criminal act of the claimant *did* break the chain of causation. This claimant had suffered physical and psychological injuries in a train crash caused by the negligence of his employer.

4.5.2 Acts of third parties

Where the intervening event is the act of a third party, that event will only break the chain where the act is unreasonable or unforeseeable, and unconnected with the defendant's breach (ie not something the defendant should have been able to foresee and therefore guard against).

In *Knightley v Johns* [1982] 1 WLR 349, there was a serious accident in a tunnel caused by the first defendant's negligent driving. Police were called to the scene, but the police inspector in charge sent two officers into the tunnel on motorbikes, without first stopping traffic from entering the tunnel. One of them, the claimant, suffered injury when he was hit by a car. The claimant brought an action against both the first defendant and the second defendant (the police inspector). The Court of Appeal found that the police inspector had been negligent and that his act (of a third party) was unreasonable and broke the chain of causation. Therefore the claim against the first defendant was dismissed.

Third party acts of medics will rarely break the chain unless those acts are deemed 'palpably wrong'. In *Robinson v The Post Office* [1974] 2 All ER 737 the claimant was injured at work due to the negligence of his employer, necessitating an anti-tetanus jab. The claimant was allergic to the injection, which exacerbated his injury. The third party (the doctor) should have carried out an allergy test before administering the injection, but this omission did not break the chain as it was not considered 'palpably wrong'. For policy reasons, this will normally be the position – after all, third party medical intervention would not have been necessary had the first defendant not been negligent to start with, and it was foreseeable. The result was that the first defendant was responsible for the original injury and the extent to which it was made worse.

4.5.3 Acts of God/natural events

Such events would include, for example, being struck by lightning, the onset of a disease or sustaining burns in a bush fire.

As you might expect, natural events will not break the chain if they could have been foreseen by the defendant. Only where the natural event is unconnected with the defendant's breach will it break the chain.

In *Humber Oil Terminal Trustee Ltd v Sivand* [1998] CLC 751, the defendant's tanker collided with and caused property damage to the claimant's dock. This was held to be negligent on the defendant's part. During repairs of the dock, further expenses were incurred by the claimant when the sea bed collapsed. The defendant tried to argue that the collapse of the sea bed was a natural event for which it should not be liable – that that act broke the chain of causation – but the court disagreed as the collapse was foreseeable as a result of the defendant's breach.

We can see how illness plays out here. In *Meah v McCreamer (No 1)* [1985] 1 All ER 367, the claimant suffered personal injury in a road accident caused by the defendant's negligence. This led to him developing a personality disorder, and as a result he went on to commit some serious criminal acts. The disorder – the natural event or act of God – was linked to the original tort and a foreseeable consequence of it, and so did not break the chain. This meant that the defendant remained liable.

However, in *Jobling v Associated Dairies Ltd* [1982] AC 794 (more usually looked at when considering aspects of factual causation but it fits just as well here), the claimant injured his back at work as a result of the defendant's negligence. Before trial, he contracted an unrelated back disease which rendered him unable to work any more. The question for the House of Lords was as to whether, and if so at what point, the defendant's liability ceased. Did the natural event break the chain? It was held that it *did* break the chain, being entirely unrelated to the breach, and something that would have happened in any event, which could not have been foreseen by the defendant nor prevented. The effect was that the claimant could only be compensated up until the point that he contracted the disease, after which the chain was broken.

4.6 Further reading

E Voyiakis, 'Causation and Opportunity in Tort'(2018) 38 OJLS 26.
S Steel, 'Justifying Exceptions to Proof of Causation in Tort Law' (2015) 78 MLR 729.

J Morgan, 'Reinterpreting the Reinterpretation of the Reinterpretation of Fairchild' [2015] CLJ 395.

J Stapleton, 'An Extended But-For Test for the Causal Relation in the Law of Obligations' (2015) 35 OJLS 697.

M Gilboa, 'Multiple reasonable behaviours cases: the problem of causal undetermination in tort law' (2019) 25(2) LT 77–104.

summary

- Causation is looked at in two parts – factual causation and legal causation.
- Factual causation always begins with the but for test and may fail at that stage.
- There are exceptions to the but for test for various types of cases, but these are exceptions and apply only to specific types of case.
- Legal causation asks whether there has been a *novus actus interveniens* that breaks the factual chain of causation.
- Events that can break the chain are acts of the claimant, acts of third parties and acts of God/natural events.
- These events will only break the chain where they are unreasonable and/or unforeseeable.

test your knowledge

Have a go at these multiple-choice questions (MCQs):

Question 1

A woman goes to hospital with stomach pains. The doctor should have run some standard tests but fails to do so. The tests would have picked up her underlying health condition for which she would have been prescribed urgent medication. The woman is told to go home and rest. She does so but in the night her condition deteriorates and she now has a long-term stomach condition. She wishes to sue the doctor in Negligence.

Which one of the following options best describes the way in which the issue of factual causation would be dealt with by the court?

A   The claimant will be able to show that the defendant's breach materially contributed to her loss, applying *Bonnington*.

B   But for the doctor's breach in failing to run the standard tests, the claimant would not have had to attend the hospital in the first place and so factual causation is satisfied.

C   But for the doctor's breach in failing to run the standard tests, the claimant would have suffered her long-term stomach condition anyway. Therefore, the breach was probably not the factual cause of the loss.

D   But for the doctor's breach in failing to run the standard tests, the claimant would not have suffered her long-term stomach condition because she would have been prescribed medication. Therefore, the breach was probably the factual cause of the loss.

E   The claimant will be able to show that the defendant's breach materially increased the risk of her harm, applying *McGhee*.

Answer

The correct answer is option D. This seems to be a fairly standard application of the but for test, albeit with an omission rather than a positive act. Factual causation would probably be satisfied here.

Question 2

A man contracts a disease in the workplace, attributable in part to his employee's breach of duty in not providing adequate hand-washing facilities.

Which one of the following statements is most accurate as to the way in which factual causation would be determined in any Negligence action the man may wish to bring against his employer?

A   The but for test would be tried first. Depending on the type of illness, how it's caused and the other medical and scientific evidence available, it's possible that an exception to the but for test may be applied to satisfy factual causation.

B   The but for test would be tried first. Depending on the type of illness, how it's caused and the other medical and scientific evidence available, an exception to the but for test will be applied to satisfy factual causation.

C   The court will not apply the but for test because this isn't an appropriate case for that.

D   The claim would simply fail at the but for stage.

E   The but for test would be tried first, but if that doesn't produce a fair answer, the court can simply find for the claimant without needing to adopt a particular approach to factual causation.

Answer

The correct answer is option A. We don't yet have enough information to draw a firm conclusion here and option A offers the best summary of the current situation.

Question 3

A woman injures her back at work due to the negligence of her employer. Shortly afterwards, whilst picking up a box, she injures her back further.

Which one of the following best describes the way in which the question of legal causation would be dealt with here?

A   Her act would only break the chain if it was palpably wrong.

B   Her act will break the chain here as she had a back injury and was doing something unreasonable.

C   Her act may break the chain if it's unreasonable and/or unforeseeable. That is difficult to gauge on these limited facts. It would help to know if she had been advised not to pick things up and as to whether she was doing this safely.

D   Her employer should have foreseen that she may need to pick up boxes and so this act will not break the chain.

E   Her act would be a *novus actus interveniens* and so would break the chain.

The correct answer is option C. We do need more information here. It's possible this act could break the chain. This looks to be either a *McKew v Holland* or a *Wieland v Cyril Lord Carpets* situation.

Question 4

A man contracts mesothelioma at work, having inhaled asbestos at some point over his working life at the premises of one or more of his employers. He wishes to claim in Negligence against all the employers.

Which one of the following options best describes which approach to factual causation is likely to be applied?

A   The but for test first, but ultimately it may be that the material increase in risk approach would be applied.

B   The but for test only.

C   The but for test first, but ultimately it may be that the material contribution to the harm approach would be applied.

D   The but for test first, but ultimately it may be that the loss of a chance exception would be applied.

E   The but for test first, but ultimately the court may simply apportion liability between the tortfeasors without the requirement to satisfy factual causation.

Answer

The correct answer is option A. Yes, this would be the test in *McGhee* and the one applied in *Fairchild*.

General Negligence – Remoteness

study points

After reading this chapter, you will be able to understand:

- what is meant by the term 'remoteness'
- where in the Negligence sequence remoteness fits
- that remoteness is about determining the scope of the defendant's liability
- that remoteness turns on reasonable foreseeability and, as such, relates to duty of care.

5.1 Introduction

Once causation has been established, the next element that the claimant has to satisfy is remoteness. In other words, the claimant must prove that their loss was reasonably foreseeable from the breach, and not too remote from it. Whether something is too remote from the breach or not is judged by the standards as they existed at the time of the breach, rather than by the standards that might exist by the time of trial. (Note: we also had this discussion at the breach stage – look back at **Chapter 3** for a reminder that breaches need to be looked at with foresight, not hindsight.)

The defendant won't be liable for *all* the losses flowing from the breach forever – this would be unfair and would lead to a policy concern you'll be aware of, namely crushing liability. Often the extent of the defendant's liability can feel like a rather arbitrary line in the sand, and undoubtedly this is at least partly because remoteness is a heavily policy-driven element.

This was summed up in *Sunny Metal and Engineering Pte Ltd v Ng Khim Ming Eric* [2007] SGCA 36, (2007) 113 Con LR 112 in this way:

> [Remoteness], unlike ... causation, presents a much larger area of choice in which *legal policy and accepted value judgment must be the final arbiter of what balance to strike* between the claim to full reparation for the loss suffered by an innocent victim of another's culpable conduct and the excessive burden that would be imposed on human activity if a wrongdoer were to be held to answer for all consequences of his default. (emphasis added)

This chapter will explore what the law says and how it has developed in this area.

5.2   The Negligence sequence – remoteness

We have reached this stage in the sequence. Do remember to include all the elements up to and including remoteness in your consolidation as you move through this chapter.

> Loss/Damage – Duty – Breach – Causation – Remoteness – Defences – Remedies

Figure 5.1   The Negligence sequence

5.3   The test of reasonable foreseeability

The current test for remoteness based on reasonable foreseeability comes from the case of *The Wagon Mound (No 1)*. It's a Privy Council case and the facts concern property damage, though the principle applies to all types of recognisable loss in Negligence.

case example

Overseas Tankship (UK) Ltd v Morts Dock and Engineering Co Ltd (The Wagon Mound No 1) [1961] UKPC 2

The defendants, who were responsible for a ship that was loading in Sydney Harbour, Australia, negligently caused an oil spillage into the water. The oil formed a film on top of the water and that spread to a nearby wharf, owned by the claimant, in which welders were working. A few days later, sparks from the welding operations ignited the oil still on the water, and this caused a fire which caused extensive property damage to the wharf and other nearby ships.

At first instance, the damage caused by the oil itself was held to be foreseeable, for example to the slipway of the wharf, but not the damage caused by fire, because the evidence suggested that when oil spread thinly on water, it rarely ignited. For that reason, the claimant was unable to claim for its property damage because the loss was too remote.

The Privy Council agreed, finding that a reasonable person would not have foreseen fire damage as a possible consequence of the breach by the defendants. The question asked, which forms the test still used today, Was: *was the kind or type of damage suffered by the claimant reasonably foreseeable at the time the breach occurred?*

The claimant did not succeed in this case, but the test has laid the basis for subsequent claimants to succeed.

Interestingly, by the time of *The Wagon Mound (No 2)*, the evidence showed that it was actually possible for oil spread thinly on water to ignite (though unlikely). It required a certain temperature to be attained, such as would be the case if a welder's spark fell onto something floating in the oily water. This is in fact exactly what happened in this case. Therefore, the issue in the later case turned not on foreseeability of damage, as this had now been established, but on whether there had in fact been a breach.

The old test of directness

Prior to *The Wagon Mound (No 1)*, a defendant could be liable for *all* the loss that was a direct consequence of their breach. There was no need for such loss to be foreseeable, and the test was essentially one of causation alone (see *Re Polemis* [1921] 3 KB 560). The Privy Council stated that *Re Polemis* was no longer good law, a fact that must have been a relief to would-be defendants as the current test is far more balanced.

5.4 The same kind or type of harm – extent need not be foreseen

Note that only the *type* of damage must be foreseeable in order for the claimant to establish remoteness, not its extent. This means that, for example, provided that property damage was foreseeable as a consequence of the defendant's breach, the extent of the property damage need not be, and the claimant could potentially claim for the full extent of their property damage, even if that was more extensive that someone else may have sustained in the same situation. This is a concept sometimes called the 'egg-shell skull rule'. Effectively, the defendant must take their victim as they find them, though see below at **5.4.1.** for the limits to that.

example

Dave is sailing a small dinghy in the sea. He is not paying attention and accidentally runs his boat into a much larger boat, causing damage to it. Unknown to him, the boat he damages is very expensive, and he is now facing the prospect of having to compensate the owners of the boat for his Negligence.

Provided that the other elements of the Negligence claim are satisfied, Dave may well find that he has to pay more damages for the property damage than he would have had to if he had crashed into a less expensive boat. This is because, at the remoteness stage, provided the claimant can show that property damage was reasonably foreseeable, then they will be able to claim for the full extent of the foreseeable loss. This is the principle of the egg-shell skull rule – you take your victim as you find them – and, because of the wording of the remoteness test from *Wagon Mound (No 1)*, is the way in which the extent of the loss would ordinarily fall to be decided.

5.4.1 A note on practicalities and procedure

On a practical note, however, the quantum of damages to be paid out still has a limit (and this is especially pertinent where the loss is personal injury); the defendant is not liable for all foreseeable losses to the defendant forever. The court discounts the damages to take into account that the claimant would have been susceptible in the future to the type of damage that they have sustained now, reflecting the 'ordinary vicissitudes of life' which the claimant, given their egg-shell skull, would one day have faced in any event. In *Page v Smith* [1996] 1 AC 155 (see **2.9.4**), the claimant's damages were reduced by 40% using this calculation.

While we're on *Page v Smith*, many judges have suggested that this case may need reconsideration in future in terms of the principle it propounds as regards psychiatric harm and the egg-shell skull rule, whereby psychiatric harm can be compensated for, so long as the claimant was at risk of foreseeable physical injury which didn't occur (look back at psychiatric harm in **Chapter 2**). For example, Lord Scott and Lord Rodger raised quizzical eyebrows at this principle in *Johnston* *v NEI Intl Combustion Ltd* [2007] UKHL 39. So far, however, nothing has yet changed.

5.4.2 Extent need not be foreseen – examples

Let's look at a couple of cases that focus on the extent of damage. In *Vacwell Engineering Co Ltd v BDH Chemicals Ltd* [1971] 1 QB 88, the defendant breached its duty by failing to give sufficient warnings about the chemicals it was marketing. As a result, there was a powerful chemical explosion in the claimant's place of work when a chemical came into contact with water. The explosion killed one of the scientists, blew the roof off the laboratory and shattered the surrounding walls. The issue was whether that loss was too remote. The Court found for the claimant, stating that once the type of loss was reasonably foreseeable (property damage caused by an explosion) then the claimant did not have to prove that the defendant should have foreseen the extent of that loss. The defendant was liable therefore for the full extent of the claimant's loss.

In *Smith v Leech Brain and Co Ltd* [1962] 2 QB 405 the defendant, through its negligence, caused the claimant to be burnt on their lip. The burn acted as a catalyst, causing a pre-existing malignant cancer to develop fairly quickly, and the claimant subsequently died. The defendant tried to argue that it should not be liable for the death because that was too remote. The Court disagreed, applying the reasoning from *The Wagon Mound (No 1)* and making reference to the egg-shell skull rule. Once the type of loss was foreseeable – and the burn was – then the defendant was liable for the full extent of the losses of the same type flowing from that breach. That included the cancer and death.

This approach was broadly followed in *Reaney v University Hospital of North Staffordshire NHS Trust* [2015] EWCA Civ 1119, though the Court of Appeal went into more detail on types of care (qualitative and quantitative) than we need concern ourselves with here.

5.5 The same kind or type of harm – narrow and wide view

The court has not always taken a consistent view as to the same kind or type of harm. The wide view is the more claimant-friendly approach; the narrower view favours the defendant.

For example, a wide view of this concept was taken in *Bradford v Robinson Rentals Ltd* [1967] 1 WLR 337. In this case, the claimant suffered frostbite as a result of having to drive a van provided by his employer that had no heating and a leaking radiator. The defendant argued that frostbite was not reasonably foreseeable and was too remote from the breach. The court took a wide view, stating that once the type of loss was foreseeable, and here that was any loss associated with the cold, then the claimant's loss could not be too remote. There may well have been policy at work here: after all, an employer has a duty to look after its employee and provide adequate materials and vehicles, etc.

Contrast this with *Tremain v Pike* [1969] 1 WLR 1556, in which a narrow view was taken. The claimant contracted Weil's disease, a disease picked up from rats' urine, whilst employed by the defendant farmer. The farmer had negligently allowed his farm to be overrun with rats. At the time, this disease was rare, there were few instances of it, and there was little evidence to suggest that the farming community had knowledge of it, or how it might be contracted (for example by handling matter contaminated with rats' urine). The Court determined that the type of damage that had to be foreseeable was disease contracted through contact with rats' urine. This was despite the claimant arguing that the approach should be wider – surely any injury caused by rats was foreseeable in the circumstances, for example a rat bite? The claimant's claim failed at the remoteness stage.

It's fair to say that the wider approach is the norm, and this accords with the wording of the test in *The Wagon Mound (No 1)*. (For more on this, refer back to some cases we have already looked at in other contexts, for example *Page v Smith* [1996] 1 AC 155 (psychiatric harm – see **Chapter 2**) and *Corr v IBC Vehicles Ltd* [2008] 2 WLR 499 (legal causation – see **Chapter 4**).)

5.6 No need to foresee the precise way in which the damage occurs

As we have seen, provided that the claimant can prove that the type of damage was reasonably foreseeable, there is no need to prove that the defendant should also have foreseen the extent of the damage. Similarly, there is no need to prove that the defendant should have foreseen the precise way in which the damage occurs.

Hughes v Lord Advocate [1963] AC 837

case example

The claimant was an 8-year-old boy who was playing near a manhole left uncovered by the defendants. The defendants had also left oil lamps surrounding the hole. The boy picked one up and then accidentally dropped it into the manhole. It exploded and, as it did so, the boy fell in and suffered severe burns.

The House of Lords held that damage from burns was foreseeable from the breach (lit oil lamps). Therefore, it did not matter that no one could have foreseen the way in which the burns came about. The claim was successful and the loss not too remote.

A different view was taken in the next case:

Doughty v Turner Manufacturing Co Ltd [1964] 1 QB 518

case example

A claimant factory worker sustained serious burns when an asbestos lid was knocked into a vat of hot liquid zinc. This caused a chemical reaction that made the liquid inside boil up and create an explosion. The defendant employer argued that this loss was too remote, in that the specific chemical reaction was not foreseeable to the reasonable person. The claimant said that, applying *Wagon Mound (No 1)*, provided some kind of physical injury was foreseeable, the precise manner in which that occurred should not matter to the success of the remoteness test.

The Court of Appeal held that the employer was in fact not liable because the explosion was unforeseeable to the reasonable man at the time at which it happened. It said that personal injury caused by splashing (when the lid fell into the vat of zinc) was foreseeable, but that the explosion was not.

The reasoning here does not necessarily align with other case law, and although this case has not been overruled, it is the *Hughes* argument which is almost always applied to similar cases.

5.7 Consolidation

Figure 5.2 may help you to consolidate this element.

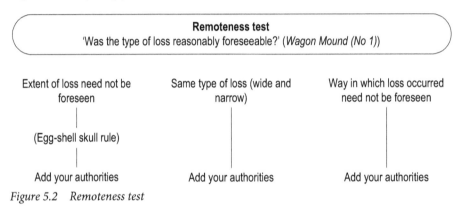

Figure 5.2 Remoteness test

5.8 The claimant's impecuniosity

In a case called *Lagden v O'Connor* [2004] 1 AC 1067, the House of Lords distinguished an earlier case (*Liesbosch Dredger v SS Edison* [1933] AC 449). In fact, *Liesbosch* has been subsequently distinguished so often that it is, for all intents and purposes, overruled. Both cases looked at claimant impecuniosity and how that affects the question of remoteness. In *Lagden*, it was confirmed that the egg-shell skull rule (or thin-skull rule) also applied to the claimant's financial health as much as to their physical wellbeing. Here, it was reasonably foreseeable that the claimant would need to borrow money in order to mitigate his losses, and therefore the defendant was liable for the full extent of those financial losses, even though the claimant had suffered to a greater extent because of his impecuniosity. We can view this as a 'thin wallet rule'.

example

Whilst reversing his tractor, Jonathan accidentally runs it into an empty barn owned by Nula. The barn is damaged and is likely to cost around £2,000 to repair. Nula's solicitor suggests she spend a small amount of money to make the barn watertight or otherwise protect it while waiting for it to be fixed. However, Nula does not have the funds to do this, and the following week, in high winds, the barn collapses. The cost of rebuilding the barn from scratch is £4,000. Jonathan states that he should only have to pay £2,000.

Provided all the other elements of Negligence are made out here, it's highly likely that, applying *Lagden*, Nula would be able to claim for the full extent of her property damage. She need only prove that property damage was reasonably foreseeable when Jonathan reversed his tractor into her barn. The 'thin wallet rule' applies, so Nula won't be penalised because she was not able reasonably to mitigate her loss due to her impecuniosity. (There *is* an expectation that losses are mitigated. So a claimant can't simply, through laziness for example, fail to do anything to help themselves when it would have been financially possible to do so, and then expect to be compensated by the defendant

5.9 Further reading

Smith LJ, 'Causation: The Search for Principle' [2009] JPIL 101.
R Cooke, 'Remoteness of Damages and Judicial Discretion' (2009) 37 CLJ 288–300.

- Remoteness is the means by which the court determines the type and extent of liability towards the claimant.
- It is based on a test of the type of harm being reasonably foreseeable.
- It's an element heavily driven by policy, though the general rules are usually followed.
- The court will take into account the claimant's egg-shell skull where appropriate, and that extends to their 'thin wallet' (impecuniosity).

Have a go at these multiple-choice questions (MCQs):

Question 1

Due to the defendant's breach, a fire causes extensive property damage to a man's neighbouring shop. He brings an action in Negligence against the defendant.

Which one of the following options best describes how the issue of remoteness will be dealt with here?

A   The test from *The Wagon Mound (No 1)* will be applied. The defendant will therefore not be liable for any losses flowing from the breach.

B   The test from *The Wagon Mound (No 1)* will not be applied as this does not apply to cases concerning property damage.

C   The test from *The Wagon Mound (No 1)* will be applied. The defendant will therefore be liable for all losses flowing from the breach.

D   The test from *The Wagon Mound (No 1)* will be applied. Unlike in that case itself, it is likely that the way in which the property damage occurs here will be held to be foreseeable.

E   The test from *The Wagon Mound (No 1)* will be applied. It is likely that the way in which the property damage occurs here will be held to be unforeseeable.

Answer

The correct answer is option D. The test from *The Wagon Mound (No 1)* would be utilised, though note that in the case itself, the claimant did not succeed due to a lack of foreseeability regarding its property damage.

Question 2

A child is playing near some factory doors. The factory owners have left open some tins of paint and bottles of chemicals. The child mixes these together and there is an explosion which causes extensive burn damage to the child's face and hands.

Which one of the following is most likely to be correct as to the approach the court will take on the issue of remoteness?

A   Given that personal injury here is probably foreseeable (mixing or playing with paint and chemicals) then the child's loss won't be too remote just because the way in which it occurs may not have been foreseen.

B   Given that personal injury here is probably unforeseeable (mixing or playing with paint and chemicals) then the child's loss will be too remote.

C   Although personal injury here is probably foreseeable (mixing or playing with paint and chemicals), the child's loss will be too remote because its extent goes beyond that which was foreseeable.

D   Although an explosion may have been foreseeable, burn damage would not be, so this claim will fail at the remoteness stage.

E   The defendant will be liable for all losses flowing from the breach

Answer

The correct answer is option A. This was the argument in *Hughes v Lord Advocate*.

Question 3

A man has a pre-existing pre-cancerous malignant growth on his face. Whilst at work, due to a breach by his employer, he is splashed in the face with a chemical. He suffers personal injury and the splash causes the cancer to develop. He later dies from cancer.

Which one of the following is correct on the issue of remoteness as to whether the man's estate will be able to claim in respect of his death?

A   Yes it probably will, as the extent of the loss needs to be foreseeable, as well as the type of injury and the way in which the injury occurred.

B   It will probably be able to claim for the initial injury but not for the death which would be seen as too remote.

C No it probably won't, as the extent of the loss needs to be foreseeable as well as the type.

D Yes it probably will, as the extent of the loss needs to be foreseeable, as well as the type, and there would be consideration of the egg-shell skull rule.

E Yes it probably will, as the extent of the loss need not be foreseeable, only the type, and there would be consideration of the egg-shell skull rule.

Answer

The correct answer is option E. This is correct applying *Smith v Leech Brain* and *Page v Smith* concerning the egg-shell skull rule.

Question 4

You are asked to deliver a presentation on the most relevant policy issues in the context of remoteness.

Which one of the following options best describes the policy concern that is most relevant in the context of remoteness?

A Defensive practices

B Insurance

C Crushing liability

D Floodgates

E Benefit/burden

Answer

The correct answer is option C. This is what *The Wagon Mound (No 1)* sought to address to an extent, with the test of reasonable foreseeability of the type of loss.

6 General Negligence – Defences and Remedies

After reading this chapter, you will be able to:
- appreciate how defences and remedies fit into the Negligence sequence
- recognise the three key defences in the context of General Negligence, namely *volenti* (or consent), *ex turpi* (or illegality) and contributory negligence
- understand the elements of each defence that the defendant must prove
- gain an overview of the types of remedy available to a successful claimant.

6.1 Scope of this chapter

We've reached the point in a General Negligence claim where the claimant has done all they can. Having suffered a recognisable form of loss, they will have tried to prove, on the balance of probabilities, that the defendant owed them a duty of care, and breached that duty, and that the breach was the factual and legal cause of their loss and was reasonably foreseeable as a result of the breach (ie not too remote). Now it's the defendant's turn: can they prove that they have a valid defence? We're going to look at the three most important defences in this context: *volenti* (or consent), *ex turpi* (or illegality) and contributory negligence. There are other, less common defences, such as necessity, but they arise relatively rarely within this tort and are therefore outside the scope of this chapter.

As for remedies, our focus here will be on providing an outline as to the principle remedy available to a claimant, ie damages. The detail as to the types of damages (be they compensatory, aggravated, exemplary and so on) and guidance on, for example, how to quantify damages will be developed as you move through your training, but that kind of depth is not relevant here, so we'll stick to the essentials.

6.2 Where in the Negligence sequence do defences and remedies fit?

> Loss/Damage – Duty – Breach – Causation – Remoteness – Defences – Remedies

Figure 6.1   The Negligence sequence

You might think of defences and remedies as the final two railway stations on a track. As is probably obvious by now, you don't reach them unless all the other 'stations' have been passed through first. In other words, each element in the Negligence sequence is arrived at only on condition that the one before is satisfied. If the claimant has suffered no loss, the claim ends there. There is no point looking at the next element because the first has not been satisfied. If the claimant *has* suffered loss, but no duty was owed by the defendant to that claimant, the claim ends there. If a duty was owed but not breached, the claim ends. And so on. By the time we reach defences, then, the claimant has satisfied all the Negligence elements thus far.

The defendant bears the burden of proving, on the balance of probability, the existence of one or more defences. (So far, of course, the *claimant* has borne this burden of proof.) To continue our train journey analogy, at this stage the train might even move backwards the way it came, perhaps only a little way – if a partial defence is accepted – or all the way back to the start – if a full defence is accepted. This is because when the defendant successfully pleads a full defence, they will not be liable at all.

Any monetary remedy for the claimant is the 'prize' at the end of the journey if no defence (or only a partial defence) is successfully pleaded.

6.3   *Volenti* (or consent)

Volenti non fit injuria (meaning 'no wrong will be done to the willing') or consent is the name of our first defence, usually abbreviated to *volenti*. (Often the term *volenti* is used in a Negligence context, with consent used for intentional torts such as battery.) Its rationale is that 'one who has invited or assented to an act being done towards him cannot, when he suffers it, complain of it as a wrong' (from *Smith v Charles Baker & Sons* [1891] AC 325). In other words, if a claimant has expressly or impliedly consented to being injured or to run the risk of the injury that they then sustain, the defendant may be able to utilise this defence to sidestep liability.

Volenti is a complete or full defence (as is *ex turpi* – see below), so if pleaded successfully, the claimant's claim fails at this stage and the defendant will not be liable for any damages at all. And because it's a complete defence, the court, as you might imagine, can be wary of allowing it, where there is even a suggestion that the defendant may have been to some degree culpable. For policy reasons (refer back to **Chapter 1** for more on policy), it can be difficult for this defence to be successful, and we'll explore this idea here and when we look at other, related torts where the defence is frequently raised, especially Employers' Liability (**Chapter 8**) and Occupiers' Liability (**Chapter 10**).

6.3.1   The elements of *volenti*

So what must the defendant prove? There are two stages to the test. The defendant must prove that the claimant:

(a)   understood the nature and extent of the possible harm or risk of harm; and

(b)   voluntarily agreed to it.

One without the other will not suffice. Importantly, the test is *subjective* (you can forget the reasonable, objective person for the moment). The particular claimant must have been aware of the nature and extent of the risk, and must have agreed to run that risk. The next case illustrates this requirement.

Dann v Hamilton [1939] 1 KB 509

Dann was the claimant passenger in a car driven by the defendant, Hamilton, who had been drinking alcohol. After a car accident caused by Hamilton's negligent driving, Dann brought an action against Hamilton's estate (Hamilton died at the scene). The defence of *volenti* was raised, and the issue for the court was whether the claimant had voluntarily assumed the risk of the defendant's negligence when she got into the car with him. Asquith J found that the claimant was aware that the defendant had been drinking (she had had a conversation with another passenger about it, who had then got out of the car) and that this would adversely affect his ability to drive safely. However, there was no evidence that she had consented to the risk that the defendant's driving might cause her injury. Knowing the risk was not enough; the claimant also had to voluntarily agree to it. The defence failed.

Note: This case pre-dates s 149 of the Road Traffic Act (RTA) 1988, which states that the defence of *volenti* is excluded where parties are travelling in a road vehicle. Instead, defendants in this situation tend to rely on the other defences we will look at below, namely *ex turpi* and contributory negligence.

You might think from *Dann v Hamilton* that *volenti* is always difficult to prove, and yet a later case, *Morris v Murray*, which seems similar on the face of it, took a different view. In this case, the defence succeeded.

Morris v Murray [1991] 2 WLR 195

The claimant and defendant spent the afternoon drinking. After drinking about half a bottle of whisky, the defendant, Murray, offered to take Morris, the claimant, for a spin in his light aircraft. (Note: this was not a road vehicle and therefore not covered by s 149 of the RTA 1988.) The claimant agreed, drove Murray to the airport and helped prepare the plane for take-off. Shortly after take-off, the plane crashed, killing the defendant and seriously injuring the claimant. The defendant's estate pleaded *volenti,* and the Court of Appeal agreed that the defence should succeed because the claimant fully understood the risk he was taking and the likelihood of serious harm, and he had voluntarily assumed the risk of injury.

How do we square *Dann v Hamilton* with *Morris v Murray*?

The above cases are difficult to reconcile, in that both had similar facts and yet, in the first, the defence of *volenti* did not succeed, and in the second it did. Various commentators have tried to analyse the reason for the differences between the cases, but, in the end, the most convincing rationale seems to be that a degree of policy drives the decisions. Where the risk of harm is glaringly obvious and/or the conduct of the claimant particularly reckless or irresponsible, the court, it would seem, is far more likely to find *volenti*.

example

Gregor, a student, gets very drunk one evening, and then decides to break into an outdoor swimming pool owned by the council. He climbs over a high fence and dives into the pool, which is almost empty. As a result, he sustains very serious injuries rendering him paralysed.

In this example, which is very similar to a real case we'll look at when we get to Occupiers' Liability (**Chapter 10**), it may well be that even if the defendant council is deemed to have been negligent (which on these bare facts is difficult to judge), it would be able to run the defence of *volenti* with a good chance of success: note that we have a drunk claimant doing an irresponsible and obviously dangerous activity and thereby perhaps consenting, albeit impliedly, to run the risk of the injuries he then sustains.

6.3.2 Other examples of *volenti*

The other key areas where this defence tends to be raised are in a medical context (we'll cover Clinical Negligence in **Chapter 7**) and in a sporting context. As to the latter, the court's view is that by willingly taking part in a sport, whether it be something mostly harmless like dominoes, or potentially more dangerous such as rugby or boxing, the claimant voluntarily assumes the risks of injury inherent in that sport. However, a claimant does not consent to a level of injury over and above that which is a normal part of the game: a dangerously late tackle or a headbutt on the football field might lead to a successful action in Negligence (or the tort of battery) with no *volenti* defence available, as discussed in *Condon v Basi* [1985] 1 WLR 866.

6.4 *Ex turpi* or illegality

Like *volenti, ex turpi* is a complete defence and heavily policy driven. Its full title – *ex turpi causa non oritur actio* – means no action may be founded on an illegal or immoral act, and its rationale is to prevent a claimant profiting where they themselves are involved in an illegal act.

In *Ashton v Turner* [1981] 1 QB 137, two men, both intoxicated, committed a burglary and then caused an accident whilst driving away in the getaway car, injuring the plaintiff who was a passenger in the car. The plaintiff sued the driver in negligence. Ewbank J found that as a matter of public policy, the defendant did not owe the plaintiff a duty of care, but that in the alternative, if a duty was owed, the plaintiff had willingly accepted the risk (a *volenti* argument pre-dating the RTA 1988) and/or could not claim on the grounds of *ex turpi*.

6.4.1 The elements of *ex turpi*

The defendant must prove two elements, though there is disagreement and inconsistency within the courts as to whether part (b) is helpful and/or forms part of the test at all. Kerr LJ restated the public conscience part (b) argument in *Euro-Diam Ltd v Bathurst* [1990] 1 QB 1, but it was rejected by the House of Lords in

Tinsley v Milligan [1994] 1 AC 340, a case concerning fraud. Here are the two parts:

(a) That the claimant was engaged in an illegal/immoral activity.

(b) That it would be an affront to the public conscience to allow the claimant to claim.

These provide, at least, a good starting point. What we do know is that this defence does not mean that a claimant who has been involved in illegal activity will *never* be able to claim against a negligent defendant. This was made plain by Bingham LJ in *Saunders v Edwards* [1987] 1 WLR 1116 who said the court cannot simply 'draw up its skirts and refuse all assistance …'. Rather it is a question of degree. What is the claimant doing in comparison with the defendant?

example

Ravi is parked on a double yellow line when a motorbike being negligently ridden by Saskia crashes into the side of his car. Ravi wants to sue Saskia in Negligence. She raises *ex turpi.*

It's very unlikely that the court would entertain this defence. Think about that issue of degree. Yes, Ravi is doing something illegal by being parked on a double yellow line, but surely to allow the rider to absolve herself of all liability would be contrary to public policy here? To put it another way, perhaps it would be an affront to the public conscience *not* to allow Ravi to claim?

6.4.2 In what circumstances will this defence actually work?

Good question. And it doesn't have a clear-cut answer. To illustrate this, let's look at *Pitts v Hunt* [1991] 1 QB 24. The claimant and defendant, both teenagers, got drunk one evening and then decided to travel home on the defendant's motorbike. The defendant (Hunt) was over the legal alcohol limit to drive, and although the claimant, Pitts, knew this, and knew that Hunt was under-age and uninsured, he rode pillion and encouraged Hunt to drive recklessly. The motorbike crashed, and Hunt was killed, with Pitts seriously injured.

Remember, this case was decided post-RTA 1988 so *volenti* would not have been an option for the defendant's estate. So, the estate pleaded *ex turpi* and contributory negligence (see below).

The Court of Appeal allowed the defence of *ex turpi*, so denying Pitts a claim, but each of the three judges applied different lines of reasoning as to why it should be applied. Dillon LJ simply relied upon the defence of *ex turpi*, stating that the claimant's injury was caused as a direct result of his being involved in an illegal activity (the joint enterprise). Balcombe LJ analysed the situation differently, stating that where parties are involved in a joint criminal enterprise, it is impossible for courts to determine the standard of care applicable, and so to determine whether the duty, if it was owed, had been breached. Beldam LJ relied on the notion that to allow Pitts to be able to claim would be an affront to the public conscience (our part (b) of the test above at **6.4.1**).

6.4.3 Has the defence evolved or changed over time?

Gray v Thames Trains Ltd **[2009] UKHL 33**

case example

In *Gray*, the House of Lords held that the claimant, who had sustained PTSD after being involved in the Ladbroke Grove rail crash, caused by the negligence of Thames Trains, and who subsequently stabbed and killed a pedestrian whilst suffering PTSD, could not recover damages in Negligence from Thames Trains. The doctrine of *ex turpi* was successfully applied. (The claimant was convicted in the criminal courts of manslaughter on the grounds of diminished responsibility.)

The rationale focused on balancing public policy concerns, and it was followed in the broadly similar case of *Henderson v Dorset Healthcare University NHS Foundation Trust* [2020] UKSC 43, in which a claimant suffering from paranoid schizophrenia was failed by the defendant NHS Trust which admitted liability in Negligence in failing to return the claimant to hospital on the basis of her manifest psychotic state. She subsequently stabbed her mother to death. *Gray* was applied, and *ex turpi* served to defeat the claimant's claim.

Between *Gray* and *Henderson* came a Supreme Court case, *Patel v Mirza* [2016] UKSC 42, which gives us perhaps the clearest indication yet that the two-stage test set out above at **6.4.1** is still the most useful approach, though it requires more examination. In *Patel* (which was not actually a tort case but involved unjust enrichment), a panel of nine Supreme Court judges heard the appeal. The facts are less important for our purposes than the discussion the judges had on the proper application of *ex turpi*. Lord Toulson gave the leading judgment in which he stated (at [120]) that it is right that the courts should assess whether it would be 'contrary to the public interest to enforce a claim if to do so would be harmful to the integrity of the legal system'. He stated (at [120]) that it was necessary in answering this question:

(a) to consider the underlying purpose of the prohibition which has been transgressed and whether that purpose will be enhanced by the denial of the claim,

(b) to consider any other relevant public policy [concerns] and

(c) to consider whether the denial of the claim would be a proportionate response to the illegality …

Although this defence is as contentious as it ever was, and difficult to distil to a consistent clear principle, at least *Patel* and subsequent cases confirm the importance of policy in driving this defence, and the particular aspects that require examination when applying the two-stage test to decide whether the defence should defeat a claim.

6.5 Contributory negligence

Contributory negligence is a partial defence that serves to reduce but not extinguish the defendant's liability. It's highly pragmatic in that it takes account of the culpability of both defendant and claimant, and it's governed by statute: s 1(1) of the Law Reform (Contributory Negligence) Act 1945, which states that the court can reduce the claimant's damages in accordance with what it considers just and equitable. This is the most common defence in Negligence and the most successful.

In practice, contributory negligence deductions normally range from 10–90% (with 20–25% the most common deduction). It is no longer possible for a claimant to be 100% contributorily negligent.

6.5.1 The elements of contributory negligence

The defendant needs to establish that the claimant failed to exercise reasonable care for their own safety and that this failure contributed to the injury the claimant sustained. This is normally relatively straightforward.

example

Atitaya decides not to wear her seatbelt as she drives her car. (Let's suppose there is as yet no statute requiring the compulsory wearing of seatbelts.) She is hit by the defendant's car as a result of his negligent driving and sustains serious injuries. The evidence shows that Atitaya would not have suffered such serious injury had she been wearing a seatbelt.

This example mirrors a real case called *Froom v Butcher* [1976] 1 QB 286. It's useful for our purposes because it neatly illustrates the requirements for this defence, namely that the claimant failed to exercise reasonable care for their own safety, by not wearing a seatbelt, and this failure, we're told, contributed to the claimant's damage. It's important to note that had the failure to wear a seatbelt not contributed to the claimant's damage, then the defence would fail. This was the position in *Stanton v Collinson* [2010] EWCA Civ 81 in which a teenager died from injuries in a car accident and was not wearing a seatbelt. It was not proven that his wearing a seatbelt would have reduced his injuries and so the partial defence failed.

The Court of Appeal in *Froom* also set out guidelines as to the appropriate reduction in damages for failing to wear a seatbelt, and these guidelines have subsequently been applied in relation to motorbike and cycle helmets in *Smith v Finch* [2009] EWHC 53 (QB) and *Reynolds v Strutt and Parker LLP* [2011] EWHC 2263 (Ch).

6.5.2 Did the claimant fail to exercise reasonable care for their own safety?

This question is viewed objectively, ie what would a reasonable person in the claimant's position have done? (See *Jones v Livox Quarries Ltd* [1952] 2 QB 608 for an early example of contributory negligence.) The classic example of contributory negligence is not wearing a seatbelt, but plenty of other scenarios can give rise to this defence, for example, crossing the road at a pedestrian crossing when the light was red and not green (*Rehill v Rider Holdings Ltd* [2014] EWCA Civ 42), jumping from a moving taxi (*Hicks v Young* [2015] EWHC 1144 (QB)) and the unforgettable but tragic case in which the intoxicated claimant stood in the middle of the road to 'moon' at passing cars (*Ayres v Odedra* [2013] EWHC 40 (QB)).

6.6 Remedies

Almost always, a claimant is seeking damages to compensate them for their loss, in other words, monetary compensation to put them in the position they would have been in had the loss not occurred. Such damages are called *compensatory*. Some commentators say that a tortious remedy in Negligence is therefore backwards-looking, as opposed to, say, contractual damages, which look forwards, in that they put the claimant in the position they would have been in had the contract been carried out.

There are other types of damages, and while we're not going to go through these in detail here, it's helpful at least to recognise them. (Note that some of these types of damages will be looked at as and when we get to the case or the tort in which they were applied. For example, contemptuous damages were awarded in a defamation case called *Grobbelaar v News Group Newspapers Ltd* [2002] UKHL 40, and we will revisit this in our chapter on Defamation (**Chapter 11**).)

Table 6.1   Types of damages

Types of damages	Effect
Special compensatory damages	Past pecuniary losses which can be quantified at time of trial (for example, loss of earnings)
General compensatory damages	Non-pecuniary losses (past and future), for example pain, suffering, loss of amenity. Future pecuniary losses, for example future loss of earnings and future medical treatment
Exemplary damages	A higher sum is paid as a punitive measure, to make an example of the defendant – rare.
Aggravated damages	A higher sum is paid to reflect that the claimant has suffered to a greater degree than expected because of the defendant's actions
Contemptuous damages	The claimant receives a very small sum to reflect the court's displeasure that such a claim was even brought by the claimant, though technically they win – a Pyrrhic victory!
Nominal damages	A legal wrong committed but no recognised harm suffered by the claimant

6.7 Further reading

Law Commission, *The Illegality Defence* (Law Com No 320, 2010).

I Field, 'Contributory Negligence and the Rule of Avoidable Losses' (2018) 38 OJLS
475.

- There are three key defences within the tort of Negligence: *volenti*, *ex turpi* and contributory negligence.
- *Volenti* and *ex turpi* are full defences, heavily driven by policy, and often difficult to predict with any degree of consistency.
- Contributory negligence is a partial defence, governed by statute. It's the most common and most successful defence of the three.
- The most common type of remedy available in Negligence is compensatory damages.

Have a go at these multiple-choice questions (MCQs):

Question 1

A man agrees to take a helicopter trip with his friend who is a pilot. The friend is obviously intoxicated. They crash due to the friend's negligent piloting of the helicopter, and both are injured.

Which one of the following options best outlines the likely outcome if the friend tries to plead the defence of *volenti* in response to any Negligence action brought against him by the man?

A. *Volenti* will not be successful here because of s 149 of the Road Traffic Act 1988.

B *Volenti* may be successful here and, as a result, the claimant man will win.

C *Volenti* will probably not be successful here because the claimant man understood the nature of the risk and agreed to it.

D *Volenti* may be successful here because the claimant man probably understood the nature of the risk and impliedly consented to it by doing something so irresponsible.

E *Volenti* may be successful here and would have the effect of reducing the defendant's liability.

Answer

The correct answer is option D. Difficult to predict for sure, but on these facts the defence is likely to succeed given that taking a helicopter ride with someone obviously drunk would be considered very risky. (See *Morris v Murray*.)

Question 2

A woman is suffering from a severe mental illness and is negligently released from hospital without the supervision she requires. She loses her job, becomes violent and stabs a passer-by in the street. She wants to sue the hospital for its negligence.

Which one of the following best outlines the likely outcome if the hospital pleads *ex turpi* in response to the negligence action brought against it?

A   The defence is likely to succeed as regards the woman's criminal act notwithstanding any negligence on the hospital's part as regards the lack of supervision.

B   The defence will not succeed because the woman's crime was so extreme.

C   The defence will not succeed because it would offend the public conscience if the woman were not able to claim.

D   The defence will not succeed because *ex turpi* is no longer recognised as a defence in this type of situation.

E   The defence will probably succeed because for policy reasons no claimant who commits a crime should be compensated.

Answer

The correct answer is option A. This follows the reasoning in *Gray* and *Henderson*.

Question 3

A woman is the passenger in a car being driven by a man. The man negligently crashes and the woman is injured. She was not wearing a seatbelt at the time. She wants to sue the man in Negligence.

Which one of the following is accurate as to the defences available to the man?

A   The man could not plead *volenti* because of s 149 of the RTA 1988. He could plead *ex turpi* and contributory negligence.

B   None of the general defences would be available to the man because of s 149 of the RTA 1988.

C   The man would only be able to plead contributory negligence because the other two defences are full and contributory negligence is partial.

D   *Ex turpi* would not be available as a defence because the woman is not doing anything illegal, but the other two defences could be pleaded.

E   Contributory negligence would likely be successful here and the woman's damages would be reduced by up to 100%.

Answer

The correct answer is option A. Either of the other two defences could be available. Contributory negligence would probably be successful provided there is evidence that the woman's injury was exacerbated because of her failure to wear a seatbelt.

Question 4

A man is injured and suffers property damage as a result of the negligence of the defendant. He wants to claim damages.

Which one of the following most accurately describes the types of damages he is likely to be awarded if successful in his Negligence action?

A   The man is likely to be awarded aggravated damages because his property was damaged as well as his person.

B   The man is likely to receive compensatory damages which may include special and general damages.

C   The man is likely to receive compensatory damages for his personal injury and exemplary damages for any other losses.

D   The man is likely to receive damages to compensate him for his losses up until the time of trial but not beyond that.

E   The man will receive only nominal damages because this is not a serious case.

Answer

The correct answer is option B. This is the most common type of Negligence remedy, and it is usual for courts to consider past and future losses so long as they are appropriate and quantifiable.

7   Clinical Negligence

study points

After reading this chapter, you will be able to:

- appreciate the overlaps between General and Clinical (or professional) Negligence
- understand how Negligence principles fit within this specific context
- apply and analyse relevant case law for each element
- analyse the more difficult areas in particular depth, especially breach.

7.1   Scope of this chapter – old and new

In a sense, this chapter does nothing new, and thereby it allows you to revise or work through the elements of a Negligence action in a specific, clinical context. (Although we will be focusing mainly on clinical cases, the principles can almost always be expanded to take in any form of professional Negligence.)

Having said that this chapter does nothing new, that's not entirely accurate. Clinical Negligence is a fascinating area in its own right (and many lawyers specialise in this one area as it is so involved), and this chapter should help you gain some insight into the particular issues that arise in a clinical context, most notably regarding breach.

There will of course be overlaps with other chapters, so do refer back to the relevant chapters on General Negligence (**Chapters 1–6**). But so as not to make this feel repetitive, you'll note we've included an 'extended written advice exercise' at **7.5.2**. This focuses in a fresh way on the issue of breach, giving you insight into not just the law in this complex area, but how to apply it, as well as showing you what a legal advice might look like on the page.

7.2   Overlaps with criminal law

A doctor can of course be found guilty of criminal offences against patients in some circumstances. The torts of assault and battery, for example, are also crimes (see **Chapter 13**, 'Trespass to the Person'), and if a doctor were to, say, proceed with an operation beyond the point at which they had obtained consent, that could in theory amount to a battery.

A doctor (and we use 'doctor' here as shorthand for any related healthcare professional, for example a nurse, dentist, etc, unless stated otherwise) could also be guilty of a crime called gross negligence manslaughter, which does not require proof of intention on the part of the defendant (as most crimes do). For this offence to be made out, however, it needs to be shown that the doctor was not 'just' negligent, but so seriously negligent that a criminal conviction is appropriate. NHS Trusts might also be convicted of manslaughter in certain circumstances by virtue of the Corporate Manslaughter and Corporate Homicide Act 2007. There are other crimes that a doctor might find themselves involved with in the scope of their role (for example assisting a suicide – see Suicide Act 1961).

However, the vast majority of litigation following medical malpractice is brought under the tort of Clinical Negligence, and that's what our focus will be on here.

7.3 Loss/damage

The same types of loss that are recoverable in General Negligence are also recoverable here, namely personal injury, property damage and consequential economic loss. As you'd expect, the main heads of loss tend to be personal injury and consequential economic loss.

7.4 Duty of care

The rules pertaining to duty of care are the same as apply in General Negligence (see **Chapter 2**). With the extra assistance we have now had from *Caparo v Dickman* (see **2.5.2**) and how duty is to be interpreted, it will be clear that most cases concerning duty will either follow precedent or else be analogous to an existing case which then determines the question of duty.

So there is little dispute that hospital staff owe a duty of care to their patients, doctors to their patients and so on. In *Cassidy v Ministry of Health* [1951] 2 KB 343, Lord Denning made clear that a duty was owed by healthcare professionals to their patients to exercise reasonable care and skill once they accept that patient for treatment.

Sometimes there are questions raised as to precisely to whom the duty may or may not be owed. For example, in *West Bromwich Albion FC v El-Safty* [2006] EWCA Civ 1299, it was held that a surgeon treating a football player did not owe a duty to that player's club (so as to make him potentially liable when that player was treated negligently). The Court of Appeal made the point that the surgeon involved had at no time assumed responsibility for the financial wellbeing of West Bromwich Albion. The club did not employ the surgeon. In *Kapfunde v Abbey National plc* (1998) 46 BMLR 176, no doctor/patient relationship of proximity arose because the doctor merely provided advice for an occupational health report.

It is not only individuals who owe a duty of care. Health authorities, hospitals and Trusts can be sued in their own right (as well as vicariously for the torts of their employees – for more on vicarious liability, see **Chapter 8**). In *Bull and Another v Devon Area Health Authority* (1993) 4 Med LR 117, the Court of Appeal found the Health Authority to owe a duty in respect of its provision of maternity services to the claimant who was in labour with twins. When assessing whether a hospital or health authority is in breach, the approach seems to be to determine whether the failings are operational failings or policy failings (as per the police case of *Rigby v Chief Constable of Northamptonshire* [1985] 2 All ER 985 – see **Chapter 2** for a reminder about duties owed by the police).

7.5 Breach of duty

Here, as with General Negligence, the court will first of all look to determine or set the standard (a question of law) before assessing whether the defendant did in fact breach that standard (a question of fact). Do look back at **Chapter 3** for a reminder of the mechanics of this.

7.5.1 Setting the standard

For professionals acting in their professional capacity, the standard (which is objective) comes from *Bolam v Friern Hospital Management Committee* [1957] 1 WLR 583. The court will expect the professional to demonstrate that they met the standard of the reasonably competent professional carrying out that particular act. Remember that the standard attaches to the task, not the person doing it ('the act not the actor'), so, for example, if a junior doctor is doing a task that requires more skill than perhaps they have yet attained, that won't serve to lower the objective standard expected of them. (This was the position in *Wilsher v Essex Area Health Authority* [1988] 1 AC 1074.)

example

Dr Kennedy is a very experienced anaesthetist. One day, whilst administering anaesthetic in a non-complicated case, a procedure he has done many times before, he carelessly administers the wrong dose, causing injury to the claimant. One of the issues for the court is the standard of care to be expected of him.

The standard of care attaches to the task, and so Dr Kennedy would be expected to meet the standard of the reasonably competent anaesthetist. He would not be expected to meet a higher standard by virtue of his experience. The standard does not move up or down – it is objective.

7.5.2 Breach of that standard

The second part of breach is to decide whether the defendant has actually fallen below the standard imposed on them. This is where we examine what went wrong. That is a question of fact, and it is open to the court to ask what happened and why. This can be particularly complex in medical settings, given that the court has to rely on the expert evidence of medical practitioners and professionals, and to make judgments in law based on what they hear.

Bolam test at the breach stage

As well as using *Bolam* to set the standard, we also use it (sometimes) to assess whether the defendant has fallen below that standard. It is appropriate where the potential breach involves a clinical decision, involving skill and judgement, for example: diagnosis of a condition, choosing between treatment options, the technique used for an operation, and so on. Essentially, where there are clinical choices to be made, and especially where there are 'two (or more) schools of thought', the *Bolam* test will be useful. It is not applied to all situations, however. For example, it would not be used in the following situations: non-medical advice, advising as to risks associated with treatment. For more on advising as to risk, see 'Breach arising through failure to warn of risk' (below).

case example

Bolam v Friern Hospital Management Committee [1957] 1 WLR 583

The claimant was a patient who was given electro-convulsive therapy without a relaxant drug and without the appropriate physical restraints. During his treatment, he fractured his hip, and this may have been caused by the lack of restraint. He had not been warned of this as a possibility. At the time, there were two schools of thought in the medical profession regarding the need to offer relaxant drugs and to restrain, and the requirement to warn patients about the risk of injury.

The Court stated that 'a doctor is not guilty of negligence if he has acted in accordance with a practice accepted as proper by a responsible body of medical men skilled in that particular art'.

The defendant doctor had not breached his duty of care because there were others in the field who would have done as the defendant did, and those others constituted a reasonable body of medical opinion.

The test for breach therefore comes from this case. Put simply, it can be very difficult for a claimant to show that a doctor (or other healthcare professional) has breached their duty of care. From an evidential point of view, it would not be enough for a claimant to adduce evidence to the effect that another professional would not have carried out the act in the way that the defendant did. Rather, it would have to be proven (on the balance of probabilities) that the body of opinion being relied upon by the defendant is not reasonable, or is unsafe – in other words, that no responsible body of medical opinion would have done as the defendant did.

How does it work?

The test for breach is perhaps best illustrated by working through a scenario. What's set out below represents a full advice on the scenario given. We can then pull out sections to discuss afterwards.

extended written advice exercise

A surgeon, Helena, opts for one technique over another when operating on the hand of a patient, Sally. There is a small risk of paralysis of the hand with the technique she chooses, even when the surgery is performed properly. The surgery *is* carried out properly, but Sally's hand is paralysed.

Sally brings an action against Helena in Clinical Negligence. There are some surgeons who would have used the technique that Helena used, but others who would not have done. The question is whether she will be in breach of her duty for choosing the technique that she used.

Standard

Helena will be judged by the standard of the reasonably competent surgeon, as that is the task she is undertaking (*Bolam*, *Wilsher*).

Breach

As to breach of that standard, we begin with *Bolam* as a starting point. Helena will presumably adduce evidence from other surgeons who would have chosen the technique that she chose, and she will argue that those others represent a responsible body of medical opinion. We know from case law that that body need not represent the majority (ie it could be that most other surgeons would not have chosen Helena's technique and yet still the minority would be seen as responsible). The authority for this comes from *De Freitas v O'Brien* [1995] EWCA Civ 28, though that case concerned niche surgery and there were only a few surgeons in the country doing the same type of operation as the defendant, so this may be distinguishable here. As a general rule, it will of course be harder to demonstrate that your body of opinion is responsible and safe if you struggle to find many others who would have done as you did.

Court would prefer not to prefer one professional view over another

The House of Lords has made clear that it would rather not arbitrate between two competing valid medical opinions (*Maynard v West Midlands Regional Health Authority* [1985] 1 All ER 635). Applying that here, much will turn on the validity of the body Helena relies upon, and we would need more information on that here.

*But court is not bound to accept expert evidence (*Bolitho*)*

However, the court will, where it sees fit, step in and find the body being relied upon to be unsafe/ unreasonable where it has good reason and sufficient evidence to do so. The court's ability to do this was discussed in *Bolitho v City and Hackney Health Authority* [1998] AC 232. It might be necessary, the court said (and this is paraphrased), to carry out an assessment of the expert evidence to see whether those experts had directed their minds to the comparative risks and benefits of any preferred procedures and whether the view arrived at was a sensible one. A judge was not bound to accept expert evidence where such assessment demonstrated that the opinion given was not supported by logic. Lord Browne-Wilkinson stated that he was looking for the body of opinion to be 'logically defensible'.

In *Bolitho* itself, which concerned an omission, the court eventually declined to find that the defendant had breached her duty. In other words, the body she relied upon was held to be reasonable, but this was the first time in which it was raised that the court could intervene and would challenge where necessary.

Bolitho *applied?*

This intervention is far more likely to happen in a non-medical, rather than a medical, context (see, for example *Re Herald of Free Enterprise*, discussed in **Chapter 3**, 'Breach of Duty', in which the common or usual practice for roll-on roll-off ferries was held to be a negligent practice). This is the equivalent of the defendant ferry company having relied on a body of opinion of others who also used the method which had been adopted by the defendant. The Court made clear that that practice was unsafe and should not have been adopted.

The *Bolitho* 'card' has been played since *Bolitho* was decided, but it is much more likely for the court to decide that a body of opinion is unsafe or unreasonable where the actions of the defendant concern decision making, or the correct process to be followed, as opposed to – as in our case – the correct surgical technique to be used. (We might query whether these even fall to be determined by reference to *Bolam* in the first place.) For example, in *Marriott v West Midlands RHA* [1999] Lloyd's Rep Med 23, Mr Marriott, the claimant, was admitted to hospital having fallen unconscious for 20 minutes. He was discharged the next day but continued to suffer from headaches and so a GP was called. The GP simply prescribed painkillers, and didn't refer the claimant to hospital, as he felt, among other things, that the risk to the claimant of further harm was low. But the claimant's condition deteriorated and he was left hemiplegic. The evidence at trial showed that there were two schools of thought in terms of what the GP could have done, and, put simply, those were to refer to hospital or not. The trial judge in *Marriott* felt, having listened to the evidence, that, due to the severity of the possible repercussions if things went wrong, the claimant should have been referred to hospital. The body which determined that this was not what they would have done, and which the defendant relied upon, was held to be logically indefensible.

Application here

Applying the above to our scenario, what we can say with certainty is that there will only be a breach of Helena's duty if the body she relies upon is determined to be logically indefensible (essentially unsafe) applying *Bolitho*. We need further evidence on that here. Whilst we can see from *Marriott* (and there are other, similar cases where *Bolitho* was applied, though again they tend to involve situations more similar to *Marriott* than to our case) that the court will step in where necessary to challenge the validity of a body of opinion being relied up on, this is unlikely to happen where the potential breach concerns, as here, a choice of surgical technique.

So there may be a breach here. It is unlikely but possible. We await further evidence on this point.

The case law – a 'mental flowchart'

You'll note that a fair amount of case law was referred to as part of the above advice. (On a practical note, when writing a legal advice, you would seek to do this too, to inform each point you seek to make with authority.) We'll have a look at the facts of *Bolitho* in more detail below, but as a starting point, you might find it helpful when dealing with discussion of *Bolam*-style breaches to imagine a mental flowchart that you work through in order to allow scope to apply some useful case law to the specifics of your scenario. Most of these cases were mentioned in the advice itself, so do read them in full for more detail.

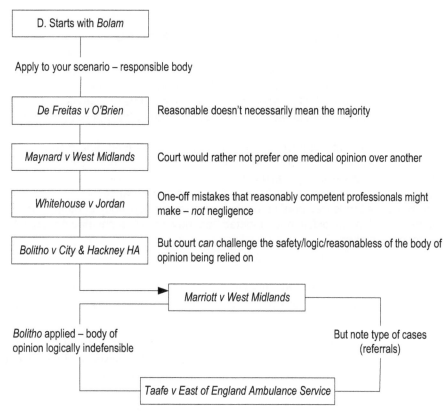

Figure 7.1   Clinical Negligence case law

Note that a couple of extra cases have been included, which may or may not assist you with the specific advice you might be dealing with, namely *Whitehouse v Jordan* [1981] 1 All ER 267 (which made the point that a one-off error of judgement by a professional is not the same as negligence – even reasonably competent professionals make errors sometimes and these should not always be construed as negligence) and *Taaffe v East of England Ambulance Service NHS Trust* [2012] EWHC 1335 (QB) (which was another application of *Bolitho* along *Marriott* lines – this case also concerned a failure to refer, this time for cardiac problems, a practice held to be logically indefensible by the court). You can also find more recent cases where *Bolitho* has been applied, and it would be a matter for your judgement as to whether they would be relevant in your advice. (Try, for example, *McGuinn v Lewisham and Greenwich NHS Trust* [2017] EWHC 88 (QB) where a doctor was found to be in breach of duty by failing to appreciate that the foetus was at risk of microcephaly. The doctor's actions 'lacked a sufficiently logical and rational basis'.)

case example

Bolitho v City and Hackney Health Authority [1998] AC 232

In this case, the claimant was the estate of a young boy who suffered brain damage and later died of a cardiac arrest after respiratory failure in hospital. The boy had experienced two serious respiratory incidents, and on both occasions the nurse had called for the doctor, who never arrived. Consequently, the boy had not been intubated (a breathing tube inserted down his throat to help him breathe). The claimant argued that intubation would have prevented his death.

The defendant doctor argued that even if she had attended, she would not have intubated the young boy because it came with risks, and for her that would not have been the right decision. She argued that, as a result, her failure to attend had not caused his death. This was therefore a complicated case revolving around omissions, breach and causation.

The House of Lords was persuaded that, as a reasonable body of other professionals would have done as the defendant did, ie not intubated had they attended, she had not breached the standard of care imposed on her.

As mentioned, this was a very important case in that it was the first where the suggestion was made that the judiciary might seek to challenge the body of opinion being relied upon:

> But if, in a rare case, it can be demonstrated that the professional opinion is not capable of withstanding logical analysis, the judge is entitled to hold that the body of opinion is not reasonable or responsible. (per Lord Browne-Wilkinson)

Subsequent case law has touched on those factors which might make a court conclude that a body of opinion being relied upon is unreasonable or illogical, and they might include: (a) where there is a dubious expert whose professional views exist 'on the fringes of medical consciousness' (*Gunapathy Muniandy v Khoo and Others* [2001] SGHC 165); or (b) where the medical expert had a 'residual adherence to out of date ideas which on examination do not really stand up to analysis' (*Hucks v Cole* [1993] 4 Med LR 393).

Using *Bolitho* and *Bolam* for breaches by omission

As can be seen above, the position can be complicated when there is a possible breach by omission in a clinical context. The House of Lords in *Bolitho* made clear that there were two questions to ask in that case itself: first, what would the doctor have recommended had she attended the boy? If the answer was that she would have recommended intubation, then that would have been evidence of a breach, with that breach causing the loss because she failed to do something which she knew she ought to have done. (Note that this involves breach *and* causation.) The doctor said she would not have intubated, so the second question was: had she attended and not intubated, would that failure to intubate have been negligent? On the facts, it was found that that decision not to intubate would not have been a breach, given the risks of intubation in a child that young (and that the failure to intubate was not the cause of death).

Therefore, regarding omissions, the questions are hypothetical but important: the court will want to know in each case whether the failure to do the thing that wasn't done (the intubation, the treatment given, etc) was negligent or not. This part can be judged using *Bolam*: would a responsible body of medical opinion also not have done that thing which the defendant did not do?

In *Gouldsmith v Mid Staffordshire General Hospitals NHS Trust* [2007] EWCA Civ 397, the alleged breach concerned a failure to refer a patient to a specialist unit for treatment on her finger. It was not known who at the unit would have seen the patient, but it was held more likely than not, if she had been so referred, that she would have received treatment for the finger because that was normal practice. Therefore, there was a breach here, and there was no need to ask whether it would be negligent for the specialists not to offer treatment. It was decided by a majority that where the alleged breach is as to a failure to refer a patient and it is not known to whom the patient would be referred, the court would conceive of a hypothetical expert in the field and consider whether it was more likely than not that that expert would treat the patient.

Breach arising through failure to warn of risk

We touched on failure to warn of the risks of treatment as it applies to causation in **Chapter 4**. However, this often arises as an issue of breach in a clinical setting. The leading case on this is now *Montgomery v Lanarkshire Health Board* [2015] UKSC 11. We will look at this case below, but before we do, it's worth noting that prior to *Montgomery,* the situation was different, the law coming from *Sidaway v Bethlem Royal Hospital* [1985] AC 871. In *Sidaway*, the surgeon had failed to warn of the very small risks of paralysis inherent in the claimant's back operation, when done correctly. Unfortunately, although properly carried out, the claimant was paralysed as a result of the operation. She said that she would not have had the operation had she been made aware of the risks.

The House of Lords, by a majority, applied *Bolam* to the question of advising on risk, accepting that a body of medical opinion (other surgeons) would not have advised on such a small risk either. There was much criticism of that decision in the years that followed, some of it focused on Lord Scarman's powerful dissent in *Sidaway*, in which he said that the courts should not 'stand idly by if the profession, by an excess of paternalism, denies its patients real choice. In a word, the law will not allow the medical profession to play God.' Subsequent cases tended to tiptoe around *Sidaway*, tacitly though not explicitly departing from it, especially *Pearce v United Bristol Healthcare NHS Trust* [1999] EWCA Civ 865 and *Chester v Afshar* [2004] UKHL 41. *Montgomery* marked an unapologetic departure from it.

Montgomery v Lanarkshire Health Board [2015] UKSC 11

case example

In 1999, the claimant, Mrs Montgomery, gave birth to a baby boy, who was born with severe brain damage having been starved of oxygen during delivery. The claimant was of small build and diabetic. Evidence shows that diabetic mothers tend to have larger babies. During delivery, her son's shoulders got stuck (a condition known as shoulder dystocia) and there was 12-minute delay in freeing the shoulders. It was during those 12 minutes that the baby sustained brain damage, as well as paralysis of one arm from the force used in pulling him out.

The claimant argued that she should have been warned by the obstetrician of the risks of shoulder dystocia, and that, had she been warned, she would have asked for a caesarean section. She claimed in Negligence against the defendant obstetrician. The defendant said she had not warned about shoulder dystocia because the risk was so small (relying on *Sidaway* and adducing evidence from others in the field who said that they would not have warned of the risk either, as per *Bolam*).

The Supreme Court took a different view, after an extensive review of *Sidaway* and other related case law. Lord Kerr and Lord Reed stated:

> The doctor is therefore under a duty to take reasonable care to ensure that the patient is aware of any material risks involved in any recommended treatment, and of any reasonable alternative or variant treatments. The test of materiality is whether, in the circumstances of the particular case, a reasonable person in the patient's position is or should reasonably be aware that the particular patient would be likely to attach significance to it.

It was also held that a doctor *is* entitled to withhold information on risks if they 'reasonably [consider] that its disclosure would be seriously detrimental to the patient's health'.

Impact of *Montgomery* on the question of breach

Montgomery was a very important case. It has been applied in many cases since it was decided and has undoubtedly changed the emphasis where failure to warn of risk is concerned in the context of breach. In *Webster v Burton Hospitals NHS Foundation Trust* [2017] EWCA Civ 62, the Court of Appeal applied *Montgomery* and concluded that the increased risks of continuing labour in the presence of ultrasound abnormalities should have been discussed with the mother, who should have been offered an induction, which she would have accepted.

However, that's not to say that *Bolam* is now redundant in this area. It still informs *Montgomery*, and there are many cases to read about here. See, for example, *Bayley v George Eliot Hospital* [2017] EWHC 3398 (QB), a case raising an issue about alternative treatment that concerned iliofemoral stenting, in which the court concluded that the only alternative treatments that the claimant needed to be informed about were those that were reasonable, not those that it was not reasonable to expect the clinicians to know about, which were not accepted practice in the UK at the time.

7.6   Causation

The same rules of factual and legal causation apply here as they do with causation in General Negligence. In fact, the chapter on 'Causation' (**Chapter 4**) covered some clinical negligence examples, so do ensure you look back at that chapter.

7.6.1   A reminder – factual causation

Here are the most important factors to bear in mind when looking at factual causation, especially in a clinical context. (For the detail, see **Chapter 4**.)

- The place to start with factual causation is always the *but for test*. The claimant must prove that but for (had it not been for) the defendant's breach, the loss to the claimant would not have happened at that time and in that way.
- This comes from *Barnett v Chelsea and Kensington Hospital* in which the claim failed at the but for stage.
- The application of the but for test can get tricky where the facts are more complex, for example, where there is more than one defendant, and/or more than one possible cause.
- That doesn't mean that the court won't apply it. It was applied in *Wilsher v Essex Area Health Authority* in which the claim failed at this stage. The doctor had breached their duty of care by carelessly administering oxygen but the breach did not, on the balance of probabilities, cause the loss. The loss (blindness) may have happened anyway.
- The *two most important exceptions to the but for test approach* (and there are others) came from industrial employer/employee cases (*Bonnington Castings Ltd v Wardlaw – the material contribution to the harm* exception, and *McGhee v National Coal Board* – the *material increase in the risk of harm* approach). Both of these have subsequently been applied in clinical contexts:
  - *Bonnington*: applied in *Bailey v Ministry of Defence*.
  - *McGhee*: applied in *Fairchild v Glenhaven Funeral Services*.

7.6.2   A reminder – legal causation

You'll recall that legal causation is about establishing whether any subsequent act that happens after the defendant's initial breach ought to break or affect the factual chain of causation that links that breach to the claimant's loss. The three events that can break the chain are:

- acts of the claimant
- acts of third parties
- acts of God.

The events won't tend break the chain unless they are unreasonable and/or unforeseeable. For our purposes in this chapter, you might recall that medical intervention (as a third party act/omission) will rarely break the chain unless it is 'palpably wrong' (*Robinson v Post Office*).

7.7 The other elements in the Clinical Negligence sequence

As with any Negligence claim, the claimant would need to establish all the elements of the claim, including those we have not concentrated on here because they are identical to those covered elsewhere in this book, ie remoteness and defences.

7.8 Apportionment

A word on who pays what, where the negligence of two professionals has caused loss to the claimant. This is where the principle of apportionment is invoked, a principle used in General Negligence claims as well – see, for example *Fitzgerald v Lane & Patel* [1989] 1 AC 328 in which damages were apportioned between the first and second defendants in relation to the loss caused to the claimant.

In a medical context, the claimant can receive the whole of the damages from either of the defendants, and it's then up to that defendant to sue the other to be reimbursed. You're not asked at this stage in your training to quantify the loss, and suffice to say that damages are divided between the defendants according to their respective degrees of culpability. In *Prendergast v Sam and Dee Ltd* (1989) 1 Med LR 36, a case concerning an illegible prescription written by a GP and then carelessly administered by the pharmacist, the pharmacist was held 70% liable, and the GP 30%.

7.9 Further reading

M Brazier and J Miola, 'Bye Bye *Bolam*: A Medical Litigation Revolution?' (2000) 8 MLR 85–114.

G Buttigieg, 'Re-visiting *Bolam* and *Bolitho* in the light of *Montgomery v Lanarkshire Health Board*' (2018) 86(1) Med Leg J 42–44.

L Sutherland QC, '*Montgomery*: myths, misconceptions and misunderstandings' (2019) 3 Journal of Personal Injury Law 157–67.

summary

- Clinical Negligence follows the General Negligence structure and is based on the same principles.
- The focus tends to be on complex areas, especially breach (and causation).
- *Bolam* is the key case when assessing the standard required of professionals acting in their professional capacity at the first stage of breach. It's often very important at the second stage, too, where the potential breach concerns a choice made by the defendant as to, say, treatment or techniques.
- In respect of breach where there has been a failure to warn of risk, the key case is now *Montgomery*.

Have a go at these multiple-choice questions (MCQs):

Question 1

A surgeon is asked by his patient to disclose and explain all the risks associated with an operation.

Which one of the following options offers the correct summary as to whether the surgeon has to disclose all the risks?

A   Only risks higher than 10% would need to be explained.

B   All material risks would need to be explained – what is material depends on what is important to the patient.

C   All risks would need to be explained to the patient, even if the patient asked not to hear about them.

D   All material risks would need to be explained – what is material is determined by what is important to the doctor.

E   Only those risks lower than 10% would need to be explained.

Answer

The correct answer is option B. This follows *Montgomery*. Material risks and alternatives need to be explained. What is material is determined by what would be important to the patient.

Question 2

A dentist is facing a Negligence action. In court, she seeks to justify her treatment option for a patient by reference to what other dentists would have done in the same position.

Which one of the following best outlines the process used in determining whether the dentist has breached her duty of care?

A   The court will decide whether the body of medical opinion she relies on is reasonable and safe. It can find the body to be logically indefensible.

B   There is no strict process to follow because the defendant is not a doctor.

C   The court will probably find the body of medical opinion she relies on to be reasonable and safe, unless the potential breach concerns an omission.

D   So long as there is a body of other dentists who would have done as this one did, she cannot be found negligent.

E   The court will start from the premise that the dentist's actions were logically indefensible, though it might be persuaded otherwise.

Answer

The correct answer is option A. This is how *Bolam* would work and how *Bolitho* might be applied.

Question 3

A man goes to hospital with chest pains. The doctor does not attend in person. He should have run some standard tests but failed to do so. The tests would have picked up the man's heart condition and treatment would have been started. Instead the man is not treated. Soon after he suffers a heart attack and dies as a result of not having been treated. The doctor claims that he would not have run the tests even if he had attended.

Which one of the following is accurate as to how the question of breach would likely be determined here?

A   As this is an omission, the court is likely to find for the claimant for policy reasons.

B   As this is an omission, the court is unlikely to ask whether other doctors in this position would have negligently failed to run the tests that were required.

C   This would be not be a breach as it is too difficult to speculate on what the defendant might have done.

D   As this is an omission, the court is likely to ask whether other doctors in this position would have negligently failed to run the tests that were required. If so, there will be no breach.

E   As this is an omission, the court is likely to ask whether, had the doctor attended and not run the tests, that would have been negligent. Here we are told he should have run the tests. So this may well be a breach.

Answer

The correct answer is option E. The wording of the question suggests the answer here and, applying *Bolitho*, this looks very likely to be a breach.

Question 4

On her way home from work, an anaesthetist comes across a man who is unconscious in the street. She puts the man in the recovery position but actually causes him injury by doing so.

Which one of the following is most likely to be correct as to the standard of care that would be imposed on the anaesthetist if a Negligence action were brought against her?

A   The standard of the reasonably competent doctor.

B   The standard of the reasonably competent surgeon.

C   The standard of the reasonably competent first-aider.

D   The standard of the reasonable man.

E   The standard of the reasonably competent anaesthetist.

Answer

The correct answer is option C as the standard attaches to the task, and this doctor appears to have carried out first aid here.

Employers' Primary Liability and Vicarious Liability

After reading this chapter, you will be able to:

- understand the difference between employers' primary and secondary (vicarious) liability
- appreciate the scope of the duty of care owed by an employer to its employee
- feel confident in navigating your way through a primary liability claim
- understand the law relating to vicarious liability
- appreciate that vicarious liability is a mechanism, not a tort.

8.1 Introduction and scope

The common law recognises the need to protect employees at work, and the tort of employers' liability reflects that. It is really just Negligence in a specific context, namely, in the workplace. The first part of this chapter will concentrate on the primary liability of employers at common law. This means we follow common law Negligence principles and won't focus on statute too much. This is an area heavily governed by statute and numerous, ever-evolving regulations, but the common law duties exist alongside statute and that will be our focus. The case law itself makes this clear. It's no defence to an employer to say that it has complied with relevant statutory provisions if it hasn't also met its common law (tortious) obligations (see *Bux v Slough Metals Ltd* [1973] 1 WLR 1358).

Note: all employers must have compulsory insurance to confer protection on employees (in other words to cover any direct and/or vicarious claims made against the employer). This requirement comes from statute – the Employers' Liability (Compulsory Insurance) Act 1969 and the Employers' Liability (Compulsory Insurance) Regulations 1998. Whenever defendants (or indeed claimants) are required to have insurance to cover their particular situation, this should always ring a policy bell in your mind! You can predict that the insured party will often be the party that will be found liable (or, if the insured party is a claimant, will not be able to bring a claim) in that that party already has a 'pot of money' to deal with exactly the eventuality that has arisen. Look out for this in other areas of Negligence, not just employers' liability.

Then, we will move on to look at employers' secondary or vicarious liability. Vicarious liability simply means 'on behalf of', and typically this will involve the employer of the tortfeasor being vicariously financially liable for the torts of that employee (and that could be Negligence but equally it could be any other tort;

whereas with employers' liability we are looking only at the defendant employer's liability in Negligence) even though the employer has not committed the tort. As we'll see, vicarious liability is not a tort; it's a mechanism or device designed to shift the financial burden across to the defendant employer, where that employer has compulsory insurance to deal with any claims arising. The employer won't be vicariously liable for every single wrongdoing of the employee. So, how do we determine when the employer should be vicariously liable and when the tortfeasor employee should simply bear the burden themselves?

8.2 Structure of an employers' primary liability claim

To be clear, the structure of an employers' liability claim is exactly the same as the structure for a General Negligence claim. We consider the elements in the correct order (and you'll hopefully feel familiar with these by now): damage or loss, duty, breach, causation, remoteness and defences (and remedies). However, as you'll see, most of the fruitful discussion is to be had at the duty and breach stages, and that is where we will concentrate our efforts. (There is also an important preliminary question to ask: is the claimant an employee of the defendant?)

What's different then? Essentially two things: first, and most importantly, the claimant in this kind of claim will always be an employee of the defendant employer. This is Negligence specially designed for the employee. For that reason, it's important to establish early on that the claimant really is an employee of the defendant. If they're not, because they're actually self-employed for example, then that claimant may still be able to bring a Negligence action, but it would be a General Negligence action, and therefore it wouldn't come with the same protections as are provided for employees.

Secondly, some of the case law that we apply here is different from the General Negligence authorities. For example, the case we use at the duty of care stage, *Wilsons and Clyde Coal Co Ltd v English* [1938] AC 57, is specific to employers' primary liability. It provides that an employer owes a duty, and it also sets out the scope of that duty. Similarly, at the breach and causation stages, we apply some specific authorities which inform those elements. This is what differentiates this area from other types of Negligence, and we'll guide you through what you need to know.

8.3 Damage/loss

Unsurprisingly, the type of loss for which a claimant employee can claim is exactly the same as for General Negligence, namely personal injury, which can extend to psychiatric harm (and did in *Walker v Northumberland County Council* [1995] 1 All ER 737 and *Barber v Somerset County Council* [2004] UKHL 13), property damage and consequential economic loss. For the usual rules applying to these, do look back at **Chapter 2**. Once the loss has been established, we then move on to consider duty of care (at **8.5**).

8.4 Is the claimant an employee of the defendant?

Usually, the answer to this question will be obvious on the facts. It is rare that this is even an issue in employers' liability claims (whereas in claims concerning vicarious liability, it is often a live issue, and we will return to this question in more detail at **8.10**).

The multiple or economic reality test

The basis for this is in fairly old but still good law. The court, when determining employment status, will use a variety of sources to help it discern the economic reality of the relationship between purported employee and employer.

case example

Ready Mixed Concrete Ltd v Minister of Pensions [1968] 2 QB 497

In this case, the court had to consider the employment status of an individual who drove a concrete mixer lorry. He was also responsible for hiring and insuring the mixer lorry, and was paid by the company on the basis of his mileage in it. The company had control over his unform and stipulated that he could not use the lorry for any other business. He had no set hours, no instructions on which routes to take and was termed an 'independent contractor' in his contract.

The driver was found to be self-employed, rather than an employee of the defendant.

As a result of that case, the court can consider relevant factors in determining employment status (though this list is not exhaustive, rather indicative). These might include:

(a) *remuneration*: including monies paid, deductions taken from salary, tax contributions and so on;

(b) *level of control* that the purported employer has over the purported employee: the higher the level, the more likely the claimant is to be an employee rather than self-employed;

(c) *all other contractual factors consistent with an employment relationship*: the gloss here would be 'anything else the court deems relevant'.

Ready Mixed Concrete was further developed in *Warner Holidays Ltd v Secretary of State for Social Services* [1983] ICR 440, in which McNeil J attempted to provide a list (again, non-exhaustive) of points a court should consider in determining the employment status of a claimant. Here is the list:

(1) Level of control

(2) Provision of tools and equipment

(3) Salary

(4) Tax/PAYE/National Insurance contributions (whether and how deductions were made for these might indicate employment status)

(5) Sick pay (where this is provided, that might be indicative of employment)

(6) Bearing the risk of profit and loss (where remuneration was linked to profitability of the purported employer, that might be indicative of self-employment)

(7) Integration within the organisation

(8) Control over hours of work

(9) Right/ability to do other work

(10) How the parties described their relationship, ie labelling. (Note that the court said it appreciates that the use of labels by either party as to a relationship is a factor to consider but is not conclusive. Otherwise, all unscrupulous employers would simply ask their 'employees' to label themselves as being self-employed and so side-step liability to avoid being sued. This need for scrutiny was confirmed in *Massey v Crown Life* [1977] EWCA Civ 12.)

As for disputes that have arisen over this issue, and a discussion of relationships 'akin to employment', see **8.10** below on vicarious liability.

8.5 Employers' duty of care

It is not in question that the employer owes its employee a duty of care. This has been provided for in the law for many years. The interesting part, once the claimant is proven to be an employee of the defendant employer, is as to the scope of that duty, which we'll look at now.

A feature of the duty is that it is personal and non-delegable. This is another way of saying that the buck stops with the employer: regardless of whether the employer delegates tasks to others (which is of course what often happens in the workplace), nevertheless that employer can't delegate legal responsibility. Lord Brandon in *McDermid v Nash Dredging* [1987] 2 All ER 878 describes the characteristics of this duty as follows:

> The essential characteristic of the non-delegable duty is that, if it is not performed, it is no defence to the employer to show that he delegated its performance to a person, whether his servant or not his servant, whom he reasonably believed to be competent to perform it. Despite such delegation the employer is liable for non-performance of its duty.

case example

Wilsons and Clyde Coal Co Ltd v English [1938] AC 57

The defendant employer employed the claimant, Mr English, to work in its mine. (Mr English actually died, so technically the claimant was his estate.) Mr English was repairing an airway to one of the mines, which was used as part of the haulage system, and was at the bottom of the pit when the haulage was mistakenly started up. He tried to evade the danger via a manhole but was trapped by machinery and crushed to death. His employer tried to claim that Mr English's own negligence led to his death: he could have taken an alternative route or alerted the employee in charge of the machinery.

At first instance, the court found for the employer, but the House of Lords held that the defendant employer had a duty to ensure a safe system of work, and this legal duty could not be delegated to another employee (though tasks and responsibilities could). Thus, they said, the employer remains personally responsible for the employee's safety, and may be vicariously liable for any negligence of another. The Lords went on to outline the scope of that duty. They said that the following should be provided by the employer: safe and competent fellow employees, a safe place of work, and a safe system of work

Note: the duties outlined in *Wilsons* are not intended to be exhaustive, as subsequent case law has shown us, but they are indicative of the sorts of things that the reasonably competent employer should provide for their employee. So, for example, providing materials might include equipment, plant, machinery, tools, uniform – whatever is relevant in the particular scenario. Providing supervision might include training, advice, hands-on supervision, a safe place and system of work and so on. Essentially, and at its heart, *Wilsons* makes the point that the employer must act as the 'reasonably competent employer', a term we're familiar with from the first stage of breach when we set the standard of care expected, and the specifics of that set out in *Wilsons* itself '… exemplify the broader duty of taking reasonable care for the safety of his workers which rests on every employer' (Lord MacDermott in *Winter v Cardiff Rural District Council* [1950] 1 All ER 819).

With that in mind, we'll break down each part of the duty to see what it has been taken to mean and how it's been applied in the common law. Having said that, sometimes the duties overlap – there aren't always bright lines between them.

8.5.1 Employers' duty to provide safe and competent fellow employees

An employer has a duty to employ competent staff in the first place, and to monitor and resolve any issues arising where a member of staff conducts themselves in a way that poses a risk to the safety of other employees. (Remember this is all part and parcel of acting as the reasonably competent employer. The court is not looking for the employer to behave perfectly, but reasonably competently in the circumstances. There are obvious overlaps with the first stage of breach here and that's fine. The difference between duty and the first stage of breach feels a semantic one in this context.)

Where a member of staff has behaved incompetently, there are various options in terms of Negligence claims. That member of staff could be directly liable, if their action amounts to, say, a tort or a criminal act. The employer could also be vicariously liable in that situation – see below at **8.10**. In addition, the employer could be directly liable, in the sense that the employer itself may have breached its duty to the claimant employee in respect of the behaviour/conduct of the 'rogue' employee. This third possibility is what we are looking at now.

in practice

The claimant employee would not be able to recover damages more than once for the same loss. This is called the rule against 'double recovery'. So, whilst the claimant might have, in the above scenario, potentially three options in terms of who to sue (directly against the tortfeasor colleague, vicariously against the employer for the tort of the tortfeasor, and directly against the employer for the employer's Negligence), in reality there would be one sum of money awarded. The court would determine the quantum and from whom that comes – that is not something you need to be able to establish at this stage in your training.

Employer hires someone who is incompetent

This happened in *Black v Fife Coal Ltd* [1912] AC 149. In this case, the employer negligently appointed a colliery manager who had no experience or insight into the dangers of carbon monoxide poisoning, in a pit where its presence was a real danger. It was held that the employer had breached its duty of care to the claimant employee in employing this individual.

'Practical jokes' at work

Whether an employer has breached its duty in terms of its employees may depend on the knowledge that the employer had or ought to have had as to the conduct of that employee. (Note that, occasionally, we are pre-empting our discussion on breach, as many cases turn, at the same time, on both the scope of duty and whether that's been breached.)

We can compare and contrast the following two cases:

---

case example

Hudson v Ridge Manufacturing Company Ltd [1957] 2 QB 348

This case involved a habitual practical joker employee. The claimant was an employee of the defendant and was injured at work as a result of his 'prankster' colleague. The colleague, who was known to the employer as being a practical joker, had been warned to desist on many occasions by the employer. However, on the day in question, the colleague played yet another practical joke on the claimant, who was pinned to ground and his wrist injured.

It was held that the employer owed a duty of care to the claimant to ensure safe and competent fellow employees. The employer was aware of the issue and so should have resolved it, for example by sacking the practical joker.

---

case example

Smith v Crossley Bros [1951] 95 SJ 655

In contrast, this was a one-off prank for which the employer was not held liable (because the duty can't meaningfully extend to protecting claimants from employees about whom the defendant knows nothing). Here, as a practical joke, two mechanic employees removed the claimant's trousers and inserted a rubber hose into his anus. The rubber hose expelled compressed air, and this caused serious injury. The Court of Appeal found that the employer was not liable for the injuries as it could not have predicted them, nor prevented against them.

This argument was followed in *Graham v Commercial Bodyworks Ltd* [2015] EWCA Civ 47, in which the defendant employer was held not directly liable for the pranks of the employee.

An employer can also be liable and owe a duty in respect of bullying and sexual harassment by an employee aimed at the claimant employee. In *Harrison v Lawrence Murphy & Co, The Chartered Secretary,* 1 March 1998, a female employee was harassed by her line manager over a period of months. The partners at the firm had been aware of this but had taken no action.

example

Anton is employed by Creatives Ltd. One day at work he opens his locker, and a bucket of oil that has been propped up inside the locker spills onto him, ruining his trousers. The bucket had been placed there by Jackie, a colleague, as a joke. Anton wants to sue Creatives Ltd.

It should be said that the practical and obvious solution here might not be a legal one, but for Anton to speak to his manager about Jackie's conduct. However, if he seeks to sue his employer for Negligence, then whether or not the employer would owe a duty and be seen to have breached that duty will depend on whether the employer knew or ought to have known of Jackie's propensity for practical jokes. Was this a one-off? If so, see *Smith v Crossly Bros* above – the employer is unlikely to have breached its duty directly (been negligent) but may still be liable vicariously, if what Jackie has done amounts to a tort.

If this act was part of a pattern by Jackie, about which the employer ought reasonably to have been aware, then the employer could be directly liable for its own negligence as in *Hudson v Ridge Manufacturing*.

8.5.2 Employers' duty to provide a safe place of work

This extends to providing safe plant and equipment. Essentially, there is a duty on the employer, as part of its overriding duty as the reasonably competent employer, to ensure that the workplace is a safe place for employees to work, so far as it's reasonable to expect an employer to do that.

In terms of a safe place, this will include the normal place of work for the employee and might extend to any third party premises, for example as used by a window cleaner, as was the position in *Wilson v Tyneside Cleaning Co* [1958] 2 QB 110, though the court did stress in that case that the employer would not necessarily be able to police third party premises in the same way that it would its own. It comes down to what is reasonable for an employer to do in the circumstances and is therefore fact specific. When the claimant window cleaner argued that the employer had failed to notice that handles on the window at the third party premises were rotten (leading to the claimant's injury), the court stated that there was no breach of duty here as it was impractical for the employer reasonably to check the safety aspects of the premises.

It's useful to remember that what it is reasonable to expect an employer to know as regards safety is something that will change over time. It is something to be judged according to the general knowledge and standards of the time (*Baker v Quantum Clothing Group Ltd* [2011] UKSC 17). On this point, in *Kennedy v Cordia (Services) LLP* [2016] UKSC 6, the Supreme Court decided that a reasonable prudent employer will conduct a risk assessment in connection with its operations so as to be able to take precautions to ensure the safety of its employees.

Safety equipment and clothing, safe machinery, plant

There are many examples of cases where claimants have sought to sue their employer in employers' liability for a failure to provide any or all of the above. Let's take a look at a few of these.

In *Yorkshire Traction Co Ltd v Walter Searby* [2003] EWCA Civ 1856, the claimant was a bus driver, who was stabbed by a passenger whilst driving his bus. He claimed that his employer had been negligent in failing to provide protective screens between the driver and passengers. Whilst there was a duty to do what was reasonable to keep drivers safe, in fact in this case the Court of Appeal found that this duty had not been breached here. This was because the defendant employer *had* introduced protective screens on some buses, but most drivers had objected to them because they reflected light at night, dazzling the drivers and were therefore dangerous. (It was also argued that the risk from passenger attack was very low; this links back to breach factors that help a court determine whether there has been a breach or not – see **Chapter 3**.)

In *Qualcast v Haynes* [1959] AC 743, it was held that the employer had not breached its duty to provide protective equipment (we say had 'discharged its duty') in that protective boots had been provided for the claimant employee, who had nevertheless been injured when he didn't wear them. These days, this case may well have been decided differently, and in the claimant's favour, though perhaps still reduced for contributory negligence. At the time, doing what was reasonable simply extended to providing equipment (which the defendant employer had done). It didn't extend to ensuring that the claimant wore the equipment, especially, where, as here, the claimant was inexperienced. In light of various health and safety statutes and regulations enacted since this case was decided (for example the Employer's Liability (Defective Equipment) Act 1969) and in light of a general shift towards a more claimant-friendly approach in the workplace, the concept of what is reasonable for an employer to do has changed somewhat – more is expected to demonstrate reasonableness on the part of the employer.

8.5.3 Employers' duty to provide a safe system of work

This has been taken to include '… such matters as the physical layout of the job, the setting of the stage, the sequence in which the work is to be carried out, the provision of warnings and notices, and the issue of special instructions' (Lord Greene in *Speed v Thomas Swift Co Ltd* [1943] KB 557).

case example

General Cleaning Contractors Ltd v Christmas [1954] AC 180

Mr Christmas, the claimant, was a window cleaner with 20 years of experience, employed by the defendant employer. He was tasked with cleaning the insides of the windows at a site and then the outside. Rather than using ladders, some employees had worked out a time-saving method of climbing onto the windowsills and holding onto the window frames whilst cleaning the windows. Mr Christmas was one of these. He had pulled open the upper half of a sash window in order to grip the bottom sash, but the top part slipped down and trapped his fingers. He then let go and fell to the ground, suffering personal injury. He claimed against his employer in employers' liability, claiming that the defendant had not acted as the reasonable employer, in that he had not received any instructions, warnings or training in relation to sash windows. The defendant argued that it was not liable because the claimant had a great deal of experience and should have recognised the risk.

The House of Lords found the defendant employer liable. It had breached its duty in that no site assessment had been done, when it would have been reasonable to do one, and no safe system of work had been put in place. It was noted: 'An employer must take into account that workmen may have disregard for their own safety. This means they [the employer] must minimise the danger of a workman's own carelessness and take reasonable care to ensure that employees comply with necessary safety instructions.'

8.5.4 Employers' duty to take reasonable care to ensure the safety of staff is not an absolute duty

We come back again to this word 'reasonable'. The duty on the employer is always to act as a reasonably competent employer, not a perfect employer. Staying with this principle of employers needing to provide a safe system of work, we can compare and contrast two cases.

In *Clifford v Charles Challen and Son Ltd* [1953] AC 643 it was held that the employer had breached its duty of care by failing to supervise staff to see that barrier cream was used. (This might be seen as relevant to a safe system or place of work. Note we said earlier that there aren't always bright lines between these duties, given that they are all part and parcel of the one duty to take reasonable care.)

In this case, Denning LJ stated that an employer '... must provide proper appliances to safeguard [his men who are asked to work with dangerous substances], he must set in force the necessary system by which they use the appliances ... and he must do his best to see that they adhere to it'.

In the slightly later case of *Woods v Durable Suites Ltd* [1953] 1 WLR 857, which also concerned the wearing of protective barrier cream, the employer had not breached its duty of care. One of the differences here was that the barrier cream was readily available on the premises, and the foreman had made known to the claimant that he should be wearing it. Also, the claimant had been provided with instructions and clear guidance on when and how to use the cream. Here, then, the defendant employer had discharged its duty of care. Singelton LJ stated: 'I do not believe it to be part of the common law of England that an employer is bound, through his foreman, to stand over the workmen of age and experience every moment they are working and every time that they cease to work, in order to see that they do what they are supposed to do.' This is a powerful reminder that what it is reasonable to expect an employer to do depends on the circumstances of the case.

It makes sense that employers would be required to do what's reasonable in terms of taking into account their employees' characteristics. For example, in *Paris v Stepney Borough Council* [1951] AC 367 (see **Chapter 3**, 'Breach of Duty' for more on this), the defendant employer should have worked harder to ensure the safety of the claimant employee welder who had only one sighted eye in the first place.

It might help, as you organise your consolidation, to picture the duty stage like this:

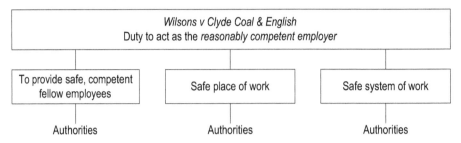

Figure 8.1   Duty of care in employers' liability

8.6   Breach of duty

You'll have noticed that we have effectively examined this element in some detail already. In analysing whether a duty is or isn't owed by an employer to an employee, in most cases we also took this one step further to try and determine whether the employer had breached any such duty.

As a reminder, there are two stages to breach: we first of all set the standard expected of the employer, and we say that is a question of law because it's an objective standard. Here we would expect employers to meet the standard of the reasonably competent employer (applying *Wilsons*). We might usefully make that more specific on occasions, depending on the type of claim, for example to pinpoint the standard of the reasonably competent employer of window cleaners, or the reasonably competent employer of mine workers, etc.

Next, we try to determine whether the employer has fallen below that standard, and that is a question of fact, in that we look at the particular circumstances of the case. This can best be illustrated by looking back at two cases, *Clifford* and *Woods* (above). The standard expected of the employer in each case was that of the reasonably competent employer (of course), and both cases concerned the provision of barrier cream. In *Clifford*, that standard was breached; in *Woods* it was not – the factual breach stage is where we get to consider what has actually happened and why.

8.7   Causation

Causation is broken into two parts, factual and legal, just as it is with General Negligence. (Look back at **Chapter 4** for a reminder.) The main difference is that, at the factual causation stage, the authority for the but for test is different. It comes from a case called *McWilliams v Sir William Arrol* [1962] 1 WLR 295. This was a case in which the claimant's estate (the wife) brought an action in respect of her husband. He was a steel erector who fell 70 feet to his death at work. His employer had failed to provide him with a safety harness. His wife sued both in common law and under statute (Factories Act 1937). The House of Lords applied the but for test and found on the evidence that but for (had it not been for) the employer's failure to provide a harness, the claimant would probably still have suffered his loss at that time and in that way because he would have refused to wear any safety harness provided. The claim therefore failed at the factual causation stage.

This case is now the authority for the but for test in employers' liability claims. Legal causation is dealt with in exactly the same way as for General Negligence, applying the same authorities and principles.

8.8 Remoteness

The usual rules of remoteness apply (see **Chapter 5**), namely that the claimant will need to prove they have suffered a reasonably foreseeable type of loss, applying *The Wagon Mound (No 1)*.

8.9 Defences

The usual general defences apply (see **Chapter 6**), namely *volenti* or consent, *ex Turpi* or illegality, and contributory negligence.

8.9.1 *Volenti*/consent

Whilst this defence can be successfully pleaded by a defendant employer, the courts are healthily sceptical of it in an employment context. This is because they are aware that sometimes a claimant employee, perhaps concerned that their job might be on the line if they refuse, will not be able, of their own free will, to give meaningful consent to run the risk of the injury that then occurs. This was first recognised as an issue in *Smith v Charles Baker & Sons* [1891] AC 325 and confirmed in *Bowater v Rowley Regis Corporation* [1944] KB 476.

Therefore, this defence is only likely to run where the claimant employee has acted in a way that's so obviously dangerous or reckless as to be tantamount to 'intermeddling with an unexploded bomb' (Asquith J in *Dann v Hamilton* [1939] 1 KB 509), such that their consent is inferred from their actions. This was the case in *ICI Ltd v Shatwell* [1965] AC 656 in which the two employees took dangerous shortcuts at work, in that they tried to check explosive detonators without following the correct procedures, resulting in injury. Their employer's *volenti* defence succeeded.

8.9.2 Contributory negligence

This partial defence is utilised a lot in the context of employers' liability claims. For the rules as to how it works, see **Chapter 6**. For some examples, see *Clifford* (already discussed above at **8.5.4** in which the claimant's damages were reduced by 50%) and *Sherlock v Chester City Council* [2004] EWCA Civ 201 where the claimant's damages were reduced by 60%. Although the employer had not given clear instructions to its employee (a joiner) and so had failed to provide a safe system of work, still the claimant, who was very experienced, could have taken the relevant safety precautions himself.

in practice
Post the Covid-19 pandemic that began in 2020, it will be interesting to note whether new types of employers' liability claims will be brought, perhaps by claimants who were caught in the first wave of illness (when arguably our knowledge as to transmission and safety wasn't as it is now) and have since recovered sufficiently to think about bringing Negligence actions against their employers. Potential claims might include supermarket check-out workers not being adequately screened or protected from customers, delivery drivers whose employers did not adequately assess or warn them as regards contact with the public, teachers and NHS staff on the frontline, and so on. What do you think?

8.10 Vicarious liability

Vicarious liability is a form of secondary liability. As mentioned right at the beginning of this chapter, it's not a tort but a mechanism or device for ensuring that the claimant has a form of recompense, if not from the tortfeasor themselves (who may not have funds to pay) then from the tortfeasor's employer.

There is no need to prove fault on the part of the defendant employer. That's because the employer is not the tortfeasor but is financially liable for the tortfeasor. As such, we say that vicarious liability incurs strict liability. Once the tort has been committed, by an employee of the defendant in the course of employment, then, without more, the defendant will be liable.

Vicarious liability most often arises between employer/employee and that will be our focus here. (It can arise through other relationships such as principal and agent but that's outside the ambit of this book.)

8.10.1 Rationale for vicarious liability

Why should the employer be financially liable for the torts of its employee? The rationale is mostly policy-based (there's a surprise!). Here is a summary of some of the justifications that various academics, commentators and judges have suggested. Do you agree with them? Can you think of any more?

(1) The 'deep pockets' theory, ie that the employer has compulsory insurance under the Employers' Liability (Compulsory Insurance) Act 1969 and so is prepared and financially able to pay out for such an eventuality.

(2) The tort was committed whilst on the employer's 'watch' and so the employer should ordinarily bear (financial) responsibility for it. This might also have the effect of encouraging or maintaining high standards from employers in terms of looking after their employees so as to avoid being sued.

(3) The 'benefit/burden' theory: if an employer gains the benefit of an employee, it is fair that it should also bear the burden when things go wrong.

8.10.2 Who can sue?

Unlike with employers' liability, where the claimant must be an employee of the defendant employer, with secondary or vicarious liability, the claimant could be anyone at all who has suffered recognisable loss as the result of a tort. Note that the tort need not be Negligence; it could be any tort. It is the tortfeasor who must be an employee of the defendant. In diagram form, that would look something like this:

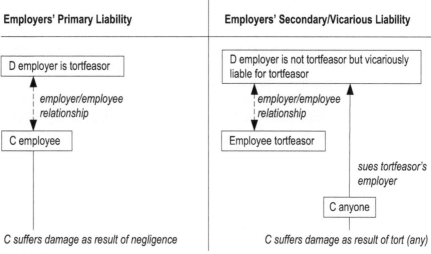

Figure 8.2   Who can sue?

8.10.3 Elements of vicarious liability

There are only three elements to be established by the claimant in order to succeed in their vicarious claim against the tortfeasor's employer. The claimant must prove that:

(a) a tort has been committed;

(b) by the employee of the defendant;

(c) in the course of employment.

A tort has been committed

This is an essential but often overlooked component! You can't sue a defendant employer for its employee's tort if the employee hasn't committed a tort. You need to establish this first. That tort could be anything – Negligence, trespass to the person, etc. To establish that a tort has been committed, you would simply follow the structure for proving that tort. For Negligence, you would go through the Negligence sequence (see **Chapters 2–6**); for trespass to the person, you would go through the necessary steps for determining whether there has been an assault or battery (see **Chapter 13**), and so on. Only once a tort has been committed can you move to the second element for a vicarious liability claim.

Note: the case law here suggests that employers could be liable both for torts and for intentional wrongful acts not all of which are torts, such as theft, harassment and misuse of private information.

By the employee of the defendant

This is something we looked at above at **8.4**. You'll see that the test is the same, when determining employment status, but we are using it for different reasons, depending on whether this is an employers' liability claim against the defendant employer, or a secondary/vicarious claim. Have another look at **Figure 8.2** above. Can you see that for a claim in employers' liability, the claimant must prove that *they are* an employee of the defendant? But for a vicarious liability claim, the claimant (who could be anyone – an employee or not) needs to prove that the *tortfeasor* is an employee of the defendant.

The point here is that if the tortfeasor is not employed by the defendant, but is self-employed, then the claimant cannot sue the employer vicariously (because the tortfeasor doesn't have an employer). The claimant's only option in that situation would be to sue the tortfeasor directly. That's possible but not ideal, in that the tortfeasor may or may not have the funds to pay.

This was found to be the position in *Barclays Bank v Various Claimants* [2020] UKSC 13. Over 100 claimants alleged that they had been sexually assaulted by Dr Bates in the course of medical examinations. He carried out such examinations for Barclays, but he was not employed by Barclays and was engaged by the bank as a 'classic independent contractor'. The Supreme Court found simply that Dr Bates was, indeed, self-employed, and so Barclays could not be vicariously liable for his actions. (This reads as a relatively straightforward case at Supreme Court level, but there was some confusion in the lower courts in that, for a while, this seemed to be examined as though it went to the third element of vicarious liability, being whether the tort happened 'in the course of employment'.)

A relationship of, or akin to, employment

It may be obvious to all parties that the tortfeasor is employed by the defendant. Have a look at this example.

example

Jose is doing his shopping in a supermarket, Chainsbury's. Norman, an employee of Chainsbury's, is stacking some shelves, but he is not following instructions from his employer as to how to do this safely. He stacks some heavy items on a high shelf. They fall on Jose, breaking his toe.

Jose is likely to bring an action vicariously against Chainsbury's for Norman's potential tort (Negligence). To bring an action vicariously, he would first of all need to show that a tort has been committed, and that is probably fairly straightforward here in that the Negligence elements look clear. (There may be a contributory negligence defence, but this isn't obvious from the facts.)

Secondly, Jose would need to show that Norman is an employee of Chainsbury's, and that seems clear here too. Apart from the fact that the questions tells us this ('Norman, an employee of Chainsbury's'), it is also apparent from the facts. Norman is stacking shelves as part of his job, has presumably signed an employment contract, is wearing a uniform, etc. For this reason, we wouldn't need to go behind that finding, and we can conclude he is an employee.

Finally, we would need to ascertain whether the tort happened in the course of Norman's employment. We haven't yet got to that part in our discussion, but it seems clear that Norman is acting on work time, doing something that is part of his job – there is a close connection between what he's doing when he commits the tort and his job – and so this part would probably be satisfied

Sometimes it will be more difficult to prove the employment status of the tortfeasor. A line of cases has explored the difficulties inherent with certain types of 'employment'.

JGE v Trustees of the Portsmouth Roman Catholic Diocesan Trust [2012] EWCA Civ 938

case example

Here, the female claimant sought damages for sexual abuse and rape perpetrated by a parish priest, while the claimant was living in a children's home run by nuns. The issue was how to classify the priest. The court accepted he was not an employee of the Roman Catholic diocese, in that there was no contract between the Trust and the priest, the Trust had no control over him and he didn't receive remuneration. The Court took the highly pragmatic (and policy-driven) decision of extending vicarious liability to include a 'relationship akin to employment' where there was no employment in the conventional sense. The test seemed to be whether the relationship of the diocese and the priest was so close in character to one of employer/employee that it was fair to hold the diocese vicariously liable. This was policy driven in that it was fair to allow the claimant a remedy for such heinous events, and also the defendant Trust was insured.

Various Claimants v Institute of the Brothers of the Christian Schools [2012] UKSC 56 ('the *Christian Brothers* case')

case example

This action was brought by 170 men who had been sexually and physically abused over a 40-year period by members ('the brothers') supplied to teach in a residential school. The brothers had been appointed by 'the Institute', an unincorporated association of lay brothers of the Catholic church.

The first problem was in establishing that there was an employment relationship between the defendant Institute and the brothers. Evidence showed that the brothers were appointed verbally, and the Institute had no right to dismiss them, nor did it pay them wages. It seemed they were neither employed nor independent contractors. The Supreme Court held that the brothers were in a relationship 'akin to employment' with the Institute. Lord Phillips stated that the policy underlying vicarious liability was simple: '… to ensure, so far as it is fair, just and reasonable, that liability for a tortious wrong is borne by a defendant with the means to compensate a victim'.

Lord Phillips then identified five specific policy reasons which supported his decision to find the Institute vicariously liable:

i)   The employer is more likely to have the means to compensate the victim than the employee ...;

ii) The tort will have been committed as a result of activity being taken by the employee on behalf of the employer;

iii) The employee's activity is likely to be part of the business activity of the employer;

iv) The employer, by employing the employee to carry on the activity will have created the risk of the tort committed by the employee;

v)   The employee will, to a greater or lesser degree, have been under the control of the employer.

This approach to employment was confirmed by the Supreme Court in *Cox v Ministry of Justice* [2016] UKSC 10, in which the prison service was found to be vicariously liable for the torts of a prisoner working in the prison kitchens of HM Prison Swansea. The female claimant, Cox, was the catering manager and had been negligently injured by the prisoner who was carrying out paid work under supervision in the kitchen when he dropped a large bag of rice onto her back.

Lord Reed stated:

Prisoners working in the prison kitchen ... are integrated into the operation of the prison, so that activities assigned to them by the prison service form an integral part of the activities which it carries out in the furtherance of its aims ... They are placed by the prison service in a position where there is a risk that they may commit a variety of negligent acts within the field of activities assigned to them ... Furthermore, they work under the direction of prison staff. Mrs Cox was injured as a result of negligence by Mr Inder in carrying on the activities assigned to him. The prison service is therefore vicariously liable to her.

This approach was again followed by the Supreme Court in *Armes v Nottinghamshire County Council* [2017] UKSC 60. It was held that the relationship between a local authority, responsible for placing children in care, and foster parents into whose homes the children were placed, was akin to employment. This ensured that the local authority was held vicariously liable for abuse perpetrated by the foster parents.

In the course of employment

This is the final element that must be proven for a vicarious claim to succeed. The rationale here is that employers should only be vicariously liable for torts committed while on the employer's 'watch'.

The close connection test

We can just go directly to the current test (the House of Lords having rejected the old law on this). It is called the close connection test and comes from *Lister v Hesley Hall* [2002] 1 AC 215. The defendant company ran a local children's home and was held vicariously liable for sexual abuse committed by one of its employees, a warden. Lord Steyn outlined that the correct approach when determining whether the torts happened in the course of employment was 'to concentrate on the relative closeness of the connection between the nature of the employment and the particular tort'. In this case, the warden's torts were closely connected with his employment, as it was precisely because of his position of trust that he was able to exploit the children. The torts were also committed on the employer's premises and during working hours.

What does the close connection test actually mean?

Whilst the result of *Lister* cannot be argued with, the meaning and wording of the test is more problematic and has proved so over the years. How closely connected to their employment do the employee's actions have to be? In the *Christian Brothers* case (see above), Lord Phillips said that the problem with the close connection test was that it 'tells one nothing about the nature of the connection'.

A Supreme Court case has looked at this question again, handing down what looks to be a very important judgment. Among other things, it affirms but also clarifies an earlier Supreme Court decision called *Mohamud v WM Morrison Supermarkets Plc* [2016] UKSC 11. Let's take a look at the case below in detail.

---

case example

WM Morrisons Supermarkets plc v Various Claimants [2020] UKSC 12

Motivated by a grudge against his employer following a minor disciplinary hearing, the former senior internal IT auditor of Morrisons, Mr Skelton, downloaded the payroll data of over 100,000 employees onto a personal USB stick. At home, he uploaded the data onto a file-sharing website and sent anonymous links to three UK newspapers. Over 9,000 of the employees whose data had been shared brought an action again Mr Skelton for, among other things, the tort of misuse of private information. The question was as to whether Morrisons could be vicariously liable, due to the tort happening in the course of employment.

The Supreme Court upheld Morrisons' appeal (the High Court and Court of Appeal both having found that Morrisons *was* vicariously liable). Lord Reed, giving the judgment of the Court, stated that the lower courts had 'misunderstood the principles governing vicarious liability in a number of relevant aspects'. The question was as follows: Was Mr Skelton's wrongful disclosure of information to be regarded as done by him while acting in the course of employment? The answer was no, having regard to the following:

(1) First, the disclosure of data on the internet did not form part of Mr Skelton's functions or 'field of activities'. It was not an act he was authorised to do.

(2) Secondly, it was not sufficient for the imposition of vicarious liability that the employment gave the employee 'the mere opportunity' to commit a wrongful act, or that the employee was 'doing acts of the same kind as those which it was within his authority to do'.

(3) Whilst there was a 'close temporal link' and an 'unbroken chain of causation' between the provision of data to Mr Skelton in the course of his employment and its subsequent disclosure, 'a temporal or causal connection does not in itself satisfy the close connection test'.

(4) Motive was not irrelevant. On the contrary: 'whether he was acting on his employer's business or for purely personal reasons was highly material.' Here, Mr Skelton was 'not acting on his employer's business but in pursuit of his own private ends ... seeking vengeance for the disciplinary proceedings some months earlier'.

It will be very interesting to see whether this judgment now clarifies this third stage of vicarious liability.

And finally ...

Remember that once those three elements are established, the defendant employer will be vicariously liable. This is a strict liability mechanism, so it's not open to the defendant to plead defences because this is not about its fault or lack of it.

8.11 Further reading

K Patten, 'Personal Injury: Step Back in Time' (2013) 163 NLJ 62.

P Gilliker, 'Analysing Institutional Liability for Child Sexual Abuse in England and Wales and Australia: Vicarious Liability, Non-Delegable Duties and Statutory Intervention' [2018] CLJ 506.

P Morgan, 'Certainty in Vicarious Liability: A Quest for a Chimaera?' [2016] CLJ 202.

- Employers' primary liability is Negligence in a specific context, namely a claim brought by an employee against their employer.
- The structure is the same as for General Negligence, though some of the authorities are different.
- Secondary or vicarious liability renders the defendant employer financially liable for the torts of that employer's employee (the tortfeasor).
- Vicarious liability is not a tort – its effect is to make the employer strictly liable once three elements are established.

Have a go at these multiple-choice questions (MCQs):

Question 1

It is a man's first day at work on a building site. He is encouraged by his foreman to wear protective barrier cream on his hands. He is shown where this is kept and given guidance on how to use it and why it's important. He fails to wear it and contracts a skin disease on his hands.

Which one of the following options offers the most likely response if the man tries to sue his employer in employers' liability?

A There is likely to be a breach here as the employer (through the foreman) should have worked harder to ensure the man wore the barrier cream.

B   There is likely to be a breach here as the employer (through the foreman) did what was unreasonable in the circumstances.

C   There is unlikely to be a breach here as the employer (through the foreman) did what was reasonable in the circumstances.

D   There is unlikely to be a breach here as the employer is not obliged to provide protective barrier creams.

E   There is likely to be a breach here as the employer should have spoken directly to the man about barrier cream and not delegated this task to his foreman.

Answer

The correct answer is option C. The duty on the employer is to do what is reasonable in the circumstances. It looks as though the foreman has done that here, and without more it seems unlikely that this would be a breach.

Question 2

A woman arrives at work on a farm and is asked by her employer to drive a tractor. She has never driven a tractor before and her employer knows this. She agrees to do it anyway, but she is then injured when she accidentally drives the tractor into an unmarked ditch.

Which one of the following best outlines how the defence of *volenti* would work in this situation?

A   Her employer probably won't succeed with this defence as her consent to run the risk of any injury was not given freely.

B   Her employer will probably succeed with this defence as her consent to run the risk of any injury was given freely.

C   Her employer will probably succeed with this defence as she did not question the employer's instruction.

D   Her employer will probably not succeed with this defence as it only applies to unexploded bombs.

E   Her employer will probably succeed with this defence as she consented to drive the tractor.

Answer

The correct answer is option A. The courts are wary of allowing this defence in all but extreme circumstances. The facts here suggest the woman may have felt compelled to agree to drive the tractor.

Question 3

An employer is facing a vicarious liability from a claimant in respect of one of its employees who was negligent. The employer wants to plead a defence.

Which one of the following is accurate as to why the employer cannot plead a defence here?

A   Because the employer should have pleaded defences at an earlier stage.

B   Because the employer was at fault in hiring the employee in the first place.

C   Because vicarious liability does not allow the defendant employer to plead defences for policy reasons.

D   Because vicarious liability is not a strict liability mechanism.

E   Because vicarious liability is a strict liability mechanism that renders an employer financially liable though that employer is not the tortfeasor. It's not for the defendant employer to plead defences.

Answer

The correct answer is option E. Yes, vicarious liability is a strict liability mechanism.

Question 4

A man is described in his contract as being self-employed. He wishes to bring an action in employers' liability against the woman he believes to be his employer, for her negligence in hiring an incompetent colleague.

Which one of the following is correct as to the man's employment status?

A   He won't be seen as self-employed because labelling in contracts is not reliable.

B   The court would accept that he was self-employed because of the wording of the contract.

C   He may be employed notwithstanding what his contract says. We would need more information to form a view.

D   He would be seen as employed because he believes himself to be.

E   He would be seen as self-employed because on the balance of probabilities his contract is correct.

Answer

The correct answer is option C. Labelling in contracts is taken into account but is not conclusive. We'd need much more information here to determine the man's employment status.

chapter

9

Product Liability

study points

After reading this chapter, you will be able to:

- appreciate that product liability encompasses claims under common law and under statute (the Consumer Protection Act (CPA) 1987)
- understand how to bring a claim for product liability in General Negligence and the limitations of such a claim
- apply relevant case law to both types of claim
- define key terms under the CPA 1987, such as product and defect.

9.1 Introduction

Product liability covers the law relating to loss caused by products. Its rationale is to hold manufacturers accountable for unsafe goods. Manufacturers, distributers, suppliers and retailers can all be held responsible, where a product or any of its component parts are defective, and that liability can arise under the Consumer Protection Act (CPA) 1987 or the common law of Negligence. We'll spend some time looking at precisely what we mean by 'product' and 'defect' shortly.

Other forms of liability

In addition to a claim under the CPA 1987 or in Negligence, a product liability claim can be based on the following grounds: contract, the Fatal Accidents Act 1976 and under criminal law. Although we won't be concentrating on these, from a practical point of view, it's good to have insight into the context of this topic. Here is a brief outline of the position in relation to each for completeness. (The contract law information has relevance for us in that some understanding of the basic principles of contract law may shed light on aspects of tortious claims made under the CPA 1987.)

In contract law, a claim for breach of an express or implied term of a contract can be brought on a strict liability basis, meaning there is no requirement to prove fault and the claimant doesn't need to prove that the retailer or producer was negligent. Also, because damages in contract are not limited to personal injury, property damage and consequential economic loss, as they are in Negligence, a claim in contract might be more attractive where a claimant wishes to be compensated for their pure economic loss (usually loss of profits).

Remember that a third party who suffers loss generally has no right of action under a contract; only the purchaser of the product who suffered the loss has that right. Note that *Donoghue v Stevenson* was a defective product claim – the bottle of ginger beer was defective – but Mrs Donoghue couldn't claim in contract because she didn't purchase the ginger beer. Which is why she brought her action against the manufacturer in Negligence. Behold! The birth of Negligence!

Next, if a product causes death, the dependants of the deceased can bring a claim under the Fatal Accidents Act 1976. As to criminal liability, manufacturers and suppliers of defective products could face criminal liability in relation to the death of the victim. This is governed by the Corporate Manslaughter and Corporate Homicide Act 2007. Individual directors cannot be convicted of an offence, only the company.

Claims under the CPA 1987 and in common law Negligence

We'll now work through the mechanics of a claim under the CPA 1987, and then consider the circumstances in which you might choose instead to bring a common law Negligence claim.

9.2 Claims under the CPA 1987 for defective products

The CPA 1987 makes the manufacturer of a product, and everyone else dealing with that product through the supply chain, *strictly liable* for damage caused to a claimant. That means there's no need to prove fault, unlike with a common law Negligence claim where the fault stage is breach – the part where we look at whether the defendant was at fault. This might make a claim through the CPA 1987 more attractive to claimants in some circumstances. That damage might be personal injury or property damage, and it needs to have been caused 'wholly or partly' by a defect in the product.

Strict liability is not absolute liability, which means that defendant manufacturers have a number of defences available to them (some of them highly technical). We'll work through the structure of a claim now. You may find it helpful to have a copy of the CPA 1987 in front of you so that you can refer back to it as we move through a claim.

9.2.1 Who can sue and be sued?

The CPA 1987 isn't crystal clear as to *who can sue*, but it would seem that anyone who was caused damage of a recognisable kind 'wholly or partly' by a defect in a product can sue (s 2(1)). This would usually be the consumer of the product, but it could be anyone else affected by it.

example

Jess buys a computer for her daughter, Sadie. They set it up together, but due a faulty component, the screen overheats, and both Jess and Sadie suffer serious burns to their hands when they touch the screen.

Here, as we will see, the product (computer) looks to be defective. Jess bought the computer, but both her and her daughter are injured as they set it up. So as both are affected 'wholly or partly' by the defect, they can both sue (provided their personal injury claims reach the damages threshold that we'll discuss below).

As to *who to sue*, there is a list of potential defendants given in s 1(2) and s 2(2)(a)–(c). This covers: manufacturers and producers, 'own-branders' (that is to say, companies who put their own name on a product made for them by someone else), as well as importers into the European Union. Claims are most often brought against the product's producer – the company or individual that has their name on the product, though if the product has been imported to the UK from outside of the European Union, then the importer is regarded as the producer. It's also possible, where there's more than one potential defendant, that they can be jointly and severally liable (s 2(5)).

2   Liability for defective products

(1)   Subject to the following provisions of this Part, where any damage is caused wholly or partly by a defect in a product, every person to whom subsection (2) below applies shall be liable for the damage.

(2)   This subsection applies to—

(a)   the producer of the product;

(b)   any person who, by putting his name on the product or using a trade mark or other distinguishing mark in relation to the product, has held himself out to be the producer of the product;

(c)   any person who has imported the product into a member State from a place outside the member States in order, in the course of any business of his, to supply it to another.

Note: the wording and application of the statute may change as a result of Brexit (for example, in terms of references to 'European Union' and 'member State(s)').

According to s 2(3), suppliers can also be sued, provided they fit the criteria set out in s 2(3)(a)–(c). The supplier can be liable for the damage if:

(a)   the person who suffered the damage requests the supplier to identify one or more of the persons (whether still in existence or not) to whom subsection (2) above applies in relation to the product;

(b)   that request is made within a reasonable period after the damage occurs and at a time when it is not reasonably practicable for the person making the request to identify all those persons; and

(c)   the supplier fails, within a reasonable period after receiving the request, either to comply with the request or to identify the person who supplied the product to him.

Essentially this tells us that a supplier can be liable if they don't provide (presumably to the claimant) information requested, within a reasonable time, about who the producer, own-brander or importer of the product is, or, failing that, if they don't provide information as to who supplied the product to them.

9.2.2 What damage can the claimant claim for?

Section 5(1) of the CPA 1987 is helpful here. It tells us that the claimant can claim for death, personal injury or property damage. Section 5(3) and (4) goes further:

(3) A person shall not be liable under section 2 above for any loss of or damage to any property which, at the time it is lost or damaged, is not—

  (a) of a description of property ordinarily intended for private use, occupation or consumption; and

  (b) intended by the person suffering the loss or damage mainly for his own private use, occupation or consumption.

(4) No damages shall be awarded to any person by virtue of this Part in respect of any loss of or damage to any property if the amount which would fall to be so awarded to that person, apart from this subsection and any liability for interest, does not exceed £275.

In other words, you can only claim for property damage if that property 'is ordinarily intended for private use' (s 5(3)(a) and (b)). This is to differentiate it from business property, to which the CPA 1987 isn't really intended to apply. If a business suffers loss as a result of a defective product, it would normally pursue a contractual or common law Negligence claim.

Section 5(4) tells us that the value of the property claimed for must exceed £275. That's the replacement value of the property, rather than the amount paid for it when the product was purchased. That's a fairly low threshold and hasn't changed since 1987 when the CPA 1987 was enacted. If the relevant property is business property and/or used as such, and/or its replacement value is less than £275 (and a claim is nonetheless worthwhile), an option would be to bring that action in Negligence. We'll look at a Negligence claim below at **9.3**.

The claimant cannot claim for pure economic loss. This is made clear in s 5(2) which talks about exclusions for the defective product itself. In other words, you can claim for damage *caused* by the defective product, but not for the defective product itself (for the latter, the claimant would bring a contract claim). Remember this is the reason why Mrs Donoghue could not claim for the defective product itself, but only for the damage caused by it – the bottle was a defective product and the economic loss must flow from damage to person or property to be recoverable in tort.

9.2.3 What is a 'product'?

Products are defined in s 1(2) and include '… any goods or electricity [including] a product which is comprised in another product' (ie component parts). The definition continues in s 45 to include 'substances, growing crops and things comprised in land by virtue of being attached to it, and any ship, aircraft or vehicle'. It's a wide definition and has been held to cover, for example, blood products provided for transfusions (*A v National Blood Authority* [2001] 3 All ER 289). Since 2000, it has also included agricultural produce as a result of the BSE ('mad cow disease') crisis.

Generally speaking, defining the product won't be the controversial part, but occasionally there are questions raised about this. Note that where a component part, incorporated into a finished product, is defective, *both* the manufacturer of the component *and* the manufacturer of the finished product are potentially liable under the CPA 1987.

9.2.4 What is a 'defect'?

The meaning of a defective product is found in s 3 (and we also have some case law to help illustrate the discussions that have been had about this):

(1) … there is a defect in a product for the purposes of this Part if the safety of the product is not such as persons generally are entitled to expect.

There are some interesting questions here. First, who are 'persons generally'? This would seem to be the claimant, of course, who would hope the court agrees with them. Is this intended to be an objective test? It's difficult to know precisely who is envisaged here. Arguments in court from defendants have often turned on their interpretation of 'persons generally', ie the defendant claims that persons would expect the product to be as it exists in its current form, and the claimant states that the product in its current form is defective as it does *not* meet the standard that persons generally are entitled to expect.

Importantly, the defect is linked to *safety* and the (objective?) expectations of the product as regards its safety. (So inherently dangerous items, such as razor blades, would not be defective *per se*.)

How do we assess whether an item is defective then? Section 3(2)(a)–(c) is helpful here (and various cases have informed how this section is to be interpreted):

(2) … all the circumstances shall be taken into account, including—

  (a) the manner in which, and purposes for which, the product has been marketed, its get-up, the use of any mark in relation to the product and any instructions for, or warnings with respect to, doing or refraining from doing anything with or in relation to the product;

  (b) what might reasonably be expected to be done with or in relation to the product; and

  (c) the time when the product was supplied by its producer to another …

Section 3(2)(a) goes to the way in which the product has been marketed. How is it packaged? Are there instructions? Warnings? What do they say? This section allows the court to look at the product as a whole and ask whether the way it's marketed meets the standards of safety that persons generally are entitled to expect. Section 3(2)(b) allows discussion of the reasonable expectation of the product – are you using it for the purpose for which it was intended? For example, if I use a hairdryer as a cricket-bat, or a turntable to serve nibbles to guests, I am not using products for the purpose for which they were intended and can't complain if the safety of the product is compromised as a result.

Let's look at some case law here.

Richardson v London Rubber Company Products Ltd [2000] Lloyd's Rep Med 280

The claimant, Mrs Richardson, failed in her claim for damages for personal injury (her pregnancy) when a condom manufactured by the defendant split during sexual intercourse with her husband. (This was an action brought exclusively under the CPA 1987 and not in Negligence.) The claimant argued that the condom was defective, as it had been weakened by ozone while at the defendant's factory. Whilst the defendant company agreed that there had been ozone weakening, it said that this had happened after the product had been used, while it had been stored in a cupboard pending trial.

The judge held that the claimant had failed to prove that the condom was defective under the meaning of the CPA 1987. He concluded that it was impossible to be certain why the condom split, as scientific research showed that occasionally they just split for no obvious reason. There was no expectation that any method would be 100% effective.

Abouzaid v Mothercare (UK) Ltd [2000] EWCA Civ 348

The claimant was a boy of 12 who was injured while helping his mother to attach a fleece-lined sleeping bag to his younger brother's pushchair (a 'Cosytoes' product). As the claimant tried to affix the product to elasticated straps at the back, it pinged off and the buckle fastener hit him in the eye, causing him a serious eye injury.

The Court of Appeal held that this case was 'close to the borderline' but that this was a defective product, applying s 3 of the CPA 1987. It said that the manufacturer could have done more to prevent accidents of this type occurring, such as by using a different method to fasten the product to the pushchair, or by providing warnings. It would have been easy for the defendant to do so and it had not chosen to do this.

In *Pollard v Tesco Stores Ltd* [2006] EWCA Civ 393, the Court of Appeal determined that the child-resistant top on a bottle of detergent was not defective, despite it having been opened by a child. The claim was dismissed on the grounds that consumers would have an expectation only that a child-proof cap was harder for a child to remove than a normal cap, and that was still the case here.

A and Others v National Blood Authority [2001] 3 All ER 289

The claimants contracted hepatitis C after being given contaminated blood during transfusions. The people who had donated the blood had been infected with hepatitis C, but at the time they donated, there was no way of testing for it. Even by the time of the transfusions themselves, whilst the medical profession knew that the disease could be transmitted in blood, they still had no way of testing for it. Therefore, it was known that some blood could be contaminated, but no one knew which blood, and the public was not warned of this risk.

The defendants argued that the blood was not defective because the public was only 'entitled' to expect the product to be as safe as it reasonably could be once reasonable precautions had been taken when handling it. There was nothing more they could have done, they said. The claimants said that to take into account whether the defendants had acted reasonably was allowing questions of fault in 'by the back door', thus eroding the strict liability tort.

Burton J found the blood to be defective, as part of what was an 82-page judgment. He said that taking into account what the defendant could or could not have done was not a relevant consideration when looking at strict liability. He asked whether it could be said that the risk of some blood being infected was one that had been accepted by the general public, concluding that the public was entitled to expect blood that was 100% safe. Therefore, the product was defective.

Many argue that this case was wrongly decided in that it was not fair that the Blood Authority was found liable, but then again this is the nature of a strict liability tort, one might argue.

An important decision was handed down on the point about defect in *Gee & Others v DePuy International Ltd* [2018] EWHC 1208 (QB). The court found for the defendant and bolstered the earlier decision of *Wilkes v DePuy International Ltd* [2017] 3 All ER 589 which also found for the defendant. In *Gee*, the Court decided that the 'inherent propensity' of a Metal on Metal (MoM) hip to shed metal debris in the course of normal use was not a defect, even though some patients may suffer an adverse immunological reaction to that.

The court took the opportunity to examine the principles of the CPA 1987 and the relevant case law, including *A and Others*. It said that the focus, when determining if a product is defective, should be on whether the product is safe, rather than on whether there had been a specific fault. Agreeing with *Wilkes*, it said that 'safety was inherently and necessarily a relative concept, because no product, and particularly a medicinal product, if effective, can be absolutely safe'.

As to 'all the circumstances of the case', the court made clear that it had to 'maintain a flexible approach to the assessment of the appropriate level of safety, including which circumstances are relevant and the weight to be given to each …'. It was important not to let notions of Negligence or other irrelevant considerations creep in, it said. Here, the court could consider a product's cost, its risk–benefit profile, avoidability (ie whether it was possible to eliminate the safety risk) and information and warnings passed onto a learned intermediary. Compliance with regulatory requirements could also have significant weight.

example

Chris fixes a stairgate onto his stairs, following the manufacturer's instructions carefully. Once set up, he tests it a few times by opening and closing it. Whilst closing it, the mechanism snaps shut on his finger, causing serious injury requiring stitches. Chris now wants to sue the manufacturer, 'FantasticProducts', under the CPA 1987.

There will be no difficulty satisfying the preliminaries here, namely that Chris as the consumer would seek to sue FantasticProducts as the manufacturer, for his personal injury caused wholly by the purported defect in the product.

The issues would be as to whether the product is actually defective and whether the defendant manufacturer would have any defences. Applying s 3(2)(a)–(c) to inform arguments as to whether the product meets the standards that persons generally are entitled to expect, we would need more information here, though we can say that Chris is using the product for the purpose for which it was intended (s 3(2)(b)). Having apparently set it up properly according to the instructions, we are not told about any warnings or guidance in relation to the mechanism that would alert us to the potential for danger here. What would persons generally expect as regards the safety of the mechanism? If there is a defect, was it the defect that caused the injury, or was the injury caused by Chris's lack of care here? Was this something that could have happened anyway?

It's difficult to know whether this product would be deemed defective. Applying *Abouzaid*, it would be, in the same way that the Cosytoes product was defective, although in *Pollard* the screw-cap was found not to be defective. However, in *Pollard,* there was an expectation (said the court) that the child-friendly screw-cap would be harder to remove for children than an ordinary screw-cap, and the point was that this was still the case, notwithstanding that the child was injured. This scenario perhaps leans more towards *Abouzaid* in terms of its facts, and so it may be that there is a defect here, though question marks remain at this stage.

If there is a defect, the defendant would seek to plead any of the defences under s 4(1)(a)–(f) (see **9.2.7** below), plus contributory negligence is available. None would seem to apply except, perhaps, contributory negligence, though again we would need more information here.

9.2.5 Causation

The CPA 1987 gives very little guidance on how causation is to be approached. It simply talks about damage 'caused wholly or partly by the defect'. Some commentators suggest that causation should be approached using common law principles of Negligence (see **Chapter 4**), though the CPA 1987 does not make this clear. Cases that discuss causation do not seem to embroil themselves in any specific tests, other than to say that the claimant must prove on the balance of probabilities that the defect caused their damage, either wholly or partly. Having said that, it seems highly likely that the usual 'but for' test for factual causation would be the starting point, and indeed in *W v Sanofi Pasteur* (Case C-621/15), the Court of Justice of the European Union (CJEU) confirmed that it was for national courts to decide on what evidential rules to apply, as long as the rules do not displace the burden of proof under the Product Liability Directive (the basis for the CPA 1987) or undermine the effectiveness of the system of liability established by the Directive.

In *Busby v Berkshire Bed Co Ltd* [2018] EWHC 2976 (QB), the claim failed because the claimant's fall was *not caused* by a defect in the bed she had bought (and more importantly there was no defect) but by her own actions in losing her balance. (In this case, Mrs Busby bought a divan bed from the defendant, whose employees assembled it at her house. A few days later, she fell backwards off the bed during sexual intercourse and sustained serious spinal injuries resulting in tetraplegia.) Shortly after the accident, the claimant's sister noticed that two feet were missing from the bed, causing a difference in level and a slight slope. The claimant was unable to prove that the defendant had supplied the bed in a defective condition, though the judge did find that the goods were not of satisfactory quality and had been poorly assembled (a breach of contract).

As there was no defect here, the peripheral discussion of causation was *obiter*, but the inference to be drawn is that it was not the state of the bed that caused her loss, and so the claim would have failed at the causation stage had it got that far.

9.2.6 Limitation period

A claimant must bring the claim within three years of the harm being suffered, except in 'latent harm' situations where the claimant only discovers the harm some time later, in which case time starts ticking from the point at which they made that discovery. Overarching that, there is a 10-year 'backstop' for claimants to claim from the time the particular product was put into circulation. The rationale here is that if a product has been on the market for 10 years, it is probably not defective.

9.2.7 Defences

Defences are provided for at s 4(1)(a)–(f):

(a) that the defect is attributable to compliance with any requirement imposed by or under any enactment or with any obligation; or

(b) that the person proceeded against did not at any time supply the product to another; or

(c) that the following conditions are satisfied, that is to say—

   (i) that the only supply of the product to another by the person proceeded against was otherwise than in the course of a business of that person's; and

   (ii) that section 2(2) above does not apply to that person or applies to him by virtue only of things done otherwise than with a view to profit; or

(d) that the defect did not exist in the product at the relevant time; or

(e) that the state of scientific and technical knowledge at the relevant time was not such that a producer of products of the same description as the product in question might be expected to have discovered the defect if it had existed in his products while they were under his control; or

(f) that the defect—

   (i) constituted a defect in a product ('the subsequent product') in which the product in question had been comprised; and

   (ii) was wholly attributable to the design of the subsequent product or to compliance by the producer of the product in question with instructions given by the producer of the subsequent product.

The most interesting of these defences from our point of view is s 4(1)(e), the so-called 'development risks' defence, and we'll focus on that in a moment. By way of a brief translation of the other defences, it would be a defence to show:

(a) that the product is defective in order to comply with domestic or EU law;

(b) that the defendant did not supply the product;

(c) that the product was not manufactured in the course of business;

(d) that the defect did not exist at the time the product was put into circulation;

...

(f) where the party is being sued because it manufactured a component of the product, that the defect was a defect within the *finished* product, and came about as a result of the way the finished product was marketed.

Note: contributory negligence is also available as a defence though not listed in s 4.

The development risks defence

The development risks defence (sometimes known as the 'state of the art defence') covers the situation where, some time *after* the product has been put into circulation, scientific or technical knowledge discovers that the product is in fact defective, such that the manufacturer could not have known at the time. This defence can only be used as a 'one-off', because after the discovery, the defendant can't say that it didn't know of the defect.

Critics have argued that this defence actually undermines the aims of the CPA 1987 in that it switches the burden of proof onto producers to show that, when they designed the product, they took the care expected of a manufacturer at that time. Does this still feel like a defence that fits the strict liability nature of this tort?

The defence was raised in *Abouzaid* (above) but failed, in essence because the court was of the opinion that the defect was as discoverable when the product was first manufactured as it was when the matter came to trial, and that it wasn't for lack of scientific or technical knowledge that it wasn't picked up on.

example

Nadim drinks an energy boost drink called Fast! After drinking it, she falls seriously ill, and contacts the manufacturer to notify it. A number of other consumers also fall ill around the same time having drunk Fast! The manufacturer pleads s 4(1)(e), stating that it is only since the product has been on the market that new tests have revealed that the drink contains an ingredient that can make some people ill.

If the issue here is as to whether the manufacturer of Fast! can utilise the s 4(1)(e) defence, there are a few questions to be asked. First, it claims that 'new tests' have revealed the problem with the ingredient, but we don't know whether the 'new' tests are new in the sense that they were not available before or that they simply hadn't been done until now. The former would more likely allow the defendant to utilise the defence of course. Secondly, we would expect to see the manufacturer withdraw the product from the market as soon as reasonably practicable after they are put on notice of the possible defect. Once they are aware of it, they can't hide behind the defence.

Aside from the above, there would be the usual evidential issues especially as to causation, which might be tricky here.

9.2.8 Summary of structure of a claim under CPA 1987

You might find it helpful to set out a clear structure for yourself, for example as in **Figure 9.1** below.

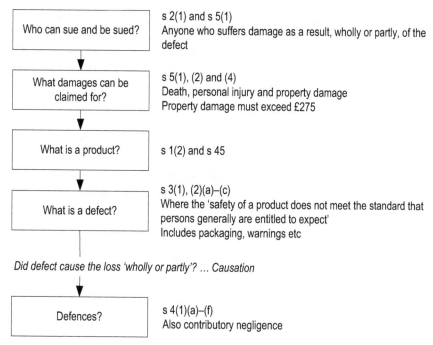

Figure 9.1   Structure of a claim under the CPA 1987

9.3 Claims in Negligence

A claim in Negligence for a defective product is less common than under the CPA 1987, because under Negligence the claimant still has to prove breach, whereas there is, as we have seen, strict liability under the CPA 1987. Due to the limitation periods, it's possible that a claimant who has sustained property damage may have longer to bring a claim in Negligence than under the CPA 1987. A claimant whose property damage is less than £275 would not be able to bring a claim under the CPA 1987 (though as mentioned this threshold is low) and so Negligence would be an option. In reality, most claimants would bring an action under the CPA 1987 and Negligence at the same time in the hope that one of them 'sticks'.

9.3.1 Damage

A claimant can claim for all the 'usual losses', namely personal injury, property damage and consequential economic loss.

9.3.2 Duty

The question of duty is determined using General Negligence principles and is owed by the manufacturer to the 'ultimate consumer' (think of *Donoghue v*

Stevenson), but it also extends beyond the manufacturer to include, for example, packers, machine operators and distributors. Any person or organisation in the supply chain could be found liable in Negligence.

The scope of the duty incorporates not just the product but also, for example, the packaging, instructions, etc. (You might think that this overlaps with what makes a product defective under s 3(2) of the CPA 1987. Certainly, the court in a Negligence action can take into account what would have been expected of the defendant in relation to this and other aspects, ie make fault-based investigations.)

9.3.3 Breach

The defendant is held to the standard of the reasonably competent defendant, and the court will look to determine whether that has been breached as a question of fact, weighing up all relevant factors.

Often, establishing fault is not that difficult, in that it can be inferred from the fact of the defect. A defendant must have fallen below the standard of the reasonably competent manufacturer in order, for example, for a snail to get inside a ginger beer bottle.

9.3.4 Causation, remoteness and defences

These elements all fall to be decided in the same way as for General Negligence (see **Chapters 4**, **5** and **6** respectively).

9.3.5 Design defects

We have so far considered manufacturing defects under *Donoghue*. However, design defects, which by their nature could potentially affect all end-users of a product, can be difficult, or even impossible, to discover, either before the product enters the supply chain or on inspection by the end-user. For that reason, it can be hard to bring a Negligence action in relation to a design defect.

Duty is not normally in issue, but for breach, it is hard to prove that the designer fell below the standard expected of it. With causation, it's a case of having to show both that the design defect *can* cause harm, and that it *did* cause the harm to that claimant. The example often given here is of a particular drug that can cause cancer due to a design flaw. Showing that it did, in fact, cause the claimant's cancer is not straightforward, given the other factors that could have come into play, such as lifestyle and genetic risks.

It was as a result of the difficulties inherent in design defect cases – nowhere more evident than in the context of the Thalidomide tragedy – that pressure for a strict liability regime grew, culminating in the European Community issuing the Product Liability Directive in 1985, requiring Member States to change and make consistent their laws on product liability. In the UK, this was reflected in the CPA 1987.

Thalidomide is a drug that was marketed from the mid-1950s to around 1961 in many countries and under many different names. It was prescribed mostly to pregnant women to help with morning sickness, but it was later discovered that

Thalidomide can cause sever birth defects when taken during pregnancy. It had been inadequately tested before being placed on the market, and around 10,000 children were born with birth defects, including severely shortened limbs, as well as developing heart and kidney problems. Life expectancy was shortened, and many children died in infancy.

In 1962, the US Congress, in response to the tragedy, enacted strict laws relating to testing of drugs for use during pregnancy, and many other countries followed suit. Though Thalidomide was not prescribed or sold for years, it was never withdrawn completely from the market, though its use these days is different – it's primarily used now to treat leprosy and some types of cancer.

9.4 Further reading

D Wuyts, 'The Product Liability Directive – More than two Decades of Defective Products in Europe' (2014) 5 JETL 1.

G Howells and M Mildred, 'Infected Blood: Defect and Discoverability: A First Exposition of the EC Product Liability Directive' (2002) 65 MLR 95.

D Fairgrieve and G Howells, 'General Product Safety – A Revolution Through Reform?' (2006) 69 MLR 59.

- Product liability is a statute-based tort, but a common law Negligence claim is also available.
- The Consumer Protection Act 1987 is a strict liability regime, whereby fault on the part of the defendant should not be relevant.
- Whether a product is defective turns on its safety, and what persons are entitled to expect as regards the safety of a product.
- Much turns on s 3(2)(a)–(c) of the CPA 1987 (on the meaning of defect), and there are also various defences available.

Have a go at these multiple-choice questions (MCQs):

Question 1

A woman buys tampons and uses them. She suddenly develops toxic shock syndrome, a serious condition, as a result of the tampon use. There was a warning and guidance inside the packaging, but the warning was very small.

Which one of the following options best describes whether the tampon is likely to be seen as defective?

A   This is probably unlikely to be a defective product as there was a warning and guidance inside the packaging. The warning is small because the packaging is small. People would probably not expect 100% safety from the product, and the condition is well documented.

B   This is probably likely to be a defective product as there was a warning and guidance inside the packaging but the warning was small.

C   This is probably unlikely to be a defective product as there was a warning and guidance inside the packaging, meaning that the product was clearly not defective.

D   This is probably likely to be a defective product as people would be entitled to expect that tampons would be 100% safe.

E   This is probably likely to be a defective product as the warning was inadequate.

Answer

The correct answer is option A. This is the likely result, especially in light of *Worlsey v Tambrands* [2000] PIQR P95.

Question 2

A man suffers personal injury as a result of a defective product, but the damage only becomes apparent two years after he uses the product.

Which one of the following best explains how long the man will have to bring a claim under the CPA 1987?

A   Three years from the date the injury was caused.

B   Three years from the date the injury becomes apparent.

C   Ten years from the date the injury was caused.

D   Ten years from the date the injury becomes apparent.

E   Two years from the date the injury becomes apparent.

Answer

The correct answer is option B. Time starts ticking once the latent damage becomes apparent.

Question 3

A man is charging his mobile phone overnight. The charging wire overheats and catches fire, and the fire spreads to the man's curtains and damages them.

Which one of the following is accurate as to whether the man can claim for his damaged curtains?

A   Yes, he should be able to claim, provided the product is defective and causes the damage to the curtains, wholly or partly. The replacement value of the curtains would need to be more than they cost to buy to bring a claim under the CPA 1987.

B   Yes, he should be able to claim, provided the product is defective and causes the damage to the curtains, wholly or partly. The replacement value of the curtains would need to be more than £575 to bring a claim under the CPA 1987.

C   Yes, he should be able to claim, provided the product is defective and causes the damage to the curtains, wholly or partly. The replacement value of the curtains would need to be less than £275 to bring a claim under the CPA 1987.

D   Yes, he should be able to claim, provided the product is defective and causes the damage to the curtains, wholly or partly. The replacement value of the curtains would need to be more than £275 to bring a claim under the CPA 1987.

E   Yes, he should be able to claim, provided the product is defective and causes the damage to the curtains, wholly or partly. The replacement value of the curtains would need to be £275 to bring a claim under the CPA 1987.

Answer

The correct answer is option D. Yes, s 5(4) discuss this point. The replacement value must *exceed* £275.

Question 4

A manufacturer, X, makes component parts for cars. A claimant seeks to bring an action against X under the CPA 1987 in relation to a car containing the component part, stating that the car is defective.

Which one of the following most accurately describes the possible defence available to the defendant?

A   s 4(1)(d): That the defect did not exist at the time the product was put into circulation.

B   s 4(1)(c): That the product was not manufactured in the course of business.

C   s 4(1)(b): That the defendant did not supply the product.

D   s 4(1)(a): That the product was defective in order to comply with domestic or EU law.

E   s 4(1)(f): Where the party is being sued because it manufactured a component of the product, that the defect was a defect within the *finished* product, and came about as a result of the way the finished product was marketed.

Answer

The correct answer is option E. There may be other defences available, and other issues with this claim generally, but this is the most likely defence on the face of it.

chapter 10

Occupiers' Liability

After reading this chapter, you will be able to:

- appreciate how occupiers' liability, though a form of Negligence, differs from General Negligence
- gain confidence in navigating your way through the relevant statutes – the Occupiers' Liability Acts 1957 and 1984
- understand how to apply common law to supplement the statutes
- appreciate the difference in law as regards visitors and non-visitors
- gain an overview of the types of remedy available to a successful claimant.

10.1 Introduction

Occupiers' liability is a form of Negligence where the claimant's damage or loss is caused by the state of the premises. It is a claim brought by a claimant, who may be a visitor or non-visitor, against the occupier of that premises. Its rationale is to provide an incentive for occupiers to keep their premises safe – their indoor and outdoor spaces (in fact, many unusual areas have been defined as premises as we'll see, including diving boards, ladders and gravestones) – and to provide a remedy for claimants who are injured or suffer other recognisable loss whilst on those premises, as a result of acts or omissions by the occupier.

However, whilst the General Negligence principles apply, this tort is distinctive in that it is largely governed by statute: the Occupiers' Liability Act (OLA) 1957 for visitors, and the Occupiers Liability Act (OLA) 1984 for non-visitors.

That means that, as lawyers, we have in mind the Negligence structure for a claim, look to the relevant Act for guidance as to how that has been formalised by statute, and then 'plug any gaps' in the wording of the statute with case law. There is quite a body of case law here, which really helps to illuminate this area of law.

The statutes were designed to simplify the common law and to make it fairer. Pre-statute, the scope of the duty owed by the occupier varied according to the circumstances surrounding the way in which and in what capacity the claimant came onto the premises. The law was confused and inconsistent in this respect. Those who were on the land by virtue of a contract (like an electrician coming to fix the wiring) were owed a higher standard of care than 'invitees' or 'licencees' (the friend you invited round for a cup of tea). For a while, there was no provision at all made for non-visitors; they were simply not owed a duty of care in any circumstances. Occupiers were under an obligation not to deliberately cause non-visitors or trespassers harm, but that just sounds like a reminder not to commit a criminal offence which was probably largely understood anyway.

There are those who argue that the desire to protect visitors and non-visitors from harm has now gone too far, and certainly there is a balance to be struck (as so often in tort law). This is what Lord Hobhouse had to say on the subject. To what extent do you agree?

> It is not, and should never be, the policy of the law to require the protection of the foolhardy or reckless few to deprive, or interfere with, the enjoyment of the remainder of society of the liberties and amenities to which they are rightly entitled. Does the law require that all trees be cut down because some youths may climb them and fall? Does the law require the coastline and other beauty spots to be lined with warning notices? Does the law require that attractive waterside picnic spots be destroyed because of a few foolhardy individuals who choose to ignore the warning notices and indulge in activities dangerous only to themselves? The answer to all these questions is, of course, no. (*Tomlinson v Congleton Borough Council* [2004] 1 AC 46)

10.2 Differences between occupiers' liability and General Negligence

To be clear from the start, these two torts are similar but not the same. The key difference, apart from the fact that occupiers' liability is statute-led, is as to the circumstances in which a claimant would claim under occupiers' liability as opposed to General Negligence. Sometimes, on paper, a scenario might look as though it could fit either tort – it may be that it could and some actions are brought in both, for example a spillage on a shop floor – but essentially:

- *Occupiers' liability*: the claimant's loss is caused as a result of the state of the premises. This might be a broken leg from falling in a hole, or down some stairs, or off a slippery seawall. (The claimant can also claim for property damage.)
- *General Negligence*: the claimant's loss is caused as a result of some activity being done by the defendant. So, for example, if you visit a farm and fall into a ditch, you might sue the farmer in occupiers' liability (injury arising because of the state of the premises). If, having pulled yourself out of the ditch, the farmer then carelessly runs you over in his combine harvester, your further action against him would be in General Negligence (injury arising because of the defendant's activity done on the land).

Here are the similarities and differences between the two torts at a glance. (The last one is rather tongue-in-cheek though accurate!)

Table 10.1   Occupiers' liability and General Negligence

Occupiers' Liability	**General Negligence**
Concerns loss caused as result of state of premises occupied by D	Concerns loss caused as result of activity/omission by D

Occupiers' Liability	General Negligence
Governed by statute	Not governed by statute (though utilises some statutes sometimes)
Reinforced with common law principles	All common law principles
Follows General Negligence structure, except no provision in the Occupiers' Liability Acts for causation or remoteness	All elements of a Negligence claim need to be proven
Divides claimants into visitors and non-visitors	Does not differentiate between claimants in this way
Key words and phrases: Tripping on paving slabs, falling down broken stairs	Key words and phrases: Crashing into other vehicles, things falling on your head

10.3 Categories of claimant and terminology

There are now just two categories of claimant, and the category determines which Act should be utilised:

- The OLA 1957 covers lawful visitors.
- The OLA 1984 covers unlawful visitors (typically trespassers).

There are three key terms we need to define before we can move on. Once we understand what these mean, we can then determine which Act best fits our claimant and work from there. The three key terms are:

- occupier;
- visitor; and
- premises.

Let's take each of these in turn.

10.3.1 Occupier

We need to understand this term because the statute imposes a duty of care on the occupier of premises. Neither Act defines the term. Where there is no definition in the Act, this is normally a sign that there is an expectation that the term or meaning is already to be found in common law. In fact, s 1(2) of the OLA 1957 makes this plain, stating that an occupier is 'the same ... as the persons who would at common law be treated as an occupier'.

The clearest definition of the term comes from the following case.

Wheat v Lacon & Co Ltd [1966] AC 552

Mr and Mrs Richardson were the live-in landlord and landlady in a pub which they rented from the defendant, Lacon & Co Ltd (a brewery). The Richardsons also had permission from the brewery to rent out the other rooms of the pub to paying guests. The claimant's husband, Mr Wheat, was killed after falling down a flight of poorly lit stairs while staying in the pub. The light bulb at the top of the stairs had been removed, which meant that Mr Wheat could not see when he had reached the top of the stairs, nor could he see that the handrail finished short of the top.

The question for the court was whether the brewery or Mr and Mrs Richardson were the occupiers for the purpose of the claimant's occupiers' liability claim. The House of Lords determined that both the brewery and the Richardsons were occupiers. As such, both owed a duty of care under the OLA 1957.

Lord Denning defined occupier as being '*anyone with a sufficient degree of control over the premises*'. That person did not need to physically occupy the premises (the brewery did not, of course).

A side issue for us, as the moment, is that in this case, neither party was found to have fallen below the standard of care required of them. The short handrail did not, of itself, make the stairs unreasonably hazardous, and neither party had removed the lightbulb. This had been done by a stranger, shortly before Mr Wheat had used the stairs.

So, *Wheat* tells us who the occupier will be. It will be a question of fact in each case as to who has a 'sufficient degree of control'. We also know that you can have more than one occupier. This was the case in, for example, *Collier v Anglian Water Authority* (1983) *The Times*, 26 March, in which the claimant, who was injured whilst walking along the seaside promenade, brought an action against both the Water Board and the local authority. The Water Board was ultimately held responsible.

It is also possible for an occupier to be an absentee who has never taken possession of a property. In *Harris v Birkenhead Corporation* [1976] 1 WLR 279, the local authority defendant was held to be an occupier, even though it had never exercised control over the premises. It did have power to secure the premises, and this was considered important.

10.3.2 Visitor

The next term we need to define is 'visitor'. The OLA 1957 tells us that an occupier of premises owes an automatic duty of care to a visitor, but who will be construed as a visitor?

Section 1(2) of the OLA 1957 tells us that 'the persons who are to be treated as … visitors are the same … as the persons who would at common law be treated as … invitees and licencees'. This means that once again we must look to the common law to 'plug the gap' in respect of this definition.

The key question will be: Does the visitor have express or implied permission to be on the premises? If so, they will be a visitor. Such permission is almost always limited in some way.

Express permission

An individual may have express permission from the occupier. If I invite you into my home, you have express permission to come into my home, and you'll be a visitor for the purpose of any occupiers' liability claim. Similarly, if you buy a ticket for the cinema, you have express permission to attend the cinema. (The OLA 1957 would construe that as contractual permission under s 5(1).)

Limiting express permission

As an occupier, I might limit your express permission, by saying, for example, you can go anywhere in the house except the study. A sign may do the same job: 'Keep Out.' As Scrutton LJ says (rather euphemistically) 'When you invite a person into your house to use the staircase, you do not invite them to slide down the banisters' (*The Calgarth* [1927] P 93 Coram).

An occupier might limit permission as follows:

- *By area:* This is what is being described above by Scrutton LJ. Sometimes occupiers attempt to limit express permission by area, but the court does not accept that they have done this sufficiently well and so they are held to have owed a duty and breached it. That was case in *Pearson v Coleman Bros* [1948] 2 KB 359. A girl accidentally found herself in the lion enclosure at a zoo, whilst roaming around to look for the toilet, and she was attacked. There were no signs indicating that this was a private area, and so the girl was considered a visitor for the purpose of her claim.

  Similarly, in *Darby v National Trust* [2001] EWCA Civ 189, the claimant Mr Darby was injured when he swam in a pond on National Trust ground. There was a sign in the carpark stating that swimming and boating was not allowed, but the sign was found to contain lots of other superfluous information and so was unclear. It was also positioned in the car park which was not next to the pond. For these reasons, the claimant was construed as a visitor because his express permission had not been limited.

- *By time:* If premises are open until a certain time but then close, then it stands to reason that you would be a visitor while the premises are open, and a non-visitor if you remain on the premises once they close. Again, sometimes occupiers are unsuccessful in their attempts to limit express permission by time. This was the case in *Stone v Taffe* [1974] 1 WLR 1575 in which the manager of a pub held a 'lock-in' to allow a party after hours. When the claimant was injured, they were construed as a visitor because the defendant occupier had not limited but extended permission by time.

- *By purpose:* If a visitor goes beyond the purpose for which they were invited, this might change their visitor status. For example, if I am invited to use the lavatory, but once I'm there I decide to redecorate the area (and let's say in the process I'm injured) then for any claim I made I would probably be construed as a non-visitor, having gone beyond the purpose for which I was invited. In *Tomlinson v Congleton Borough Council* [2004] 1 AC 46, it was made clear that visitors could use the lake for canoeing, fishing and windsurfing only. By swimming, which was not permitted, the claimant became a non-visitor.

Implied permission

As the name suggests, this is permission to be on the occupier's premises, but that is implied rather than express. I don't directly invite the postman to walk up to my letterbox and post letters, but he has implied permission to do so (and so when on the premises – the garden path – he would be construed as a visitor). If the postman decided to come into my house and have a bath, he would no longer have any kind of permission to be on those premises, express or implied.

The burden of proving the existence of implied permission rests with the person who alleges it exists (normally the claimant). Sometimes the claimant will be unable to do this and so their claim would fall to be treated as a non-visitor rather than visitor claim. This is what happened in *Edwards v Railways Executive* [1952] AC 737. One part of the railway, where the fence was down, had been used a shortcut by members of the public for years. The fence was repaired whenever it was reported broken. On the day in question, the fence was in a good state of repair. When the claimant was injured, he was construed as a non-visitor because he did not have implied permission to be there.

Sometimes, the assertion by an occupier that permission has been revoked altogether (which is allowed, where appropriate) will fail, as it did in *Snook v Mannion* [1982] Crim L Rev 601 (a criminal case). In this case, an occupier motorist told a policeman, who had followed him up his driveway to breathalyse him, to 'fuck off'. The court held (unsurprisingly) that these words were not sufficient to revoke the implied permission the policeman had to be on the occupier's driveway.

Anyone with lawful authority to enter premises can do so and would be construed as a visitor (with implied permission) for the purpose of any claim. This is provided for under s 2(6) of the OLA 1957 and would include, for example, police officers with a warrant to search a home, or gas board officials, who would be allowed by statute to enter premises to check for gas leaks.

10.3.3 Premises

We now know that an occupier owes a duty of care to visitors, and we have defined both terms. That duty is to visitors who are on the 'premises' (over which the occupier has a sufficient degree of control). So how do we define 'premises'?

We start with the statute. The term is defined in the same way in both Acts and, frankly, is normally obvious. If you slip on a floor, the floor where you slipped would be the premises for the purpose any claim. The Act defines premises as '*any fixed or moveable structure, including any vessel, vehicle or aircraft*' (OLA 1957, s 1(3)(a) and OLA 1984, s 1(2) which refers us back to the OLA 1957). This wide definition includes obvious places such as buildings, driveways, stairs, and less obvious and less permanent structures, such as scaffolding, a derelict boat, a ladder, and a splat wall (*Gwilliam v West Hertfordshire Hospitals NHS Trust* [2002] EWCA Civ 1041).

example

George falls over and is injured when he falls through a rotten piece of decking. The decking is in Rahim's garden. Rahim had invited George for a drink in the garden, and when George needed the toilet, Rahim had told him to walk through the back door and into the house. This necessitated George walking across the decking that led to the back door. George wants to sue Rahim in occupiers' liability, but Rahim says that George did not have permission to be on the decking.

It looks like George had express permission to be in Rahim's garden and implied permission to cross the decking to get to the house. For any claim in occupiers' liability, George would be construed as a visitor, and the premises would be the decking. Rahim would be the occupier as he has a sufficient degree of control over the premises.

10.4 Claims under the OLA 1957

Let's now turn to how we might navigate our way through a claim under the OLA 1957.

10.4.1 Which Act?

Provided a claimant can prove that they have suffered recognisable loss on the occupier's premises, and that they were a visitor, then we know that the correct statute would be the OLA 1957. So, the first step is to define the three terms and establish that they apply (occupier, visitor, premises).

10.4.2 Duty of care

Section 2(1) of the OLA 1957 states that 'An occupier of premises owes the same duty, the "common duty of care", to all his visitors …'. This means that a visitor is owed an automatic duty of care under the OLA 1957. (This is different under the OLA 1984 as we'll see.) Claims can be made for personal injury or property damage.

10.4.3 Breach – setting the standard

As with all Negligence claims, we first of all set the standard expected of the defendant occupier. As you might expect, the occupier is expected to meet the standard of the reasonably competent occupier. We can either ask whether the defendant has breached their duty of care, or we can ask whether the defendant has 'discharged their duty'. Those terms deal with the same issue. You may see one or the other in the authorities you read.

This standard of the reasonably competent occupier is found at s 2(2) of the OLA 1957:

> The common duty of care is a duty to take such care as in all the circumstances of the case is reasonable to see that the visitor will be

reasonably safe in using the premises for the purposes for which he is invited or permitted by the occupier to be there.

Note: *it is the visitor and not the premises that need to be kept safe*. This means that an occupier is free to run dangerous activities on their land if they wish, for example pot-holing weekends, but they would need to work hard in that case to ensure that they meet the standard of the reasonably competent occupier in keeping the visitor safe, so far as it's reasonable to expect them to do so.

Where the occupier is aware of a particular vulnerability of a visitor, they must take reasonable steps to keep that visitor safe. That might include a blind person with implied permission to use the highway, as was the case in *Haley v London Electricity Board* [1965] AC 778. A blind visitor was also able to claim in *Pollock v Cahill* [2015] EWHC 2260 (QB), a case in which the claimant visitor suffered serious injury after falling out of the window at a friend's house.

Has the standard been breached?

This is where the court would ask what has gone wrong and why, just as under General Negligence. The OLA 1957 gives some guidance as to particular situations that might constitute a breach, and this is where we would also bring in any case law that might inform the advice we are drafting. Lord Hoffman in *Tomlinson v Congleton* made clear that we can look at all the same factors that are considered in General Negligence. He stated, when determining whether there has been a breach, that the court would assess

> ... as in the case of common law negligence, not only the likelihood that someone may be injured and the seriousness of the injury which may occur, but also the social value of the activity which gives rise to the risk and the cost of preventative measures. These factors have to be balanced against each other.

Laverton v Kiapasha [2002] EWCA Civ 1656

After a night out, the inebriated claimant broke her ankle after slipping over in the defendant's busy kebab shop. It had been raining earlier and the shop floor was wet and slippery. The question was whether the defendant occupier had breached his duty or not.

The majority of the Court of Appeal held that there was no breach. The occupier had done what was reasonable in the circumstances: he had re-laid the floor using slip-resistant tiles and he had a system for mopping up the excess water regularly.

Similarly, in *Tedstone v Bourne Leisure Ltd* [2008] EWCA Civ 654, there was no breach when a woman slipped on a patch of water on her way from the jacuzzi to the swimming pool. The defendant occupier had taken reasonable care to ensure the area was safe. As with breach generally, whilst the occupier owes a duty to keep visitors reasonably safe, there is also an expectation that the visitor will take reasonable care for their own safety.

The OLA 1957 focuses, in particular, on children and professionals.

Children – OLA 1957, s 2(3)(a)

Section 2(3)(a) of the OLA 1957 states that 'an occupier must be prepared for children to be less careful than adults'. Some commentators view this as saying that occupiers owe a higher standard of care to children, but a clearer interpretation, which aligns with our discussions on breach in General Negligence (see **Chapter 3**), is simply to say that what is reasonable to expect from an occupier changes according to who the visitor is. It's not so much a higher standard as a need to do more to reach that reasonable threshold. Much will turn on the age of the child and the circumstances in determining whether there has been a breach.

case example

Jolley v Sutton London Borough Council [2000] 1 WLR 1082

A boat had lain abandoned on council land for two years. It appeared to be in good condition but was actually rotten. The claimant was a 14-year-old boy who decided to repair the boat with a friend. As he lay underneath to push it up, it fell and crushed him, causing severe injuries that left him paralysed. He brought an action under the OLA 1957.

The House of Lords found that there had been a breach. It was or should have been reasonably foreseeable to the occupier that children might approach the boat and be tempted to climb on it. Lord Hoffman said that 'children's ingenuity in finding unexpected ways of doing mischief to themselves and others should never be underestimated'. (The claimant's damages were reduced by 25% for contributory negligence.)

An occupier is, where appropriate, entitled to assume that parents will take responsibility for young children. In *Phipps v Rochester Corporation* [1955] 1 QB 450, the claimant, a 5-year-old boy, went blackberry picking with his sister. They walked across a large area of land that was part of a housing estate being developed by the defendant occupier. The claimant fell down a large trench that had been dug by an employee of the occupier. Although the trench would have been obvious to an adult, it wasn't to a child. It was held that prudent parents would not have allowed a young child to walk across that area. There was no breach as the occupier was entitled to expect that children would not come onto the premises (because their parents would stop them). As Devlin J stated: 'It would not be socially desirable if parents were, as a matter of course, able to shift the burden of looking after children from their own shoulders to those of persons who happen to have accessible bits of land.'

In *Simkiss v Rhondda Borough Council* (1983) 81 LGR 460, a 7-year-old child was seriously injured when playing with a friend on a steep hill. The child's father did not consider the bank to be dangerous, and this was important, because the Court of Appeal said that the occupier shouldn't be held to a higher standard than the parent. In other words, if the father didn't think the hill was dangerous, then why should the council? There was no breach.

Persons in the exercise of their calling – s 2(3)(b)

Section 2(3)(b) preserves the common law prior to the OLA 1957. It states that 'an occupier may expect that a person, in the exercise of his calling, will appreciate and guard against any special risks ordinarily incident to it, so far as the occupier leaves him free to do so'.

This means that an occupier will not have breached their duty when a professional, doing their job, is on the occupiers' premises and injures themselves, when that professional should have known better.

Roles v Nathan [1963] 1 WLR 1117

Chimney sweeps were called in by the defendant to come and clean out the flues of an old coke-burning boiler in the Manchester Assembly Rooms. They were found dead in the chimney area the next morning having been poisoned by carbon monoxide. The occupier had in fact asked them twice to take precautions, telling them to leave the boiler room (at one point trying to pull one of them away) but they continued to work.

The Court of Appeal by a majority said that there was no breach here. The occupier had done what was reasonable to keep the (professional) visitors safe, and those visitors should have known how to look after themselves as per s 2(3)(b).

In *Salmon v Seafarer Restaurants Ltd* [1983] 3 All ER 729 and *Ogwo v Taylor* [1987] 3 All ER 961, the claimant visitors were firemen actively fighting fires. In both cases, the firemen had taken all reasonable safety precautions. Their injuries arose from the risks that the occupiers had created on the premises. Those risks remained despite the skill of the firemen, so in each case there was a breach and the defendants were liable.

Warning notices

An occupier can discharge their duty of care (ie demonstrate they have reached the standard expected of them) by virtue of a warning notice. This is provided for in s 2(4)(a) of the OLA 1957, which states that any attempt to warn a visitor of danger will only be sufficient if '*in all the circumstances it was enough to enable the visitor to be reasonably safe*'. This means the warning sign needs to do enough to satisfy s 2(2) of the OLA 1957. The court will ask: has the occupier, by warning of the danger, done enough to keep the visitor '*reasonably safe in using the premises …*'.

The classic warning sign will actually include an attempt to warn and an attempt to exclude liability. You have probably seen something along the following lines many times:

USERS OF THIS CAR PARK DO SO AT THEIR OWN RISK.
THE MANAGEMENT WILL NOT ACCEPT RESPONSIBILITY FOR ANY DAMAGE, ACCIDENTS OR LOSSES.

Where you have an attempt both to warn ('Users of this car park do so at own risk') and to exclude ('The management will not accept responsibility for any damage, accidents or losses') then it's best to deal with these one at a time. We'll look at the warning part here, under breach. You *can* also look at attempts to exclude here, but they are perhaps best dealt with at the defences stage, because it would act as a quasi-defence for the occupier if successful.

It will be a question of fact in each case if the warning sign does enough to keep the visitor reasonably safe. The more specific the sign as to the problem, the more likely it is to discharge the occupier's duty of care. Lord Denning talks about the specificity required in *Roles v Nathan* when he considers a sign that would be acceptable in allowing the visitor to be reasonably safe: *'Do not use this footbridge. It is dangerous. There is a safe one further upstream.'* Note also that the size of the sign, its location in relation to the danger, and so on, will all have a bearing on the extent to which it enables the visitor to be reasonably safe.

case example

Darby v National Trust [2001] EWCA Civ 189

In this case (discussed at **10.3.2** above), the claimant's husband died whilst swimming in a pond in Derbyshire owned by the National Trust. Visitors often swam or paddled in the pond and the occupier did very little to discourage this. There was a sign near the car park but that was some distance from the pond, and the sign was inconspicuous and contained a fair amount of wording about other things. It prohibited swimming and boating. In addition, wardens occasionally patrolled the ground, warning members of the public not to swim, in case of contracting Weil's disease.

The claimant stated that the lack of 'No Swimming' signs next to the pond was a breach of the occupier's duty of care, as was the lack of signage warning of Weil's disease. The Court of Appeal held that such notices would have told the claimant 'no more than he already knew' about the general risks of swimming in open water. There were no special or hidden dangers in this particular pond and therefore no duty on the National Trust's part to warn the claimant of the obvious dangers. The Trust had done all that could be reasonably expected of it. May LJ said: 'It cannot be the duty of the owner of every stretch of coastline to have notices warning of the dangers of swimming in the sea. If it were so, the coast would have to be littered with notices in places other than those where there are known to be special dangers which are not obvious. The same would apply to all inland lakes and reservoirs.'

A warning sign could be written, but warnings could extend to a tape to cordon off an area, or they could be oral. Sometimes, the *lack* of a warning sign will be indicative of a breach, as it was in *English Heritage v Taylor* [2016] EWCA Civ 448. Here the claimant was able to recover damages for the serious head injury he sustained after falling over a sheer drop at Carisbrooke Castle on the Isle of Wight. The defendant occupier had failed to provide a sign to warn of the drop, which was not obvious. (However, damages were reduced by 50% for contributory negligence.)

Discharge of liability for the work of subcontractors

Section 2(4)(b) of the OLA 1957 covers a situation where the occupier hires independent contractors to do work on the premises, and the claimant visitor is then injured. It states:

> (b) Where damage is caused to a visitor by a danger due to the faulty execution of any work of construction, maintenance or repair by an

independent contractor employed by the occupier, the occupier is not to be treated without more as answerable for the danger if in all the circumstances he had acted reasonably in entrusting the work to an independent contractor and had taken such steps (if any) as he reasonably ought in order to satisfy himself that the contractor was competent and that the work had been properly done.

Therefore, the occupier can discharge liability provided they can prove that they acted reasonably in:

(a) *Hiring an independent contractor in the first place:* This will depend on the complexity of the task and will be a question of fact. It's not normally controversial.

(b) *Selecting the independent contractor:* This might include checking references and the insurance position of the independent contractor. In *Gwilliam v West Hertfordshire Hospitals NHS Trust* [2002] EWCA Civ 1041, the Court of Appeal stated that it is not the responsibility of the occupier to check that the independent contractor has insurance, though where they have so checked, that might be indicative of doing what's reasonable to discharge this part of s 2(4)(b) (though there was no requirement to check the policy in detail, which is why the claim failed in this particular case).

(c) *Supervising and checking the work so far as was reasonable:* What is required here will depend on the complexity of the work being done and how reasonable it would be to expect the occupier to be able to check or supervise this. In *Haseldine v Daw* [1941] 2 KB 343, the claimant visitor was injured, whilst on the occupier's premises, in using a lift that had been negligently installed by independent contractors. The court said that it would not have been reasonable to expect the occupier to supervise that technical work.

However, we can contrast that with *Woodward v Mayor of Hastings* [1945] KB 174 in which a pupil at the defendant occupier's school slipped on an icy step and was injured. The step had been left in a dangerous condition by a cleaner (the independent contractor). The occupier tried to argue that this was not work it could reasonably have been expected to inspect. The court disagreed, stating that anyone could and should have noticed that the step was icy and unsafe. The occupier had not discharged its duty and so was liable.

example

Daniel is a headteacher and hires independent contractors to do excavation work in the grounds of his school, ready for builders to come in and lay foundations for a new building. The independent contractors dig a large hole which is left uncovered for two weeks. Daniel sees this and thinks it might be dangerous but fails to do anything about it. The school's security guard, Monty, whilst patrolling the grounds at night, falls into the hole. It was dark and there were no barriers or warnings. He breaks his toe and his watch is smashed.

Monty will seek to bring an action against the occupier or occupiers for his personal injury and property damage in occupiers' liability. As a visitor, presumably with express permission to be on the premises (the school grounds) at night, he will bring an action under the OLA 19857. He could sue both Daniel, the headteacher, and the independent contractors, as both might be said to have a 'sufficient degree of control over the premises'. Both will owe Monty a duty of care automatically under s 2(1) of the OLA 1957.

The issue will be whether Daniel has discharged his duty of care under s 2(4)(b) in terms of his hiring and supervising of the independent contractors. If so, he will not be liable, but they will be. If he can't show that, potentially they both remain liable.

Looking at the three stages of s 2(4)(b), there don't look to be any problems as regards Daniel hiring independent contractors in the first place, and we have no evidence to suggest that they are not capable, or as to his checking their competence, so we can assume there is no issue there. The concern will be as to the third stage: did Daniel do what was reasonable to supervise/check the work being done so as to ensure visitors were reasonably safe? There is a question mark here. Whilst we wouldn't expect Daniel to be able to supervise or check on the technical aspects of the excavation work, we are told he'd seen the large hole and 'thinks it might be dangerous'. As the hole has been there for two weeks, it would be reasonable to expect Daniel to have taken some steps, whether by speaking to the independent contractors about putting up barriers, or by doing so himself. By doing nothing, he's almost certainly breached his duty here and so has not discharged his duty.

10.4.4 Defences and attempts to exclude

As mentioned, neither the OLA 1957 nor the OLA 1984 make provision for causation or remoteness, there being an assumption that these are made out once duty and breach are satisfied. Occasionally, you will find judges discussing these elements, but this tends to be where the claim is being brought in both Negligence and in occupiers' liability. So we can move on to defences.

Volenti

This is provided for in s 2(5) of the OLA 1957, which states that an occupier will not be liable where a visitor's injuries arise from *'risks willingly accepted as his by the visitor'*. The defence works in exactly the same way as for General Negligence, so do refer to the chapter on defences (**Chapter 6**).

The defence was successfully pleaded in *Geary v Wetherspoons plc* [2011] EWHC 1506 (QB) in which the claimant fractured her spine and was paralysed after falling 4 metres onto a marble floor while trying to slide down a banister. Coulson J said:

> [T]he claimant freely chose to do something that she knew was dangerous … she was therefore the author of her own misfortune. The defendant owed her no duty to protect her from such an obvious and inherent risk. She made a genuine and informed choice and the risk that she chose to run materialised with tragic consequences.

Contributory negligence

The is provided for in s 2(3) of the OLA 1957, which states that when determining the common duty of care, 'the degree of care, and want of care, which would ordinarily be looked for in such a visitor' is taken into account. This has been taken to mean that contributory negligence applies here. Again, the normal principles will apply.

Attempts to exclude liability under the OLA 1957

We said above (at **10.4.3**) that warning notices often include an attempt to exclude liability. By s 2(1) of the OLA 1957, an occupier can effectively attempt to exclude or limit liability 'so far as they are free to do so'.

Where the premises are occupied for business purposes, an occupier's ability to limit their liability is restricted by s 2(1) and 2(2) of the Unfair Contract Terms Act (UCTA) 1977. Section 1(1)(c) of UCTA 1977 specifically refers to notices that seek to exclude or limit liability under the OLA 1957. What s 2(1) and 2(2) of UCTA 1977 say is that an occupier cannot exclude liability for death or personal injury arising from negligence. For other types of damage, for example property damage, whether or not the occupier can exclude liability will be subject to a test of reasonableness. If the premises are in private use then, in theory at least, the occupier is free to restrict or exclude liability as they see fit, subject perhaps to a base level of 'common humanity' required as a result of *British Railways Board v Herrington* [1972] AC 877.

Attempts to exclude liability for non-visitors under the OLA 1984 are dealt with differently, as we'll see at **10.5.5**.

10.5 Claims under the OLA 1984

The OLA 1984 is intended to provide some, albeit limited protection for non-visitors or trespassers who suffer personal injury. It's not possible to claim for property damage under the OLA 1984 (s 1(8)).

10.5.1 How do we define non-visitor or trespasser?

We'll define the term 'non-visitor or trespasser' in a moment, but let's pause for a moment. Do you think it's right that before the OLA 1984 there was no provision made for trespassers at all? After all, they're not supposed to be where they are, so why should they be able to claim? Does it make a difference if you ask yourself who you picture when you think about a 'trespasser'? A burglar? Someone breaking into premises at night? What about a drunk student wandering about in a cordoned-off area? Someone taking a shortcut across a field? Someone who is lost and has inadvertently strayed into the wrong room? A child retrieving a ball from a railway track?

Let's define 'trespasser' and then we can consider the background to the OLA 1984 and why the court felt that it was right to allow trespassers to claim for injury in certain circumstances.

A trespasser was defined, in *Robert Addie & Son (Collieries) Ltd v Dumbreck* [1929] AC 358, as '... he who goes on to the land without invitation of any sort and whose presence is either unknown to the proprietor or, if known, is practically objected to'. This definition pre-dates the OLA 1984, and you might feel that the impression it gives of a trespasser is of someone 'up to no good', rather than someone falling into the other categories we've suggested above.

For completeness, a 'non-visitor' would simply be defined as someone who does not fit any of the categories of visitor that we discussed under the OLA 1957. Essentially, we're defining this category of claimant by what they are not, and in practice, it doesn't matter whether someone is termed a trespasser or a non-visitor. If the claimant is not a visitor, then they can't utilise the OLA 1957 and can only bring an action under the OLA 1984, which offers much more limited protection.

10.5.2 Background to the OLA 1984

The OLA 1984 came about largely as the result of a case called *British Railways Board v Herrington* [1972] AC 877. In this case, a boy suffered serious burn injuries while playing on an electrified railway track. The defendant railway board knew about the gap in its fence, and it knew that this was regularly used by children to gain access to the track and to play on it, but it took no action. It argued that, as a trespasser, the boy was simply not permitted to bring an action.

The House of Lords took a more humane view. It held that the claimant should be able to recover, because the defendant knew of the risk of children playing near the railway tracks and had failed to fix the fences, something which it would have been easy for it to do. Therefore, the defendant had breached its duty of care. However, what was the level of duty owed to trespassers? It was, the court decided, a duty of 'common humanity', a base level of care that ought to be provided for everyone, even where those people were not visitors. This thinking formed the basis of the OLA 1984 which codified what was said in this case. Let's look at the Act now.

10.5.3 Duty of care under the OLA 1984

You'll recall that a visitor is owed an automatic duty of care under the OLA 1957 once they can prove they are a visitor, they have established who the occupier is and what the premises are. Not so for the trespasser, who has to prove that they are owed a duty by satisfying three criteria.

(You'll note that at every stage of the OLA 1984, there are extra hurdles for the claimant, the rationale being that they shouldn't have been where they were in the first place, so why should they easily be able to claim? Most claims fail under the OLA 1984. Many of the judgments we read will discuss why, for example, a claim failed at the duty stage, though often the judges will take the opportunity (*obiter*) to talk about how and why the claim would have failed at a later stage if it hadn't already done so! Look out for this when you are reading cases concerning trespassers.)

The trespasser needs to prove the following under s 1(3)(a)–(c) of the OLA 1984:

> (3) An occupier of premises owes a duty to another (not being his visitor) in respect of any such risk as is referred to in subsection (1) above if —

(a) he is aware of the danger or has reasonable grounds to believe that it exists;

(b) he knows or has reasonable grounds to believe that the other is in the vicinity of the danger concerned or that he may come into the vicinity of the danger (in either case, whether the other has lawful authority for being in that vicinity or not); and

(c) the risk is one against which, in all the circumstances of the case, he may reasonably be expected to offer the other some protection.

You might find it helpful to abbreviate the above criteria using the initialism DPP for 'Danger, Proximity, Protection'. The duty is to act reasonably in light of what the occupier knows or ought to have known. Only if all three conditions are met will the claimant be owed a duty (and then only as regards personal injury).

Most cases in this area look at why a duty wasn't owed. In *Rhind v Astbury Water Park Ltd* [2004] EWCA Civ 756, the claimant suffered head injuries when he hit his head on a fibreglass container when diving into a lake. The container was not visible from the surface and so the defendant occupiers had no knowledge of it, nor was it reasonable for them to suspect that it might be there, and so no duty was owed.

A key case in this area is *Tomlinson v Congleton Borough Council* [2004] 1 AC 46, in which a duty was not owed (but, as described above, the court took the opportunity to discuss some of the other elements too).

case example

Tomlinson v Congleton Borough Council [2004] 1 AC 46

The claimant attempted a shallow dive into a lake which was in the grounds of a public park managed by the defendant borough council. He broke his neck and was paralysed. Although boating and fishing were allowed, swimming was not, and several prominent notices made this clear stating: 'Dangerous water: no swimming.' Also, rangers patrolled the area making clear that swimming was not allowed. However, visitors frequently ignored the signs and there had been several accidents where people had tried to swim. The council knew about this and had planned to plant vegetation on the beach areas to prevent people swimming from there, but had not yet done so due to financial constraints.

The claimant sued the council as a trespasser under the OLA 1984. It was early on accepted that his visitor status had been limited by area (see above at **10.3.2**) so that as soon as he entered the lake he was construed as a trespasser, but he still maintained that he should be owed a duty under s 1(3)(a)–(c) of the OLA 1984.

The House of Lords rejected the claimant's claim, overturning a majority Court of Appeal decision. This was because, it said, there was no risk to the claimant due to 'the state of the premises or anything done or omitted upon the premises' (from the preliminary s 1(1) of the OLA 1957) and therefore no risk of the type that would give rise to a duty (under *either* of the Acts).

The House of Lords said it made no difference that the defendant council had intended to take steps to prevent the danger by covering the beach area with vegetation. This was evidence that the council was aware of the danger and had reasonable grounds to believe that people were in the vicinity, but, focusing on s 1(3)(c), the risk was not one against which they could reasonably be expected to offer protection.

Lord Hoffman made clear: 'It will be extremely rare for an occupier of land to be under a duty to prevent people from taking risks which are inherent in the activities they freely choose to undertake upon the land ...' He went on to: '... even if swimming had not been prohibited and the Council had owed a duty under section 2(2) of the 1957 Act, that duty would not have required them to take any steps to prevent Mr Tomlinson from diving or warning him against dangers which were perfectly obvious. If that is the case, then plainly there can have been no duty under the 1984 Act. The risk was not one against which he was entitled under section 1(3)(c) to protection.'

This demonstrates just how difficult it is for a claimant to get over the duty threshold. In *Donoghue v Folkestone Properties Ltd* [2003] 3 All ER 110, the trespasser claimant's claim failed at s 1(3)(b) of the OLA 1984 because whilst the defendant was aware that people swam in the harbour during the summer, it was not aware that people would be swimming in winter.

10.5.4 Breach

If the claimant manages to prove they ought to be owed a duty of care (and as we have seen, this is rare) then s 1(4) of the OLA 1984 sets out the standard of care expected of the occupier. This is a modified version of what we find under the OLA 1957 and states that the duty is to 'take such care as is reasonable in all the circumstances to see that [the claimant] does not suffer injury on the premises by reason of the danger concerned'.

Therefore, we are looking for the standard of the reasonably competent occupier but only in relation to personal injury. And, as we'll see, it is arguably easier for a defendant to discharge that duty than it is for an occupier under the OLA 1957. All the usual factors can be taken into account at this stage. The OLA 1984 doesn't give much more guidance except as to warnings.

Warnings

Section 1(5) states that the defendant occupier can discharge their duty of care in respect of any risk of danger by 'taking such steps as are reasonable in all the circumstances of the case to give warning of the danger concerned or to discourage persons from incurring the risk'.

Note that all the occupier has to do here to discharge their duty is to take reasonable steps to make the trespasser aware of the danger ('give warning of the danger'). The standard attaches to the awareness, not to fixing the danger itself. In contrast, the OLA 1957 equivalent (s 2(4)(a)) requires occupiers to do all that's reasonable to keep visitors safe, which is a far more onerous and wide-ranging duty.

Table 10.2   Warnings and discharging liability – the two Acts in a nutshell

OLA 1957, s 2(4)(a)	**OLA 1984, s 1(5)**
Occupier must demonstrate that the warning *'in all the circumstances was enough to enable the visitor to be reasonably safe'*	Occupier must take *'such steps as are reasonable in all the circumstances of the case to give warning of the danger concerned or to discourage persons from incurring the risk'*

Perhaps the rationale here is that whilst visitors may not have any choice as to whether to be on the premises or not, a trespasser can choose. From the outset, they are choosing to be somewhere they shouldn't be (though think back to all the categories of trespasser we touched on earlier and consider whether that rationale is sound). Physical barriers, or signs warning the trespasser not to trespass, can be sufficient here (see *Titchener v British Railway Board* [1983] 1 WLR 1427 where fences were considered sufficient warning).

10.5.5   Defences

Both *volenti* and contributory negligence are available under the OLA 1984, and, as with every aspect of a claim under the OLA 1984, the defences are more likely to succeed than under the OLA 1957 (if the case even gets as far as the defences stage).

Volenti

It would seem that the court is more likely to infer consent from the conduct of the claimant where that claimant is a trespasser bringing an action under the OLA 1984, than when the claimant is a visitor.

case example

Ratcliff v McConnell [1997] EWCA Civ 2679
The claimant was a 19-year-old student who had been drinking one night with friends on campus. They decided to break into the student swimming pool, by climbing over a locked gate. There were signs indicating where the deep and shallow ends were, and stating the opening hours, but the students didn't see these because it was dark. All three dived into the pool, but it was shallower where the claimant dived in, and, as a result, he was paralysed from the neck down.

At first instance, the court found that the defendant occupiers had breached their duty but reduced the claimant's damages by 60% for contributory negligence. On appeal, the Court of Appeal held that there was no breach in that the defendants had done what was reasonable to protect the claimant. They said, even if there had been a breach, that the claim would have failed as the defendants had a full defence of *volenti*.

Contributory negligence

Revill v Newbery [1996] QB 567

case example

In this case, the claimant trespasser ultimately had his damages reduced by two thirds when he was found to be contributorily negligent. The defendant occupier was a 76-year-old man, William Newbery, who was sleeping in the shed of his allotment to protect his property at night. The claimant trespasser, Revill (plus an accomplice), attempted to break into the shed whereupon Newbery fired a twelve-bore shotgun through a hole in the shed, intending to frighten the claimant. However, Revill was shot and brough an action against the defendant, both in Negligence and under the OLA 1984.

The circumstances thereafter were very interesting, garnering much attention in the press. The defendant was acquitted of a criminal charge of assault. The claimant pleaded guilty to burglary but sued the defendant in tort. The court decided that Mr Newbery was not liable under the OLA 1984 because this wasn't even an occupiers' liability claim, given that the injury had arisen as a result of an activity done on the land (the shooting), not as a result of the state of the premises themselves. However, the court effectively utilised the OLA 1984 as a means by which to demonstrate that the claimant was owed a duty in General Negligence. Mr Newbery was therefore found liable in Negligence, but, as mentioned, the claimant's damages were reduced by two thirds for contributory negligence.

Attempts to exclude liability under the OLA 1984

Unlike the OLA 1957, the OLA 1984 is silent on whether it's possible to exclude or limit liability. There is some debate as to why and the effect of this. Some commentators argue that an occupier can simply exclude or limit liability to trespassers as they see fit. Except, if that's the case, why have an Act in the first place if an occupier can simply side-step liability through an exclusion notice? The other argument is that an occupier cannot exclude liability entirely, *because* of the Act which lays down a bare minimum standard of care, below which an occupier cannot go (ie, an occupier can't simply exclude liability for injury). But if that's the case, then this would potentially put trespassers in a more advantageous position that visitors (in that trespassers would always recover *something*), which seems contrary to the intention of Parliament in drafting the two statutes. Perhaps, in reality, it doesn't matter a great deal because claims brought by trespassers are so often unsuccessful that meaningful consideration of exclusion notices is never relevant, given that the claim will probably have failed at an earlier stage in any event. But it's a moot point, and one to give some thought to.

10.5.6 Do claims under the OLA 1984 *ever* succeed?

Such claims do succeed, but rarely, and usually where they concern children. Of course, the claimant in *Herrington* (see **10.5.2**) succeeded, and this was the basis for the OLA 1984. Another example is *Young v Kent County Council* [2015] EWHC 1342 (QB). Here, the claimant was a 12-year-old boy who was at a youth club on the school's premises. He climbed onto the roof, as some other children had also done in the weeks before, using the flue of an extractor on one side of the building. He then fell through a brittle skylight, suffering personal injury.

The court determined that he was owed a duty under the OLA 1984 which had been breached. The state of the premises was inherently dangerous given the brittleness of the skylight, and the area was a known meeting place for children. The solution to the problem was low cost and would have been easy for the defendant occupier to put in place. It was held that the defendant had a duty to protect and that, almost certainly, if the claimant had been an adult, he would not have succeeded in his claim. The claimant's damages were reduced by 50%, however, due to contributory negligence.

10.6 Differences between the OLA 1957 and the OLA 1984

Now that we've considered both Acts, you might find it helpful to utilise a table which reminds you of the differences between them.

Table 10.3   Differences between the OLA 1957 and the OLA 1984

	OLA 1957	**OLA 1984**
What can the claimant claim for?	Personal injury and property damage (as per common law pre-OLA 1957)	Only personal injury (s 1(8))
'Premises', 'occupier'	Defined the same way in each Act	Defined the same way in each Act
Duty of care	Owed automatically under s 2(1) once visitor status established	Claimant needs to prove all three elements from s 1(3)(a)–(c)
Standard of care	From s 2(2): Duty to keep the visitor safe on the premises so far as is reasonable	From s 1(4): Duty to prevent only personal injury to the trespasser so far as is reasonable

	OLA 1957	**OLA 1984**
Discharge of duty	Ordinary factors to be considered – Visitor should take reasonable care for their own safety (s 2(3)). Note children and professionals (s 2(3)(a) and (b)) – Re warnings: may be discharged by taking reasonable steps to give warnings that enable visitors to be reasonably safe – Re independent contractors: generally no liability where contractors have done work on premises provided the occupier can satisfy the three requirements at s 2(4)(a)	Ordinary factors to be considered – Re warnings: may be discharged by taking reasonable steps to give a warning about the danger (s 1(5))
Defences	*Volenti* and contributory negligence apply to both Acts	*Volenti* and contributory negligence apply to both Acts
Attempts to exclude liability	Occupier can attempt to exclude, via a notice (s 2(1)) so far as free to do so. This will be subject to UCTA 1977, s 2(1) and (2).	Act is silent on whether this is possible.

10.7 Further reading

S Hepburn, 'Occupiers' liability and open water swimming' (2021) Prop LB 170, 5–6.

J Elvin, 'Occupiers' liability, free will, and the dangers of a "compensation culture"' (Case Comment) (2004) 8(1) Edin LR 127–32.

M Lyons, 'Occupiers' liability – Occupiers' Liability Act 1984 – trespass – duty of care – causation (2001) JPI Law 1, 91.

summary

- Occupiers' liability is a form of statute-based Negligence but that also looks to case law.
- Visitors are afforded a high degree of protection when injured on premises as a result of the Occupiers' Liability Act 1957.
- Non-visitors or trespassers have some but limited protection as a result of the Occupiers' Liability Act 1984.
- Most cases brought under the Occupiers' Liability Act 1984 fail at the duty stage.

test your knowledge

Have a go at these multiple-choice questions (MCQs):

Question 1

A partially sighted man is injured at a gallery when he trips on the wires of an art installation. The wires were exposed and there were no signs or warnings about them.

Which one of the following options best describe the man's chances of success as regards proving duty and breach in occupiers' liability?

A   The man will probably be construed as a trespasser on the gallery premises, with the gallery as occupier. He will therefore not be owed an automatic duty of care under the OLA 1957.

B   The man will probably be construed as a visitor on the gallery premises, with the gallery as occupier. He will therefore be owed an automatic duty of care under the OLA 1957 and this looks like a breach by the gallery.

C   The man will probably be construed as a visitor on the gallery premises, with the gallery as occupier. He will therefore be owed a duty of care under the OLA 1957 provided he can satisfy s 1(3)(a)–(c).

D   The man will probably be construed as a visitor on the gallery premises, with the gallery as occupier. He will therefore be owed an automatic duty of care under the OLA 1957 but there is probably no breach by the gallery.

E   The man will probably be construed as a trespasser on the gallery premises, with the gallery as occupier. He will therefore need to prove he was owed a duty, by satisfying s 1(3)(a)–(c) of the OLA 1984.

Answer

The correct answer is option B. Yes, the gallery would need to ensure that it acted reasonably to keep visitors safe, including visitors who may be partially sighted, applying, eg, *Haley v London Electricity Board*.

Question 2

A woman is burned when she accidentally walks into a store cupboard in an unfamiliar building on her first day at work. The room is marked 'private – keep out'. It contains corrosive chemicals at floor level and the woman steps into a tray containing chemicals.

Which one of the following best outlines whether the woman would be seen as visitor or trespasser, and why?

A   She may be seen as a trespasser on entering the private room, as any express permission as a visitor looks to have been restricted by area. (She may be able to claim if so under the OLA 1984 however.)

B   She may be seen as a visitor on entering the private room because she is presumably allowed into the building if she works there.

C   She may be seen as a visitor because the occupier should know she would enter the room.

D   She may be seen as a trespasser on entering the private room and so would not be able to claim.

E   She may be seen as a visitor because she has express or implied permission to be in the room.

Answer

The correct answer is option A. This is the best option here, though even as a trespasser, she may be able to claim if the room is inherently dangerous with chemicals on the floor? It is dependent on facts we don't have yet.

Question 3

A sign on a wall states that the occupier excludes all liability for any loss or damage caused to trespassers.

Which one of the following is accurate as to whether the occupier can exclude liability under the OLA 1984?

A   The OLA 1984 is silent on this point. The occupier may be able to exclude liability.

B   The occupier would be able to exclude all liability.

C   The occupier would not be able to exclude liability for personal injury but may be able to exclude liability for property damage.

D   The occupier would be able to exclude liability for personal injury but not property damage.

E   The OLA 1984 is silent on this point so we would need to refer to the OLA 1957.

Answer

The correct answer is option A. This is correct though feels unsatisfactory.

Question 4

Independent contractor electricians are doing some work for an occupier. They do it badly and a woman is injured on the premises as a result.

Which one of the following most accurately describes whether the woman should sue the occupier or the independent contractors?

A   If the work is complex (and it probably is here) then, on the face of it, it looks as though she should sue both the independent contractors and the occupier as both will be liable.

B   If the work is complex (and it probably is here) then, on the face of it, it looks as though she should sue the occupier as the occupier under s 2(4)(b) of the OLA 1957.

C   If the work is complex (and it probably is here) then, on the face of it, it looks as though she should sue the independent contractors as the occupier may have discharged liability under s 2(4)(a) of the OLA 1957.

D   If the work is complex (and it probably is here) then, on the face of it, it looks as though she should sue the independent contractors as the occupier may have discharged liability under s 2(4)(b) of the OLA 1957.

E   If the work is complex (and it probably is here) then, on the face of it, it looks as though she should sue the occupier under s 2(4)(b) of the OLA 1957.

Answer

The correct answer is option D. The duty to supervise and check work would apply only so far as is reasonable, as per *Haseldine v Daw*.

11 Defamation

After reading this chapter, you will be able to:

- define defamation, and appreciate the similarities and differences between libel and slander
- understand the relationship between the common law and statute (especially the Defamation Act 2013) as to the substantive claims and defences in defamation
- recognise and explain key terms in defamation, such as 'serious harm', 'sting', 'innuendo', 'publication'
- work through the structure of a defamation action, identifying what the claimant needs to prove, the defences available to a defendant, and possible remedies.

11.1 Defamation – definition and background

Defamation is fundamentally different in nature from all the other torts we look at in this book. It protects a claimant's reputation. Specifically, it protects a claimant's reputation from *untrue* statements that would harm them in the eyes of others. A basic distinction between defamation and the law of privacy, which is outside the ambit of our discussion here, is that defamation is designed to protect a person against *untrue* statements which are or might become *public*, and privacy protects against statements which are *true* but *private*.

(Where a statement is untrue and does not damage reputation, but does cause some commercial harm, for example the erroneous suggestion that a trader has ceased trading, this might be covered by a related tort of malicious falsehood, again not something we cover here.)

The original definition of defamation comes from *Sim v Stretch* [1936] 2 All ER 1237, in which Lord Atkin describes it as the publication of a statement: '... *which tends to lower the claimant in the estimation of right-thinking members of society generally, and in particular to cause him to be regarded with feelings of hatred, contempt, ridicule, fear and disesteem.*'

Defamation law is about balancing public and private rights. You might say it's an attempt to allow public interest in freedom of expression to co-exist with private interest in maintaining personal reputation. You might have a sense already that this is going to cause friction, and you'd be right. Throw into the mix that defamation law can get highly technical (indeed, lawyers tend to specialise solely in this area for this reason) and that it is 'governed' by statute – most recently the Defamation Act (DA) 2013 which came into force in January 2014 and codifies but does not obliterate the importance of the common law, which is now to be regarded as persuasive rather than binding – and you begin to see how fascinating and sometimes complex this tort can be. Indeed, the DA 2013 not only develops many of the common law principles but provides, in its Explanatory Notes, for the fact that some of the DA 2013 provisions are intended to mirror the common law position. What this means for lawyers is that we have to understand *both* the common law and the DA 2013.

Interestingly, the DA 2013 itself came about as a result of much campaigning from those who felt that the common law on defamation was far too complicated. It does introduce reforms which we'll look at, for example a seriousness threshold and so-called new defences, which are arguably just the old defences in new clothes, but as to whether these reforms simplify the law remains to be seen.

Finally, though we won't focus much on this here, the importance of the Human Rights Act (HRA) 1998 will no doubt continue to be of significance to defamation lawyers as they attempt to interpret the DA 2013 in light of its provisions. If this is an area that interests you, then you might wish to explore, for example, how Article 10 of the European Convention on Human Rights (incorporated into the HRA 1998) has a bearing on defamation law in the UK, in that it both guarantees freedom of expression but also contains an exception as regards protecting the reputation of others, and as to how to square that with Article 8 which guarantees the right to private and family life, including reputation. How will that impact on the future direction of defamation law?

11.2 Libel and slander

Defamation is really the umbrella term for two torts, libel and slander. Historically at least, though less so now perhaps with the DA 2013, it was important to distinguish between the two for procedural reasons.

11.2.1 Libel

Libel is the publication of a defamatory statement in a permanent form. This would normally be something written, but it also includes films, recordings, pictures and even statues. Broadcasts recorded for radio or television would be potentially libellous rather than slanderous because of their permanency under the Broadcasting Act 1990, as would theatrical performances in public according to the Theatres Act 1968. Material posted on the internet is potentially libellous, too, due to its perceived permanency: see *Godfrey v Demon Internet Ltd* [2001] QB 201, as is material posted on Facebook and other social networking sites, according to *Applause Stores Productions Ltd and Another v Raphael* [2008] EWHC 1781 (QB). Even material posted on, for example, Snapchat, a multimedia mobile messaging application whose messages might be visible for a few seconds only, is considered potentially libellous.

Monson v Madame Tussauds Ltd [1894] 1 QB 671

A waxwork of a man was held to constitute libel because of where it was placed within the exhibition and the meaning attributable to that. The man had been tried for murder but the jury had returned a verdict of 'not proven' (an option in Scottish law and a form of acquittal but with a twist – you might say it's a half-way house verdict: we can't prove that you did it but we think you did!). The defendant placed the wax statue, holding a gun, in a room next door to the Chamber of Horrors section of the waxwork museum. Naturally, visitors viewing it would think badly of the individual, notwithstanding the verdict, and the Court of Appeal found this to be libellous.

11.2.2 Slander

Slander, in contrast to libel, is defamation in a temporary or transitory form. The most obvious example would be speech (that hasn't been recorded), but it could include sound, gestures, or anything regarded as transitory in nature.

In fact, the distinction between libel and slander is not always easy to determine and sometimes even the judges can't agree. For example, voicemail messages were held to be potentially slanderous in *Reachlocal UK Ltd v Bennett* [2014] EWHC 3405 (QB) but libellous in *Cooper v Turrell* [2011] EWHC 3269 (QB).

11.2.3 Does the distinction between libel and slander matter?

Well yes and no. In the grand scheme of things, no, not really, in that both broadly run along similar lines, and defamation is defamation. But technically, yes, for this reason: for *all* cases, whether libel or slander, the claimant needs to demonstrate that the publication of the statement has caused or is likely to cause serious harm (see **11.3.2** below). In addition, for slander, the claimant must normally prove material loss flowing from this (special damage) unless an exception applies. There are two exceptions to the slander rule, ie two situations whereby the claimant can claim without proof of special damage:

(a) Where the statement of the defendant alleges that the claimant has committed an imprisonable offence.

(b) Where the statement of the defendant alleges that the claimant is incompetent or unfit in any office, profession, calling, trade or business. See, for example, *McManus v Beckham* [2002] EWCA Civ 939 where Victoria Beckham wrongly and loudly accused the claimant of selling fake signed photos of her husband, David Beckham, in the claimant's memorabilia shop.

11.2.4 Difference between defamation and mere abuse

Mere abuse is not normally defamatory, but there is a fine line between what is abuse and what tips over into an actionable claim.

Berkoff v Burchill [1996] 4 All ER 1008

case example

Steven Berkoff, theatre director and (then) actor, sued journalist, Julie Burchill, for libel after two comments she made about him in *The Sunday Times*, in which she referred to him as 'hideously ugly' and compared him to Frankenstein's monster (the monster coming out of it marginally more favourably). Berkoff complained that such abuse tipped over into damaging his reputation, that he would be offered fewer auditions as no-one would want to work with an actor who was perceived to be hideously ugly. Burchill countered that she may have caused hurt feelings or annoyance, but that these statements did not amount to defamation.

The Court of Appeal narrowly (by a majority of 3 to 2) found for Berkoff, deciding that the statement was capable of being defamatory, 'even though [the words hideously ugly] neither impute disgraceful conduct to the claimant nor any lack of skill or efficiency in the conduct of his trade or business or professional activity, if they hold him up to contempt, scorn or ridicule or tend to exclude him from society'.

At the time, it was for a jury to decide if the words were actually defamatory. This is no longer the case, as jury trials have mostly been abolished – one of the changes that has been brought about by s 11 of the DA 2013.

11.3 Structure of a claim

Let's take a look at the requirements needed for a claimant to bring an action in defamation against a defendant.

11.3.1 Who can and cannot sue?

Table 11.1   The claimant

Who can sue	Who cannot sue
All 'natural and legal persons', in other words, living individuals. Interestingly, unlike with Negligence, where the claimant's estate could bring any action on behalf of the claimant were they to die, with defamation, if the claimant dies, the claim dies with them.	**Governmental bodies**. This was confirmed by the House of Lords in *Derbyshire County Council v Times Newspapers Ltd* [1993] 1 All ER 1011 on the basis that to allow a local authority to sue would inhibit freedom of speech, something that it is particularly important to preserve in a democracy. This has also been applied to political parties, though individual Members of Parliament may be able to sue.

Who can sue

Trading corporations. For example, McDonalds succeeded in a libel action against environmentalists in the longest running libel trial in England, *McDonald's Corporation v Steel and Morris* [1997] EWHC 366 (QB) (the so-called 'McLibel trial').

As a result of s 9 of the DA 2013, there is a further limitation on who can sue. Section 9 provides that the court will not have jurisdiction to hear a defamation claim where the defendant is resident outside of the UK, European Union or Lugano Convention states (Iceland, Norway and Switzerland) unless it is satisfied that England and Wales is the most appropriate place to bring the action. This provision was enacted so as to combat so-called 'libel tourism', that is, litigants from overseas bringing libel claims in the UK when they had only peripheral association with the UK, because it was perceived as easier to win there than in their home country. It will be interesting to note how Brexit will affect prospective EU litigants.

11.3.2 The requirement of serious harm

Section 1(1) of the DA 2013 has added an initial requirement for a claimant to prove, in that it states: 'A statement is not defamatory unless its publication has caused or is likely to cause serious harm to the reputation of the claimant.'

This was introduced to prevent trivial claims being brought, and it has attracted perhaps more judicial attention than any other new provision within the DA 2013. The question of what is 'serious' continues to be in issue. It appeared early on that the threshold for bringing an action had risen considerably.

For example, in *Cooke & Another v MGN Ltd* [2014] EWHC 2831 (QB), it was suggested that the claimant would need to prove specific reputational harm, such that libel could no longer be said to be actionable *per se*, and that in all but the most serious cases, where allegations of, say, paedophilia or terrorism were levelled at the claimant in a national newspaper, the claimant would find it difficult to meet the evidential requirement. (This was *obiter* in that a prompt apology prevented the potentially defamatory statement from constituting serious harm.)

In *Ames v Spamhaus* [2015] EWHC 127 (QB), Warby J (who had just replaced Sir Michael Tugendhat as the primary specialist media law judge) suggested that the threshold might not be as high as *Cooke* had suggested. The same Justice found the serious harm threshold to have been reached by the claimant in *Monroe v Hopkins* [2017] EWHC 433 (QB) in relation to two tweets sent about the claimant that had caused her 'real and substantial distress', as well as injuring her feelings, and leaving her upset and horrified about what people would think, to the point that she feared online abuse. This was made worse in that the defendant did not apologise in the two years prior to this case going to court. Warby J stated that the 'serious harm requirement is satisfied, on the straightforward basis that the tweets complained of have a tendency to cause harm to this claimant's reputation in the eyes of third parties, of a kind that would be serious for her'.

Having swung towards the claimant, the pendulum swung back a little towards the defendant in *Lachaux v Independent Print Ltd & Another* [2019] UKSC 27, in which the Supreme Court stated that the meaning of s 1(1) of the DA 2013 is such that the question of whether serious harm has been suffered must be determined by reference to actual facts, rather than inference. However, the Court also acknowledged that inferences of fact can be drawn from the context of the publication, including consideration of, for example: (i) the scale of publication, (ii) evidence that the publication came to the attention of identifiable individuals, and (iii) the gravity of the statements made against the claimant. All of which tells us, in short, that whether the serious harm threshold has been reached will be a question of fact for the court. This might fall to be determined by way of preliminary trial, or it may be better left for the trial itself (*Hamilton v News Group Newspapers Ltd* [2020] EWHC 59 (QB)).

By contrast, s 1(2) of the DA 2013 has passed with little scrutiny. It states that 'harm to the reputation of a body that trades for profit is not serious harm unless it has caused or is likely to cause the body serious financial losses'.

11.4 Elements of defamation

The claimant must establish that:

(1) a defamatory statement was made;
(2) the statement referred to the claimant; and
(3) the statement was published to a third party.

We'll look at each of these in turn.

11.4.1 A defamatory statement was made

We use 'statement' throughout to mean the potentially defamatory material in question, whether that be written, spoken or communicated via some other medium. The question to be asked at this stage is whether the statement was defamatory. Sometimes the easiest way to do that is to split this into two questions: (a) what is the meaning of the statement, and (b) is that meaning defamatory, to this claimant?

The meaning of the statement

Sometimes the meaning of a statement is obvious on its face. 'John Smith has a contagious disease/is a paedophile/stole from his employer' would all be clear examples of potentially defamatory statements whose meaning is obvious to all. All of the above would cause the claimant to be lowered in the 'estimation of right-thinking members of society' (from *Sim v Stretch*) applying the ordinary and natural meaning of the words. In other words, a literal interpretation of the words used is all that is required to get at what we call the 'sting' of the statement, ie the harmful part for the claimant. This is always where we start, when pleading meaning, with a literal interpretation of the statement. Importantly, it is for the claimant to plead the meaning, or sometimes range of meanings, they say are attributable to the statement. Lord Tenterden, CJ said in *Harvey v French* (1832) 1 Cr & M 11 that a court must 'read the words in the sense in which ordinary persons … would understand them'.

Sometimes, meanings are capable of being defamatory but would or would not be to that particular claimant.

example

An allegation is made that Joe Bloggs does not pay his TV licence. Joe Bloggs is the current Director General of the BBC. Gordon Bleu is a famous chef who publicly berates those who buy ready meals instead of cooking from scratch. He is secretly filmed late at night buying a basket full of ready meals.

Can you see that we have two potentially defamatory situations here? In the first, it would perhaps not of itself be defamatory to allege that someone doesn't pay their TV licence. To watch TV without a licence would be against the law but probably not construed by most people as a serious offence. However, where that person is the Director General of the BBC, the sting of the allegation is clear: that Bloggs is dishonest and/or hypocritical in not paying his TV licence when he heads the BBC. But imagine if Joe Bloggs was not Director General of the BBC but was instead an axe-murderer serving a life sentence. The same statement about his not paying his TV licence, whilst capable of being defamatory, would not be defamatory *to him* (his reputation already being pretty low and not capable of being lowered any further by this kind of allegation). This was the argument raised in *Williams v MGN Ltd* [2009] EWHC 3150 (QB).

Similarly, with Gordon Bleu, it is the fact of his apparent dishonesty and hypocrisy in buying ready meals, when publicly berating those that buy them, that would, if it were true, damage his reputation.

A statement where the literal meaning is unclear

Stocker v Stocker [2019] UKSC 17

In this case, the defendant, Nicola Stocker, posted numerous comments on the Facebook wall of her ex-husband's new partner, claiming that her ex-husband, Ronald Stocker, had, among other things, 'tried to strangle me'.

At first instance, in finding for the claimant, Mitting J had relied on the *Oxford English Dictionary* in his determination of the meaning: he said that either Mr Stocker had tried to kill his wife, or he had constricted her throat/neck in such a way as to cause pain. The fact that Mrs Stocker said that her husband had tried to strangle her precluded the latter meaning; therefore, the only possible meaning was that Mr Stocker had tried to kill her, something which Mrs Stocker was unable to prove.

In the Supreme Court, a unanimous panel decided that the trial judge and the Court of Appeal were wrong in law. Lord Kerr stated:

Mitting J fell into legal error by relying upon the dictionary definition of the verb 'to strangle' as dictating the meaning of Mrs Stocker's Facebook post … In consequence, he failed to conduct a realistic exploration of how the ordinary reader of the post would have understood it. … If Mrs Stocker had meant to convey that her husband had attempted to kill her, why would she not say so explicitly? And, given that she made no such allegation, what would the ordinary reasonable reader, the casual viewer of this Facebook post, think it meant? In my view, giving due consideration of the context in which the message was posted, the interpretation that Mr Stocker had grasped his wife by the neck is the obvious, indeed the inescapable, choice of meaning.

Context

Mentioned in the above passage is the importance of context. When searching for the meaning the claimant pleads, the court will always consider the matter in context. So, for example, if a statement is made up of words and a picture, the court will look at both, rather than simply one or the other.

Charleston v News Group Newspapers Ltd [1995] 2 All ER 313

case example

Here, the defendant tabloid newspaper published a photograph in which it appeared that the claimants (the actors who played Harold and Madge in Australian soap 'Neighbours') were engaged in sexual intercourse. The headline read: 'Strewth! What's Harold been up to with our Madge?' However, the wording underneath the photograph and the rest of the text made clear that the photograph was fake, in that it had been computer-generated without the consent of the actors, who had not had sex with one another. The House of Lords held that this was not defamatory because of the context: the words negated what the picture suggested. The ordinary, natural reader would have looked at both the picture and the words. (Does this seem likely to you?) Lord Nicholls did say that, had the explanatory text been hidden away, then the court may have taken a different view.

Innuendo

Sometimes the meaning of a statement needs unearthing, it being implied or veiled rather than obvious on its face. The law of defamation takes this into account, and that makes sense because otherwise would-be defendants would permanently sidestep liability simply by ensuring that their statements' meanings were sufficiently hidden. We call this hidden meaning innuendo, and it is for the claimant to plead the hidden meaning or range of meanings attributable to the statement.

False or popular innuendo

If you imagine the sting being hidden under the surface where innuendo is concerned, then false or popular innuendo is simply where the meaning is hidden just under the surface. You might say that all the reader has to do is 'read between the lines' to get at the meaning, without needing any extrinsic knowledge of the facts to do this. Examples of false innuendo might include slang, colloquialisms, puns and so on.

An example of false innuendo as slang comes from *Allsop v Church of England Newspaper Ltd* [1972] 2 QB 161 in which the claimant, a television presenter, was accused by the defendant of having a 'preoccupation with the bent'. The case was less about the meaning of the word 'bent' itself (which was taken by the claimant to mean dishonest/disingenuous and accepted as being capable of bearing that meaning) and more about the requirement that the claimant plead the meaning he says is there, even where that meaning is fairly easily understandable.

True or legal innuendo

True or legal innuendo is where the meaning is hidden more deeply. Such innuendo relies on some extrinsic knowledge on the part of the reader to get at it, and for that reason it can be more difficult for the claimant to convince a judge on the meaning they say is attributable to the statement. A good example of true/legal innuendo is *Tolley v JS Fry & Sons Ltd* [1931] AC 33. In this case, a cartoon image of the claimant, who was a very well-known amateur golfer, was used, without his knowledge, in an advert for the defendant's chocolate. Without any extrinsic knowledge about the difference between amateur and professional sporting status, this may have seemed innocuous. However, for those with knowledge that amateur sportspersons could not accept money from their sport, the fact that Tolley had apparently done so was serious. Indeed, 16 of the most prestigious golf clubs in the country had banned him as a result of having seen this advert, so it clearly carried the defamatory meaning (that Tolley pleaded was there) for many. Therefore the claimant was able to prove, on the balance of probabilities, that there were persons who knew of him as an amateur golfer and who read into the statement the meaning he alleged.

It is a requirement for the claimant, when attempting to demonstrate that the statement is defamatory by way of true innuendo, to show that someone to whom the statement was published (see below at **11.4.3** for what is meant by 'published') actually had the extrinsic knowledge to make sense of the innuendo (and the greater the number who have that knowledge, potentially the higher the damages would be).

example

The year is 1929. A picture appears in a tabloid newspaper showing a man at a race track with his arm around a mystery woman with the caption suggesting that they are engaged. In fact, this is wrong, the man is already married, and his wife sues the paper for libel saying that people who know her will assume that she's 'living in sin', or condoning his bigamy.

This scenario comes from a real case called *Cassidy v Daily Mirror Newspapers Ltd* [1929] 2 KB 331. The claimant wife (who was not mentioned or pictured in the article – see below at **11.4.2** 'The statement referred to the claimant') succeeded in her libel action, and pleaded the meaning using true or legal innuendo. Those who knew her would put two and two together and make an assumption about her.

Interestingly, this is also an example of the fact that what might be considered defamatory is a concept that changes over time. In 1929, such an allegation was arguably more serious than it would be now in the Western world.

Is the statement defamatory to that claimant?

Having established the meaning or range of meanings attributable to the statement, the claimant must prove that that meaning is actually defamatory. We've discussed already the sometimes fine line between defamation and 'mere abuse' (see above at **11.2.4**) and how some statements might be capable of being defamatory but will or won't be in relation to that particular claimant (see the Example above featuring Joe Bloggs and Gordon Bleu).

What we haven't yet discussed in detail is *how* the court decides whether a statement is defamatory. The basic test, as mentioned, comes from *Sim v Stretch*: a statement which tends to lower the claimant in the estimation of right-thinking members of society would be a potentially defamatory statement. There are two other useful cases here that give us alternative tests for what is defamatory. The first is *Yousopoff v MGM* (1934) 50 TLR 581 which tells us that defamatory statements are those which 'tend to cause the claimant to be shunned and avoided'. The second is *Berkoff v Burchill* (see above) which states that statements that expose the claimant to 'ridicule, hatred and contempt' are defamatory.

So, we have three tests or markers to use as a basis for determining whether the statement is defamatory. The claimant would not need to prove that their situation satisfies *all* of them, but just one of them. If the test is as to 'right-thinking members of society' then the suggestion is that it's objective. (It used to be that right-thinking members of society were the jury who would determine the outcome of the trial, but jury trials have now been abolished by the DA 2013 in all or most cases.) In reality, you might argue that the test is subjective to the extent that it is the judge who determines the outcome. This is perhaps most clearly illustrated in *Byrne v Dean* [1937] 1 KB 818 in which the accusation that the claimant had informed the police about a criminal offence (a fruit machine in a golf-club bar where there was no licence for gambling) was held by the judge not to be defamatory, because all right-thinking people would not think less of someone who reported a crime to the police. (This perhaps highlights the gap between what judges, as opposed to the public, might feel to be acceptable.)

The court has made the important point that it's necessary to take into account the societal and cultural norms of the readership of a publication in determining who the 'ordinary reader' is and how they might feel. This was made clear in *Al-Fagih v HH Saudi Research & Marketing (UK) Ltd* [2002] EWCA Civ 1634 whose readership was made up largely of people from the Saudi Arabian community.

11.4.2 The statement referred to the claimant

The claimant must next prove that the statement referred to them. That can be easy where the claimant is named in the statement or otherwise made obviously identifiable. For more obscure references, it can be more difficult to show that the reasonable person would understand the statement as referring to the claimant. Where this is the case, perhaps there is a clue or indication within the statement, or evident as part of the context, that identifies the claimant. The test then becomes whether the hypothetical reasonable reader, having knowledge of the circumstances, would believe that the article was referring to the claimant. (Note: can you see that this is essentially the same rationale as underpins the concept of legal innuendo? Look again at *Cassidy v Daily Mirror* above, where reference to the claimant is satisfied because of innuendo.)

Reference to the claimant can be satisfied even where the claimant is referenced unintentionally.

Hulton v Jones [1910] AC 20

case example

The defendant newspaper published a fictional account about a motor vehicle festival in France featuring a made-up character, 'Artemus Jones', a church-warden from Peckham. Unknown to the defendants, there existed a real Artemus Jones, a barrister living in Wales. He successfully sued for libel, claiming that a number of his friends had read the story and assumed it referred to him. The House of Lords said there was sufficient evidence to suggest a jury could reasonably conclude that a reasonable person would believe the story referred to the claimant.

It's also possible that a true statement about one individual might inadvertently defame another with the same name, as was the case in *Newstead v London Express Newspaper Ltd* [1940] 1 KB 377. In this case, the newspaper ran a story about Harold Newstead, a 30-year-old barman from Camberwell in London who had been convicted of bigamy. It was *not* true of the claimant, a man in his 30s called Harold Newstead from Camberwell! You may have noticed that many gossip-style magazines and online publications seem to give very detailed descriptions of individuals, including name, age, hair colour, shoe size, and so on. This is precisely so as to avoid the kind of defamation action against them that happened in *Newstead* – the more specific the description, the less likely that a different claimant could sue.

However, not every unintentional reference will be the basis for a claim, as was discussed in *O'Shea v MGN Ltd* [2001] EMLR 40, in which a model in an advertisement for pornography running in the *Sunday Mirror* looked very similar to the claimant. The court held that the statement did not refer to the claimant, who had sued for libel given, she said, that others who knew her would assume she had consented to appear in such an advert. Morland J held that, although the image was on the face of it defamatory, to hold the newspaper liable would be contrary to Article 10 of the ECHR and would place an 'impossible burden on a publisher if he were required to check if the true picture of someone resembled someone else who, because of the context of the picture, was defamed'.

Reference to a group or class of claimants

The general rule is that it is not possible to defame a group or class of claimants. So, for example, the statement 'all politicians are corrupt' is not actionable. This general rule comes from the House of Lords in a case called *Knupffer v London Express Newspaper Ltd* [1944] AC 116, in which Lord Porter said: 'No doubt it is true to say that a class cannot be defamed as a class, nor can an individual be defamed by general reference to the class to which he belongs.'

The exception to this rule is where the group or class is so small that the claimant can establish that the statement can be said to apply to all members of that group, or it indicates a particular member of that group. This happened in *Aspro Travel Ltd v Owners Abroad Group plc* [1996] 1 WLR 132. The defendant told hotels and travel agents in Cyprus that Aspro Travel was insolvent but still trading. This was not true. Aspro Travel was made up of only four members (three brothers and their father) and therefore the words were held to apply to all four members.

To go back to the example given above, whilst the statement 'all politicians are corrupt' is not actionable, the statement 'all the politicians in the running for the position of Chancellor are corrupt' (where there are only, say, three) might be.

11.4.3 The statement was published to a third party

This is the third and final requirement for the claimant to prove and often the simplest. 'Published' simply means communicated to a third party, and the same requirement applies to both libel and slander.

A private conversation or letter seen only by the claimant and defendant would not be deemed to have been published to a third party and so would not be actionable. However, sending a letter in circumstances where it is reasonably foreseeable that this will be opened by a third party (for example a secretary or administrative team, or a spouse) would suffice, as was the case in *Theaker v Richardson* [1962] 1 WLR 151 in which the defendant wrote and hand-delivered a letter to the claimant, in which he described her as 'a lying low-down brothel-keeping whore and thief'. This was opened by her husband who assumed it was an election address. The claimant successfully sued for libel.

A postcard would be deemed published to a third party as it's foreseeable that the postman would see/read it. Other examples of publication to a third party might include: speaking in a loud voice so that others close by can hear (*White v J & F Stone (Lighting and Radio) Ltd* [1939] 2 KB 827) and publication on the internet (*Godfrey v Demon Internet Ltd* [2001] QB 201). This would extend to, among other things, tweets and retweets, online blogs and Facebook posts.

Republication

Every fresh publication of a statement will give rise to a new cause of action. So, in theory at least, a claimant can sue the writer of a statement, the editor, publisher and even the newsagent.

However, s 8 of the DA 2013 provides an exception to this through a 'single publication rule', which applies to the republication of the statement by the same author. This prevents an action being brought in relation to publication of the *same material* by the *same publisher* after a one-year limitation period from the date of the first publication of that material to the public or a section of the public. In other words, the single publication rule states that time starts ticking on the one-year limitation period 'clock' from the date of the first publication to the public, and isn't reset, regardless of any subsequent publication which is substantially the same.

It would seem that, save perhaps for some litigation regarding publication that was ongoing at the time the DA 2013 came into force (for example *Richardson v Facebook* [2015] EWHC 3154 (QB)), there have been few reported disputes as to s 8.

11.5 Defences

There are many defences to a defamation action, and we'll look at the most important of these now.

11.5.1 Truth

There can be no liability in defamation for a truthful statement. However hurtful or damaging a statement about an individual might be, if it's true then that provides an absolute defence for the defendant. Section 2(1) of the DA 2013 has established a statutory defence of truth, and by s 2(4) the previous defence of justification has been abolished and s 5 of the DA 1952 repealed. In fact, as was suspected by lawyers when the DA 2013 came into force, the defence of truth is essentially identical to the old justification defence, and courts are applying the principles that applied to a plea of justification to a plea of truth.

Section 2(1) states: 'It is a defence to an action for defamation for the defendant to show that the imputation conveyed by the statement complained of is substantially true.' The defendant does not have to prove that every word published was true, only that the libellous part (the sting) was substantially true.

Alexander v North Eastern Railway Co (1865) 6 B&S 340

case example

The defendant published a poster at all of its stations to the effect that the claimant had been found to have travelled without a ticket and had been punished with a fine or 3 weeks' imprisonment. In fact, the claimant had been sentenced to only 2 weeks' imprisonment. The claimant stated that the defendant's mistake made his offence seem more serious than it was. The court disagreed: the defence of justification (as it then was) had been made out, and the small error made no difference to that.

Grobbelaar v News Group Newspapers Ltd [2002] UKHL 40

case example

The allegation here was that a footballer, Bruce Grobbelaar (Liverpool and England goalkeeper), had accepted money in return for match-fixing. He was covertly videoed by the *Sun* confessing to having fixed matches in the past, and he took money (£2,000) to fix future matches. The claimant was then arrested (though the criminal case was eventually dropped after the jury could not agree on whether he had taken bribes).

The claimant then brought a defamation action against the newspaper, which pleaded the defence of truth. That defence failed. Why? Because even though there was clear evidence of Grobbelaar confessing to past and future match-fixing, and taking money (and therefore evidence as to conspiring to fix matches), there was no evidence of match-fixing itself. The *Sun's* headline had been: 'Grobbelaar took bribes to fix games.' *That* was the sting, rather than conspiracy to fix matches, and that was found to be untrue.

Having said that, having initially been awarded £85,000 in damages, the Court of Appeal overturned this as perverse, and the House of Lords awarded just £1 in light of the fact that Grobbelaar had been shown to be corrupt.

11.5.2 More than one statement made?

Where a number of defamatory statements have been published, or, to adopt the wording of s 2(2) of the DA 2013, where the 'statement complained of conveys two or more distinct imputations', the claimant can choose only to sue in relation to one, or in relation to more than one. Section 2(3) states that 'if one or more of the imputations is *not* shown to be substantially true, the defence under this section does not fail if, having regard to the imputations which *are* shown to be substantially true, the imputations which are shown to be substantially true *do not* seriously harm the claimant's reputation' (emphasis added). The effect of this is twofold. First, the defendant may still be able to use the defence of truth, even where one or more of the allegations is not true, so long as the ones that are true constitute the sting. Secondly, and related to this, the defendant will not be able to defend themselves in relation to the untrue statements, by establishing the truth of the other claims. This is explained very well by Brooke LJ in *Cruise and Kidman v Express Newspapers plc* [1999] QB 931 in which he says: 'It is no defence to a charge that "you called me A" to say "Yes but I also called you B on the same occasion, and that was true".'

11.5.3 Honest opinion

Section 3 of the DA 2013 replaces the old common law defence of honest or fair comment with the statutory defence of honest opinion. In *Butt v Secretary of State for the Home Department* [2017] EWHC 2619 (QB), Nicol J stated that much of s 3 codified the old defence of fair comment and that previously established common law principles still apply. However, as we'll see, there are some differences here between old and new, most significantly in that the requirement that the comment be on a matter of public interest was abolished.

Honest opinion provides a defence where three conditions are met:

(1) The defamatory statement is one of opinion (not fact).
(2) The statement indicates, whether in general or specific terms, the basis of the opinion.
(3) An honest person could have held that opinion on the basis of true facts or facts alleged to be true under privilege. (We will look at the defence of privilege at **11.5.4** below.)

Opinion not fact

Of course, it can sometimes be hard to differentiate between opinion and fact. As a crude guide, facts tend to be descriptive, and capable of verification, whereas opinions are evaluative and not capable of verification as being true or false, dependent as they are on a person's values and preferences. That my cat is black is a fact. That he is friendlier than all the other cats in the street is an opinion. The courts have struggled with this concept on occasion, in that the same statement could be fact or opinion depending on the context. (In terms of procedure, whether a statement is one of fact or opinion is normally determined at a pre-trial hearing called a meaning hearing).

Statement indicates the basis of the opinion

It's important to note that a defendant can't simply couch their statement in terms of opinion rather than fact and hope that that protects them in law. That won't work. The defence of honest opinion will only be available where the opinion is based on facts, and where those facts are sufficiently identified (DA 2013, s 3(3)).

In *Kemsley v Foot* [1952] AC 345, the defendant expressed the opinion that Kemsley Press was of bad quality. He based this opinion on facts, namely that some of the reporting was inaccurate and the tone used was not neutral. The defence succeeded.

Opinion based on facts which are either true or privileged

The defendant must prove that there is a true factual basis on which the opinion is built. Not all the facts on which the opinion is based need to be true, just enough such that an honest person could reasonably have held that opinion, either 'on the basis of any fact which existed at the time the statement complained of was published' (s 3(4)(a)) or 'on the basis of anything asserted to be a fact in a privileged statement published before the statement complained of' (s 3(4)(b)). In other words, the defendant's opinion must be based on fact, and that fact must either be true or privileged (protected even if not true). We will look at privilege below.

11.5.4 Privilege

Privilege is another word for legal protection, or immunity, and the defence of privilege allows defendants to publish statements without fear of defamation proceedings. In other words, this defence offers the defendant the right to be wrong in certain circumstances. In a sense, this is freedom of expression taking priority over an individual's right to protect their own reputation.

There are different types of privilege, and we'll consider them now.

Absolute privilege

Key situations which are privileged absolutely (offering complete protection to certain statements no matter how untruthful or malicious they might be) are as follows:

(a) parliamentary proceedings, including statements made in Parliament and in reports published by Parliament;

(b) reporting of judicial proceedings made contemporaneously;

(c) court proceedings in the UK and international domestic courts, the Court of Justice of the European Union, the European Court of Human Rights and UN international tribunals, as well as communications between lawyer and client in relation to those court proceedings.

Qualified privilege at common law

This goes much wider than absolute privilege and is, as the name suggests, a form of qualified protection or immunity. It is qualified in that it only protects statements made without malice. A malicious statement is one made with the intention of damaging the claimant's reputation, where the defendant has no belief in the truth of the statement or does not care whether the statement is true or not. An example of this would be *Lillie and Reed v Newcastle City Council & Others* [2002] EWHC 1600 (QB) in which the defendant council set up a team to investigate complaints of child sexual abuse against the claimants, two nursery nurses. In its report, the team concluded that there had been sexual abuse of children at the nursery, despite there being no evidence to support this. Whilst the review team were on the face of it entitled to qualified privilege, they lost this protection because they acted maliciously, in that they knew their findings were untrue. Honest belief in the truth of the statement enables the defendant to utilise this defence.

Qualified privilege offers a defence 'where the person who makes a communication has an interest or duty, legal, social or moral, to make it to the person to whom it is made, and the person to whom it is made has a corresponding interest or duty to receive it. The reciprocity is essential.' (*Adam v Ward* [1917] AC 309)

This means that there must be a duty on the part of the publisher to impart the information to the audience, and a duty on the audience's part to receive the information. These forms of privilege can usefully be divided into two kinds: publications to limited audiences (for example, job references) and publications to the public at large.

Statutory qualified privilege – two examples

One example of statutory qualified privilege is codified in s 15 of the DA 1996 (read with Part I of Schedule 1) and this hasn't changed with the DA 2013. It covers fair and accurate reports of parliamentary proceedings, and fair and accurate reports of judicial proceedings. The rules here can get a little technical, and this takes them outside of the depth required here, but, by way of example, the defence would apply to fair and accurate reports of public meetings of local authorities (but is lost if the claimant asks the defendant to publish a reasonable statement by way of explanation or contradiction, and the defendant has failed to do this).

The DA 2013 (in s 6) has created a new category of statutory qualified privilege, that of 'peer reviewed statements in a scientific or academic journal'. This defence is aimed at fostering academic debate, following *British Chiropractic Association v Singh* [2010] EWCA Civ 35, in which a scientific journalist was sued by the defendant Chiropractic Association for accusing the claimant of promoting bogus treatments. The defamation action failed, but the case highlighted the difficulties individuals may have in defending defamation claims. It's also an interesting case on fair comment/honest opinion should you wish to read it in that light.

As such, the defence provides a niche category of the qualified privilege defence to those publishing in a scientific or academic journal (provided the statement relates to scientific or academic matters (s 6(2))). Where the privilege arises, the publication of a fair and accurate copy, extract or summary of the statement is also privileged. As with all qualified privilege, the defence is defeated by malice.

There doesn't yet seem to exist a reported case in which s 6 has been argued, so it remains to be seen how it might play out as a defence.

11.5.5 Publication on a matter of public interest

Section 4 of the DA 2013 abolished the common law defence of '*Reynolds* qualified privilege' and replaced it with a new, pithily titled statutory defence called 'publication on a matter of public interest'. This can best be seen as a form of statutory qualified privilege, though it differs from other forms of privilege, in that whilst, with other forms, the privilege attaches to the *occasion*, with *Reynolds*/s 4 it attaches to the *statement itself*.

As has been the pattern so far with the so-called new defences, this one is being interpreted in line with the principles of the old *Reynolds* defence, as confirmed in *Economou v De Freitas* [2018] EWCA Civ 2591 (discussed below). Having said that, there continues to be some debate in relation to the proper weight to be attached to the old *Reynolds* criteria.

case example

Reynolds v Times Newspapers Ltd [2001] 2 AC 127

Libel proceedings were brought against the defendant *Sunday Times* newspaper by the claimant, Albert Reynolds, the former Prime Minister of the Republic of Ireland.
The allegation was that he had misled the Irish Parliament. The article did not put the claimant's side of the story, but the newspaper claimed that it was protected by qualified privilege. Though the defendant lost in the House of Lords, nevertheless the case marked a huge shift in the law of defamation in favour of media freedom. Lord Nicholls devised 10, non-exhaustive factors (see below) to be taken into account in determining whether publication of the relevant information was in the public interest and whether the defence should be available.

In essence, this defence protected responsible journalism, allowing journalists a defence in relation to statements published in the general media, which later were found to be untrue, so long as the discussion could be said to contribute to informed public debate.

Lord Nicholls's *Reynolds* criteria

The following criteria (paraphrased here) were designed to help the court decide whether the untruthful allegations made by the journalist should be privileged:

(1) The seriousness of the allegation. The more serious the charge, the more the individual is harmed (and the public misinformed) if the allegation is untrue.

(2) The nature of the information, and the extent to which the subject-matter is of public concern.

(3) The source of the information.

(4) The steps taken to verify the information.

(5) The status of the information. Had it already been the subject of a previous investigation that commands respect?

(6) The urgency of the matter.

(7) Whether comment was sought from the claimant (though not always necessary).

(8) Whether the article contained the gist of the claimant's side of the story.

(9) The tone of the article. Does it adopt allegations as statements of fact?

(10) The circumstances of the publication including the timing.

The wording of the statutory defence

This comes from s 4(1) of the DA 2013, which states:

> It is a defence to an action for defamation for the defendant to show that—
>
> (a) the statement complained of was, or formed part of, a statement on a matter of public interest; and
>
> (b) the defendant reasonably believed that publishing the statement complained of was in the public interest.

Even though fundamentally important, the DA 2013 does not define 'public interest' because this has been well established in common law. A starting point definition comes from *London Artists v Littler* [1969] 2 QB 375 in which Lord Denning said: 'wherever a matter is such as to affect people at large, so that they may be legitimately interested in, or concerned at, what is going on, or what may happen to them or others, then it is a matter of public interest ...'

While it is clear (from cases such as *Flood v Times Newspapers Ltd* [2012] UKSC 11) that Parliament's intention was to codify and reflect the *Reynolds* defence, it should be noted that there are differences. For example, public interest is approached from a different angle in each limb of the test. In the first it goes to the subject matter: was this a matter of public interest? In the second, it goes to the fact of publication: was it in the public interest, in the circumstances, to publish the defamatory material?

How to square *Reynolds* with the statutory defence

Section 4(2) of the DA 2013 states that in determining whether the defendant has satisfied s 4(1)(a) and (b), the court should have regard to all the circumstances of the case, and this has been interpreted as allowing courts to reflect on the *Reynolds* criteria. Perhaps the *Reynolds* criteria (1) and (2) (see above) most obviously go to help determine s 4(1)(a), and the remaining criteria go to responsible journalism, thus helping to inform s 4(1)(b).

Economou v De Freitas [2018] EWCA Civ 2591

The claimant, Alexander Economou, was the ex-boyfriend of Eleanor De Freitas, the late daughter of the defendant. Ms De Freitas accused Economou of raping her, and Economou was subsequently arrested but not charged. Eight months later, he brought a private prosecution – the CPS eventually took this over – against Ms De Freitas claiming she had sought to pervert the course of justice by falsely accusing him of rape. Four days before the trial, Ms De Freitas, who suffered from bipolar affective disorder, committed suicide. Mr De Freitas wanted the inquest into his daughter's death to include examination of the role of the CPS and was advised to raise the issues publicly. He did this, writing and/or authorising the writing of seven articles. These articles formed the basis of the claimant's claim.

It was held at first instance that only two of the articles were actionable, as the others failed to meet the 'serious harm' threshold from s 1 of the DA 2013. The key issue was not simply whether the articles raised issues of public interest (they did), but also whether the defendant 'reasonably believed that the publication of the particular statement was in the public interest'. It was argued by the claimant that the defendant's conduct fell 'far short' of the *Reynolds* criteria, and yet the s 4 defence succeeded. Warby J considered that it would be wrong to have expected the defendant to meet the *Reynolds* criteria given that he was not himself a journalist. This approach was approved by the Court of Appeal.

Economou is helpful to us for a number of reasons. First, it gives us a recent example of how the courts have squared *Reynolds* with the s 4 public interest defence (namely to use *Reynolds* as a helpful template but also to consider the specific wording of s 4(1)(a) and (b)). From a legal point of view, it seems to suggest that 'mere contributors', such as the defendant, bloggers and other writers who are not trained journalists, will not be held to the same standards as professional journalists and yet might still be able to benefit from the s 4 public interest defence. The question is whether this is fair: does it tip the balance too far towards freedom of expression and away from the protection of an individual's reputation?

11.5.6 Distributors, including operators of websites

For the purposes of defences to defamation actions, a distinction is made between those who publish or republish defamatory material, such as authors, editors and publishers, and those who merely disseminate the materials, such as booksellers, newsagents, libraries and so on.

That second category, the 'innocent disseminators', are provided with a defence (called 'innocent dissemination') in s 1 of the DA 1996 (which obviously pre-dates the DA 2013) where the defendant is able to show that:

(a) he was not the author, editor or publisher of the statement complained of,

(b) he took reasonable care in relation to its publication, and

(c) he did not know, and had no reason to believe, that what he did caused or contributed to the publication of a defamatory statement.

This defence would also cover broadcasters of live programmes under s 1(3)(d) (such as phone-ins regarding statements made live on air by persons over whom the defendant broadcaster has no control).

Section 10(1) of the DA 2013 adds a further layer of protection for so-called secondary publishers. It states that the court does not have jurisdiction to hear a defamation claim against a person who was not the 'author, editor or publisher' of the statement complained of, unless satisfied that it is not reasonably practicable for an action to be brought against the author, editor or publisher.

The effect of this provision is to, for example, prevent a claimant suing Facebook in respect of postings on its platform (assuming it were possible to identify the person who posted the statement) and may save internet intermediaries from much legal wrangle.

Section 5 of the DA 2013, together with the Defamation (Operators of Websites) Regulations 2013, extends the protection offered to website operators, so that it is a defence 'for the operator to show that it was not the operator who posted the statement on its website' (s 5(2)). This provides website operators with immunity where they can show they have followed a procedure for responding to defamation complaints regarding third party content. The defence is defeated by evidence of malice (s 5(11)).

Arguably the danger here is that this defence allows internet operators to provide a forum for internet 'trolls' without being held accountable. In any event, there do not appear to be any reported cases so far in which a s 5 defence has been run at a hearing. It may be that, as a complicated procedure, it is not actually an attractive defence to website operators who will often be able to rely on other substantive defences in any event.

11.5.7 Offer of amends

This has the effect of a defence but is in reality more of a damage limitation exercise. The defence is provided for in ss 2–4 of the DA 1996. It is most often used, but not exclusively, where the defamatory statement is unintentional (see *Hulton v Jones* above at **11.4.2**). Here, the defendant can choose to make an offer of amends, which normally comprises an apology, a correction and appropriate damages. The apology and correction should be commensurate with the original statement. In other words, if a tabloid newspaper splashes a story on its front cover and then wishes to make an offer of amends in relation to that story, that apology and correction should also appear on the front page, rather than being tucked away in tiny font on page 12.

Timing is everything. The offer of amends must be made before the service of a defence to the claim. In other words, the defendant must choose whether to admit they were wrong or to defend the claim. If the defendant's offer of amends is accepted, the action stops there and then, and damages are agreed between the parties, or assessed by the court if they cannot be agreed. However, if the offer is *not* accepted, the defendant can, applying s 4 of the DA 1996, use the fact of the offer in their defence (though the defence will not be successful if the claimant can prove that the defendant knew the statement was false and defamatory – the Court of Appeal has clarified that the 'innocent' requirement is a subjective test of what the defendant knew).

In practice, what this means is that, should the claimant lose at trial, having rejected the defendant's offer of amends, they become liable for the costs that accrued from the point at which the action could have been stopped.

in practice

The *Daily Express* and *Daily Star* published allegations on their front pages that suggested that the McCanns were implicated in the death of their daughter, Madeleine McCann. They then made offers of amends which were accepted, including front page apologies.

This is an example of an offer of amends that was accepted, thereby stopping the claim in its tracks. (BBC News, 'McCanns welcome papers' apology', 19 March 2008)

example

The claimant feels she has been defamed in a series of tweets made by the defendant. She tweets the defendant saying 'public apology + £5k to migrant rescue and I won't sue. It'll be cheaper for you and v satisfying for me.' The offer was later repeated in a letter to the defendant from the claimant's solicitor. It was not accepted.

This was exactly the position in *Monroe v Hopkins*. The trial judge, Warby J, said: 'The case could easily have been resolved at an early stage. There was an open offer to settle for £5,000. It was a reasonable offer.' In the event, the claimant, Monroe, was awarded £24,000 in compensation and the costs were reported to be in excess of £300,000. (The defendant's application to appeal was refused.)

11.6 Remedies: damages and injunctions

Whilst injunctions are available to prevent further publication of a defamatory statement, the key remedy is damages.

It used to be that the jury were left to assess damages, and this led to a very wide range of awards, particularly when compared to those awarded for personal injury. (This is partly to do with the respective rationale of damages awarded for personal injury and defamation. The purpose of personal injury damages is compensatory, whereas damages for defamation, as well as being compensatory, also incorporate material losses, and feelings of distress or hurt caused by the statement.) After a Court of Appeal case called *John v Mirror Group Newspapers Ltd* [1996] 2 All ER 35, in which the jury's initial award to Elton John was reduced from £350,000 to £75,000 in relation to an article entitled 'Elton's diet of death', judges were allowed to inform juries of the levels of damages awarded in personal injury claims as a way of guiding them as to appropriate levels. As a result of the DA 2013, s 11, the presumption of jury trials has now been abolished, and the judge now determines the amount of damages.

As to injunctions, an award of damages can be accompanied by a final injunction prohibiting further publication of the defamatory material in question. A defendant who fails to comply can be imprisoned for contempt of court. Injunctions can be obtained quickly – within days or even hours.

More difficult for the courts are super-injunctions which seek to pre-empt a decision, and to prevent publication until trial. Moreover, a super-injunction is designed to prevent reporting of the fact that an injunction exists at all. Media outlets cannot therefore report on who has obtained an injunction without being in contempt of court. The courts tend to be reluctant to grant such injunctions, and critics of them argue that they can in any event be breached due to the relative ease of searches on social media. It's difficult to be certain, because of their nature, how many super-injunctions have in fact been granted. One confirmed super-injunction was issued in 2008 in relation to journalist Andrew Marr (and revealed by him in an interview he gave in 2011). The injunction was granted in relation to an extramarital affair Marr had had with another journalist.

11.7 Further reading

A Mullis and A Scott, 'Tilting at Windmills: the Defamation Act 2013' (2014) 77 MLR 87.

E Craven (Matrix Chambers), 'The ECHR and Defamation' (Westlaw, 30 September 2019).

L McNamara, *Reputation and Defamation* (OUP, 2007).

summary

- Defamation is the generic term for two torts: libel (for defamatory statements in permanent form) and slander (for defamatory statements in temporary form).
- Defamation protects reputation against untrue statements.
- A claimant must prove three elements: the statement was defamatory, referred to the claimant and was published.
- Defamation is a complicated tort that requires understanding of both statute, in particular the Defamation Act 2013, and common law.

test your knowledge

Have a go at these multiple-choice questions (MCQs):

Question 1

A man draws a picture depicting a woman that he knows holding a bloodied knife and standing over a dead person. The woman has recently been cleared of murdering the dead person. The woman now wants to sue the man in defamation.

Which one of the following options best describes whether her action is likely to be for libel or slander?

A   This would be a claim for slander as the statement (the drawing) is a potentially defamatory statement in a permanent form.

B   She would be allowed to bring her action as either libel or slander.

C   This would be a claim for slander as the statement (the drawing) is a potentially defamatory statement in a temporary form.

D   This would be a claim for libel as the statement (the drawing) is a potentially defamatory statement in a temporary form.

E   This would be a claim for libel as the statement (the drawing) is a potentially defamatory statement in permanent form.

Answer

The correction answer is option E. The answer can only be E here as both the type of defamation and the reasoning are correct.

Question 2

A woman fails to accept an offer of amends made to her by the defendant tabloid newspaper regarding a potentially defamatory article about her.

Which one of the following best describes the effect of the woman failing to accept the offer of amends?

A   Provided the defendant acted in good faith, this becomes a shield for the defendant in that, if the woman were to lose at trial, she would be liable for the costs from the point at which she could have stopped proceedings and failed to do so.

B   Provided the defendant acted in good faith, this becomes a shield for the woman in that, if she were to lose at trial, she would not be liable for the costs from the point at which she could have stopped proceedings and failed to do so.

C   At trial, having rejected the offer, the woman will be liable for costs whether she wins or loses.

D   At trial, the defendant will be liable for the costs whether the claimant wins or loses.

E   Having rejected the offer of amends, the woman cannot now win at trial.

Answer

The correction answer is option A. This is an analogous situation to *Monroe v Hopkins* (albeit no offer of amends was forthcoming). The offer of amends, once rejected, becomes a defence of sorts for the defendant at trial if the claimant loses.

Question 3

A poster pasted on a public wall in Smalltown says: 'Corruption is Ryfe in Smalltown!' Local councillor, Steven Ryfe, is thought by some to be behind a corrupt scheme whereby he is said to be profiting directly by taxing local businesses.

Which one of the following best describes how, as a claimant, Steven Ryfe would seek to plead the meaning he says is attributable to the words on the poster?

A   He would plead the meaning by reference to the literal meaning of the words.

B   He would plead the meaning by reference to false or popular innuendo.

C   He would plead the meaning by reference to true or legal innuendo.

D   He would plead the meaning by appealing to the ordinary reader.

E   He would plead the meaning by using a dictionary – Ryfe is a spelling mistake.

Answer

The correction answer is option C. If the meaning he seeks to plead is that people will read the words and assume he is implicated in corruption, then he would need to do this by reference to true or legal innuendo, in that only those with knowledge of his name and perhaps with knowledge that he is a local councillor would make the connection between the allegation of corruption and him. The other options simply wouldn't unearth the hidden meaning – see *Tolley v Fry.*

Question 4

A journalist writes an article for a newspaper about a Member of Parliament, Mr X, stating that Mr X, although Minister for Monogamy, is actually a bigamist. The journalist uses, as his only source, the ex-wife of Mr X, who bears ill-will towards Mr X.

Which one of the following offers the most likely explanation of the chances of success for the journalist of pleading the s 4 defence of public interest in the Defamation Act 2013?

A   The defendant journalist is unlikely to succeed because Mr X's activities would not be a matter in the public interest to report.

B   The defendant journalist is unlikely to succeed because, although Mr X's activities would probably constitute a matter of public interest, it was not appropriate to release the article into the public domain without acting responsibly in terms of researching the allegation.

C   The defendant journalist is likely to succeed because the s 4 defence is considered more media-friendly than the old *Reynolds* defence.

D   The defendant journalist is likely to succeed because there was no evidence of malice on his part.

E   The defendant journalist is unlikely to succeed because his conduct in researching the allegation did not meet all the criteria from *Reynolds* which have been codified in the s 4 defence.

Answer

The correct answer is option B. This is the most likely explanation/summary of how s 4 would work in relation to a journalist in this situation, who has clearly not acted responsibly in researching the allegation. The matter, given Mr X's post, is likely to be one of public interest.

Nuisance and the Rule in *Rylands v Fletcher*

After reading this chapter, you will be able to:

- define nuisance and understand the interests it seeks to protect
- appreciate that nuisance is the umbrella term for three separate torts: private nuisance, public nuisance and the rule in *Rylands v Fletcher*
- understand the similarities and differences between the three nuisance torts
- work through the structure of each nuisance tort: what the claimant needs to prove, the defences available to a defendant, and possible remedies.

12.1 What is nuisance?

Nuisance is an old tort. It pre-dates Negligence by more than 100 years, which might perhaps explain its archaic language ('sensible personal discomfort') and even, as regards *Rylands v Fletcher* at least, the question marks that sometimes surround its continued existence.

But first things first: what *is* nuisance? It is actually an umbrella or generic term for three separate torts, and those are private nuisance, public nuisance, and the rule in *Rylands v Fletcher,* the latter tort being named after the case itself.

12.1.1 What interests does nuisance protect?

All three types of nuisance are land torts, and broadly speaking they all protect use and enjoyment of land. Note that nuisance doesn't protect the *land itself*; that would be the ambit of a tort called trespass to land (which we don't cover in this book) or other areas of law, such as land law.

The way to determine the interests protected by a tort is to consider the damage or loss for which you can claim. We will consider this area in more detail as we arrive at each nuisance tort, but, in outline, for private nuisance, a claimant can claim for property damage, specifically where the amenity value of the property has been affected by the nuisance caused by the defendant, and/or for 'sensible personal discomfort'. For public nuisance, a claimant can claim for almost anything at all, including personal injury, pure economic loss, or even annoyance, so long as the loss is 'material'. For the rule in *Rylands v Fletcher*, the claim would be for damage to the claimant's property. Consequential economic loss is also recoverable for all three torts.

12.1.2 Remedies

We're dealing with injunctions and damages here. Claimants in a private nuisance action will almost always seek an injunction – an order which stops (full) or limits (partial) an activity being carried out by the defendant. For more on the law relating to injunctions (an equitable remedy), which we don't consider in detail here, you can consult a textbook on equity or more specialist works. Sometimes, damages will be awarded as well, or in lieu of an injunction. For the rule in *Rylands v Fletcher,* which tends to focus on things spilt from the defendant's land onto the claimant's, an injunction may be of use, and/or damages. An injunction and/or damages are also available in public nuisance.

12.1.3 Order of play

It makes sense for us to consider private nuisance first, it being the most important of the three torts for common law lawyers, in that there is much to say and discuss; new private nuisance cases are being heard on a fairly regular basis, and we'll consider the most important of those. Next, we'll consider the rule in *Rylands v Fletcher,* because it is in some ways closely related to private nuisance. It was described by the House of Lords as a 'subset' of (private) nuisance in *Transco plc v Stockport MBC* [2003] UKHL 61. As we'll see, both torts require the claimant to have a legal interest in the land affected, and neither allow for the claimant to recover for personal injury. (There are other overlaps, too).

We'll consider public nuisance last. It's so different from the other two as to feel in some ways completely unrelated. It's a crime as well as a tort, it doesn't require the claimant to prove that they have an interest in the land affected, and personal injury, among other things, is recoverable.

You should be aware that nuisance is heavily governed by statute as well as common law. An alternative to bringing a private nuisance action might be to bring a statutory nuisance action utilising, for example, the Environmental Protection Act 1990. However, the focus of this chapter will be on the common law.

12.2 Private nuisance

Private nuisance is unlawful interference with a person's use or enjoyment of land. 'Interference' will usually mean some indirect and continuous activity or state of affairs, be it noise, fumes, smells, vibrations and so on. (*Direct* interference would give rise to a trespass to land claim.) 'Unlawful' in this context simply means unreasonable. From this it can be seen that private nuisance is essentially about balance: the balance between the defendant's right to carry out activities on their land as against the claimant's right to use and enjoy their own land in peace. This was described as 'give and take, live and let live' in *Bamford v Turnley* (1862) 122 ER 25.

12.2.1   What can the claimant claim for?

The claimant in a private nuisance action must show that they have suffered reasonably foreseeable and recognisable loss/damage, as the tort is not actionable *per se*. The damage may be either 'sensible personal discomfort' and/or physical damage to property. As this is a tort that relates specifically to land, then any claim must relate to the diminished use or enjoyment of land. Therefore, it is not possible to claim for personal injury in private nuisance. Should the claimant sustain personal injury, their recourse might be to Negligence rather than nuisance.

Sensible personal discomfort

Sensible personal discomfort was defined in *St Helen's Smelting Co v Tipping* (1865) 11 HL Cas 642, as '... the personal inconvenience and interference with one's enjoyment, one's quiet, one's personal freedom, anything that discomposes or injuriously affects the senses or the nerves'.

example

Meredith can't enjoy any peace and quiet in her garden because of the constant noise coming from the nearby factory. In addition, the noxious fumes being pumped out are interfering with her sense of smell.

This example would be precisely the ambit of sensible personal discomfort in a private nuisance claim. We're concerned with some kind of interference with the senses. You might call this type of damage amenity damage, in that it goes to the enjoyment value of property as opposed to its pure monetary value.

Not everything that arguably affects use and enjoyment of land can be claimed for in private nuisance. This was made clear in the key case of *Hunter v Canary Wharf Ltd* [1997] 2 All ER 426 in which the court rejected residents' claims for interference with television reception caused by the erection of the Canary Wharf tower block.

Fearn & Others v The Board of Trustees of the Tate Gallery [2020] EWCA Civ 104

case example

In this case, the claimants, who were residents of newly designed flats featuring floor to ceiling windows, complained that their right to privacy and to quiet enjoyment of their properties was being affected by the fact that they were overlooked by visitors to Tate Modern, some of whom, from a viewing platform within Tate Modern, were waving, gesturing and taking photographs. Staff at the gallery had put up signs to dissuade visitors, but residents complained that this was insufficient and they sought an injunction requiring the closure of part of the walkway on the platform. (The claimants also claimed that their right to privacy under Article 8 of the ECHR had been infringed.) The claim was dismissed at first instance and in the Court of Appeal. A Supreme Court Appeal is pending.

Property damage

Any claim for physical damage to the property must be more than *de minimis*, according to *Mitchell v Darley Main Colliery* [1886] App Cas 12. Consequential loss, flowing from damage to the property, is also recoverable, according to *Hubbard v Pitt* [1976] 1 QB 142.

It used to be the case that the claimant could only claim once the damage had occurred. However, a case called *Network Rail Infrastructure Ltd v Williams* came to a different conclusion.

---

case example

Network Rail Infrastructure Ltd v Williams [2018] EWCA Civ 1514

Here, the claimant, who lived next to land owned by Network Rail, brought an action against Network Rail, which had Japanese knotweed (a highly invasive, fast-growing weed) growing on its land. No damage had yet occurred to the claimant's land, but his argument, accepted at first instance and on appeal, was that the mere presence of Japanese knotweed interfered with the amenity value of that land without proof of further damage. As a result, the claimant was able to obtain a final mandatory injunction (the onus being on the defendant to destroy/ treat the knotweed).

12.2.2 Structure of a private nuisance claim

One of the factors that links private nuisance with the rule in *Rylands v Fletcher* (and distinguishes these types of nuisance from Negligence) is as to who can sue and who can be sued. Let's work through the structure of a private nuisance claim.

Who can sue?

In order to sue, the claimant must prove that they have a legal interest in the land affected, whether that be possessionary or proprietary (freehold or leasehold). This was confirmed in *Hunter v Canary Wharf*, in which several of the claims failed for lack of *locus standi* – the claimants did not have the requisite interest in the land – for example because they were family members living with the home owner, or lodgers, rather than the owners of the properties affected. This rule came under scrutiny in *McKenna v British Aluminium* [2002] Env LR 30 following the implementation of the Human Rights Act 1998, the question being whether there was an infringement of Article 6 (right to a fair trial) and/or Article 8 (right to respect for private and family life), but the case of *Dobson v Thames Water Utilities Ltd* [2009] EWCA Civ 28 confirmed the position in *Hunter*.

Who can be sued?

Again, this is a factor that needs to be established before the claim can continue. Where possible, the claimant will want to sue the *creator of the nuisance*, even if that defendant may not be the occupier of the land (*Thomas v National Union of Mineworkers (South Wales Area)* [1986] Ch 20).

It is very common for the claimant to sue the *occupier* of the land from which the nuisance emanates. That occupier may be the creator of the nuisance, or the nuisance may happen on their land, not caused by them, but not prevented by them, and so deemed to be within their control.

Leakey v National Trust [1980] 1 All ER 17
The defendant National Trust was liable when a huge mound of earth, which it had accumulated on its land, collapsed onto neighbouring land. The National Trust was aware of the hazard but had done nothing to prevent it.

Note: this case is used here as authority for the potential liability of an occupier in private nuisance, but it is also a good example of a *Rylands v Fletcher* claim, in that it concerns an 'escape' of a substance (see **12.3** below).

Note also that occupiers will only be liable for naturally occurring nuisances on their land so far as it is reasonable to expect them to prevent such nuisances. The court will look at the circumstances, including the financial and other resources available to the defendant (see, for example, *Vernon Knight Associates v Cornwall County Council* [2013] EWCA Civ 950, in which it was held that the defendant council had sufficient resources to carry out flood prevention works and so was found liable when it did not).

Independent contractors on the occupier's land may be liable for nuisance, where they have created it, unless the occupier has asked the independent contractor onto the land to perform certain tasks and those tasks create an inevitable or reasonably foreseeable nuisance.

Trespassers causing nuisance on the land would ordinarily be liable, unless the occupier continued or adopted the nuisance.

Finally, *landlords* will normally not be liable for private nuisance at their property, but a claimant might be able to sue a landlord if they have created or authorised the tort, or if they knew or ought to have known of the nuisance at the time they let the property.

Coventry v Lawrence (No 2) [2014] UKSC 46
This issue was discussed in *Coventry* in which the claimant, who owned a property around one kilometre from a noisy motor-racing stadium, sued the occupier and landlord in private nuisance. The Supreme Court decided that the landlord was not liable because he had not authorised the nuisance (the noise) by, for example, leasing the property when he knew or ought to have known of the high probability that the lease would result in that nuisance being created. It was held that the noise had not been inevitable, and the landlord being aware of the nuisance and not doing anything to stop it was not of itself enough to establish liability.

12.2.3 Other elements of the claim
Once the claimant has established that they have the right to sue, and chosen the right defendant to sue, it's then a case of proving three key elements, namely:

- indirect interference;

- reasonably foreseeable damage of a recognised kind; and
- unlawful/unreasonable interference.

We've explored the issue of damage in sufficient detail, so let's concentrate on the other two elements.

Indirect interference

Almost always, as already mentioned, indirect interference will take the form of something intangible, be it smells, fumes, vibrations, noise, etc. In a classic case of private nuisance, *Sturges v Bridgman* (1879) 11 Ch D 852, noise and vibrations coming from the defendant's confectionery factory were the basis of a successful claim.

That interference will emanate from the defendant's land and adversely affect the claimant on their own land. Most of the time, the interference would need to be a continuing problem: a one-off interference might be actionable in public nuisance but wouldn't be in private.

Unlawful/unreasonable interference

The claimant must prove that the defendant's interference is 'unlawful'. However, this really just means unreasonable. If the activity being carried out by the defendant is deemed to be unreasonable in the circumstances, it will be a nuisance, and we move on to consider any possible defences and remedies. If the activity is held to be reasonable, there is no nuisance and the claim fails at that stage.

example

The factory next door to Connor uses heavy machinery that sometimes causes the walls of Connor's property to vibrate. One day, whilst this is happening, a valuable painting falls off Connor's wall and is damaged when it hits the floor.

Here, Connor is likely to bring an action in private nuisance against the defendant factory owner/creator of the nuisance for the property damage he has sustained.

Claims for property damage are usually relatively straightforward in that there is not much to consider in terms of balance: the court's view tends to be that if an activity by the defendant has caused physical damage to the claimant's property, then without more it is probably unreasonable. The court has made explicit that it wouldn't consider the locality/character of the neighbourhood when looking at property damage claims, whereas these would always be important where the damage is sensible personal discomfort (*St Helen's Smelting Co v Tipping*).

Factors the court will consider where the damage is 'sensible personal discomfort'

The court will look at any relevant factors to help determine whether the defendant's activity is reasonable or not. The following is not an exhaustive list, nor is it a checklist. The court might consider any or all of these, or other relevant factors, in determining whether that balance we discussed has tipped towards making the activity unreasonable or not. The factors include the following:

Locality/character of the neighbourhood

The key case here is an old one, *Sturges v Bridgman* (1879) 11 Ch D 852, in which Thesiger LJ famously commented: 'What would be a nuisance in Belgrave Square wouldn't necessarily be so in Bermondsey.'

What he meant was that it's all about context: put a factory belching fumes in an already highly industrialised area, and chances are those fumes would not be considered a nuisance because of the locality. Put the same factory in the middle of the countryside, and suddenly those fumes might constitute a nuisance. Specifically, Thesiger LJ was referencing the rarefied air of Belgrave Square (an exclusive and expensive area) as against the industrial, noisy, smelly Bermondsey, as it then was, complete with several tanning factories (which used urine in the tanning process).

Time and duration

When does the interference take place? For how long and how frequently? These will be important considerations. (Noise at 3am is perhaps more likely to constitute a nuisance than at 3pm.) See *Kennaway v Thompson* [1981] QB 88 which concerned noise created by motorboats racing on Lake Windermere.

Malice

Where the claimant can prove that the defendant's activities are motivated by spite, or malice, aimed at annoying the claimant, this of itself could be evidence of nuisance, even if ordinarily that activity would not be a problem.

Hollywood Silver Fox Farm v Emmett [1936] 2 KB 468

case example

In this case, the claimant owned a fox breeding farm next door to the defendant's land. After an argument with the claimant, the defendant got his son to fire gun shots close to the claimant's land over several nights, with the purpose of disrupting the foxes breeding. (When frightened by noise, the vixen would miscarry or eat their young!) The claimant was granted an injunction which stopped the defendant making loud noises during the breeding season, on the basis that the defendant's interference (the noise), whilst not of itself a nuisance, became so once it was proven to be motivated by malice.

Abnormal sensitivity

This factor holds less weight than it used to. The premise is that if it can be shown that the claimant or their property is 'abnormally sensitive' then that would defeat a nuisance action, the interference not being unreasonable in those circumstances.

Compare and contrast *Robinson v Kilvert* (1889) 41 ChD 88 and *McKinnon Industries v Walker* [1951] 3 DLR 577. In *Robinson*, the claimant and defendant shared business premises. The heat emitted from the defendant's property damaged the claimant's heat-sensitive paper, but it was held that that paper was 'abnormally sensitive' and that ordinary paper would not have been so affected. The claim failed. But in *McKinnon*, where the defendant tried to use the same argument when fumes from its factory damaged the claimant's precious and expensive orchids, that argument failed, because the orchids were not found to be abnormally sensitive: *all* the plants (trees, hedges) had died as a result of the fumes. Therefore, the claimant was able to claim for the full extent of the loss.

This does raise the question of what precisely the claimant or the property should be measured against: other orchids; other flowers; all plants; a piece of A4 paper? It seems that this test is moving more towards its Negligence equivalent of reasonable foreseeability, at least according to this next case:

Network Rail Infrastructure Ltd v Morris [2004] EWCA Civ 172

In this case, the claimant argued that a railway signalling system installed by Network Rail interfered with electric guitars being used in the claimant's recording studios. The defendant raised abnormal sensitivity (think of guitars gently weeping), but Buxton LJ and Phillips MR were unconvinced that abnormal sensitivity should be relied upon as a concept. They felt that such cases should be viewed in terms of foreseeability of damage. Abnormal sensitivity, they said, was evidence that the loss was not foreseeable. The claim failed. *Robinson* was disapproved by the Court of Appeal, though not overturned.

Defendant's lack of care

If the defendant's activities are carried out carelessly, or without due care and skill, then that might constitute a nuisance (see *Andreae v Selfridge and Co Ltd* [1938] Ch 1 concerning building works carried out shoddily, causing undue noise and dust).

12.2.4 Defences

Should the interference be considered unlawful/unreasonable, then it is deemed a nuisance, and we now ask whether the defendant might have a defence. Here are the most important defences.

Prescription

This is a defence peculiar to private nuisance and it is rarely successfully pleaded. It works like this: if the defendant's activity has been an actionable private nuisance for 20 years or more and the claimant, during that time, has not complained, then they will be held to have acquiesced to the nuisance should they then attempt to bring an action. The important thing seems to be the length of time during which the claimant could have complained but did not (not the time during which the activity has been going on *per se*).

In *Sturges,* this defence was unsuccessfully pleaded. The defendant's confectionery factory had been in operation for well over 20 years, but it only became an actionable nuisance to the claimant when that claimant's medical consulting rooms were built close to the factory, causing vibrations and noise. Time started ticking from that point for the purpose of the prescription defence, which did not therefore succeed.

Statutory authority

The defendant can avoid liability completely provided that the activity being carried out is authorised by statute *and* that the nuisance is an inevitable consequence of that defendant carrying out that work, exercising reasonable care in doing so. That activity might be, for example, the expansion of an oil refinery causing noise and vibrations, as in *Allen v Gulf Oil Refining* [1981] 1 All ER 353, in which, by a majority, the House of Lords found the refinery's operations to be protected by this statutory defence.

Note that planning permission does not, of itself, authorise or provide a defence to a nuisance. Planning permission, granted by a council, is not the same as statutory authority (*Wheeler v JJ Saunders Ltd* [1995] 3 WLR 466).

Contributory negligence and consent (*volenti*)

Despite its name, contributory negligence also applies to private nuisance, and the usual Negligence rules apply (applying s 1(1) of the Law Reform (Contributory Negligence) Act 1945). The same is true of consent or *volenti* (see **Chapter 6** for more on this defence in Negligence).

What will not constitute a defence?

example

Ingrid is about to move to a new area to live. She hasn't done much research on her new neighbourhood and in fact is not aware that motorboat racing takes place every weekend near her new home. This attracts hundreds of visitors and is noisy. After moving, Ingrid wants to sue the defendant organisers of the motorboat racing, but they claim that they have a defence, in that she moved to the area when she knew or ought to have known that this activity was going on.

In fact, whilst it might be wise to check out the area to which you plan to move, in case, for example, there are noisy or antisocial activities carried out there, you would not be precluded from bringing an action as a claimant if you failed to do this. Many cases make this point, and it was confirmed in *Coventry v Lawrence (No 2)* [2014] UKSC 46 in which it was no defence that the claimant had acquired the property after the nuisance (motor racing) had started.

What about where the *defendant's activity benefits the community* – would that offer a defence? The answer is no. In *Adams v Ursell* [1913] 1 Ch 269, despite the court recognising that the defendant's fish and chip shop provided a public benefit for the local community, especially at a time when cheap, hot food was a rarity, nevertheless the activity was still considered a nuisance due to the noise and smells in a residential area.

However, whilst the public benefit argument doesn't provide a defence, it is a factor that can be take into account at the remedies stage (see **12.2.5** below).

Dennis v Ministry of Defence [2003] EWHC 793 (QB)
Here, the taking-off and landing of Harrier Jump Jets owned by the Ministry of Defence was held to be a nuisance for the local neighbours because of the huge noise levels and the fact that this happened at all times of night and day. The fact that the public benefit/defence of the realm argument was obvious did not provide a defence. However, given the exceptional circumstances, the court awarded damages in lieu of an injunction. It was effectively allowing the activity to continue but compensating the claimants, who, through no fault of their own, were now unable to sell their property. (The claimants received around £950,000 in recognition of the depreciation value of their house.)

12.2.5 Remedies

Injunction
Where a claimant establishes a private nuisance to which the defendant has no defence, the usual remedy will be an injunction, either full or partial (controlling or limiting but not stopping the activity). Sometimes the court might award damages in lieu of an injunction (see *Dennis* above), but this should only be done in 'exceptional circumstances' according to the Court of Appeal in *Watson v Croft-Promo Sport Ltd* [2009] EWCA Civ 15.

Damages
Where the private nuisance causes property damage, then damages can be claimed to cover the cost of repair or renewal, and also any consequential economic loss. Damages can also be awarded for sensible personal discomfort.

12.3 The rule in *Rylands v Fletcher*

If the basis of private nuisance is that the defendant has caused interference with the claimant's use and enjoyment of their land, then the basis of *Rylands v Fletcher* is similar, albeit that the 'thing' causing damage to the claimant's land will have escaped from the defendant's land and caused property damage. *Rylands v Fletcher* actions tend to concern an isolated escape rather than an ongoing state of affairs, and they arose as a result of, and in response to, the increasingly industrial landscape of the mid-19th century. With industry came risk: the risk of water or chemicals or other substances leaking from the defendant's land onto the claimant's land.

The seminal case of *Rylands v Fletcher* (1868) LR 3 HL 330 concerned water flooding from the defendant's reservoir into the claimant's underground mineshafts and thereby flooding the land. Though the defendant had not been negligent in allowing the water to escape, nevertheless he was found to be liable, and from this case came the rule in *Rylands v Fletcher*, formulated as follows:

> … the person who for his own purposes brings on his lands and collects there anything likely to do mischief if it escapes, must keep it in at his peril, and if

he does not do so, is prima facie answerable for all the damage which is the natural consequence of its escape. (per Blackburn J)

The House of Lords introduced the requirement that the defendant's use of their land should be 'non-natural'. We'll look at each part of this rule, but first let's consider strict liability.

12.3.1 Strict liability

Rylands v Fletcher created so-called strict liability for escapes, in other words, liability is assumed without fault having to be proved. This isn't the same as absolute liability – after all, a defendant may have a defence, and they are only liable for reasonably foreseeable damage as a result of the escape – but it is correct that the claimant need not prove that the *escape* was foreseeable, and to that extent this is a strict liability tort.

12.3.2 Who can sue and be sued?

The claimant, as with private nuisance, must have a legal interest in the land affected in order to sue. This was confirmed in *Transco plc v Stockport MBC* [2003] UKHL 61, which also made the point that *Rylands v Fletcher* is a 'sub-species' of private Nuisance. The defendant will be the creator of the nuisance, ie the person who accumulates on their land the thing that escapes, and/or an owner/occupier with control over the land in question.

12.3.3 Loss/damage and remedies

The claimant can claim for property damage only (not personal injury) plus any consequential economic loss. (Historical cases used to allow for personal injury claims but this is no longer the case.) The usual remedy would be damages but an injunction is possible, too.

12.3.4 Elements of the tort

'Brings on his land and collects there'

This requires the defendant to have voluntarily brought something onto the land that wasn't existing there already, whether that be water, chemicals, or anything else that might escape (thistles in *Giles v Walker* (1890) 24 QBD 656 were already naturally growing on the land).

'Anything likely to do mischief if it escapes'

This requirement would be fulfilled by obviously dangerous things such as chemicals, but it has also been applied to water (in *Rylands* itself), electricity, noxious fumes and colliery spoil, for example.

Transco plc v Stockport MBC [2003] UKHL 61

Transco concerned a leaking water pipe which saturated an underground embankment, causing it to collapse over time. This in turn exposed a high-pressure gas pipeline owned by Transco (formerly part of British Gas) which had to take expensive preventative measures to prevent the pipe from cracking. Had the defendant brought something onto its land likely to do mischief? Lord Bingham thought not, making clear that the thing that escapes (here, water) had to be reasonably recognised as having an 'exceptionally high risk of danger or mischief' were it to escape. The claim failed. (It would have failed anyway, as there was no escape as such, the water having stayed on the defendant's land throughout.)

Non-natural use of land

What does this mean? Well, in *Rickards v Lothian* [1913] AC 263, Lord Moulton stated that non-natural use of land was use 'bringing with it increased danger to others …'.

Interestingly, what is considered non-natural use of land is a concept that has changed over time. In 1919, when cars were still a rarity, parking a car full of petrol in a garage was considered a non-natural use of that land (*Musgrove v Pandelis* [1919] 2 KB 43). Water storage in *Rylands v Fletcher* was also a non-natural use, perhaps because there had been a reservoir disaster shortly before this case was decided and this was still in the public consciousness.

In *Cambridge Water Co Ltd v Eastern Counties Leather Plc* [1994] 2 AC 264, chemicals were stored on the land by the defendant (in a factory on an industrial estate). The defendant did not realise that the chemicals had been escaping and polluting the claimant's water supply, and in any event sought to argue that this was not a non-natural use of the land. The House of Lords disagreed, stating (*obiter*) that the storage of chemicals on industrial premises is an 'almost classic case' of non-natural use of land.

Escape

The things must escape from the defendant's land onto the claimant's land. (Remember this did not happen in *Transco*, in which the water stayed on the defendant's land.) The escape could be a one-off, isolated incident, or a slow escape over time, as it was in *Cambridge Water*.

Causing foreseeable harm

Following *Cambridge Water*, the defendant will not be liable for all damage caused by an escape, but only for *reasonably foreseeable* damage. In this case, the claim failed. The defendant owned and operated a leather manufacturing business. Over many years, a chemical had seeped through the defendant's concrete floor, polluting the water system below. The water found its way to a borehole owned by the claimant 1.3 miles away, and this borehole was supplying water to local residents. As a result, the claimant had to relocate its pumping station, costing over £1 million. However, Lord Goff stated that it was not foreseeable that chemicals spilt on a concrete floor would cause pollution damage to the claimant's water. (See **12.3.1** above for a discussion of how this does or doesn't erode the concept of strict liability.)

12.3.5 Defences

Some of the same defences apply here as in private nuisance, for example consent (or common benefit, where the claimant derives a benefit from the escaping thing), statutory authority and contributory negligence.

In addition, the defendant may plead:

(a) *Act or default of the claimant:* the defence was recognised by Blackburn J in *Rylands v Fletcher*. If the escape is caused wholly by the claimant, then they won't be able to claim. In *Dunn v Birmingham Canal Co* (1872) LR 8 QB, the claimant dug underneath the defendant's canal, causing it to flood his own land!

(b) *Act of third party:* If the escape arises through the unforeseeable act of a third party, over whom the defendant had no control, then that provides a defence.

(c) *Act of God:* This provides for a situation where the escape and subsequent damage is the result of a natural event, and it is not reasonably possible to prevent (*Transco*). This covers only exceptional and unforeseeable natural events, for example unexpected flash flooding or earthquakes. In *Nichols v Marsland* (1876) 2 Ex D 1, the defendant was not liable when exceptionally heavy rainfall caused his ornamental ponds to flood the neighbouring property.

12.4 Public nuisance

Public nuisance is a crime, as well as a tort, and most cases are dealt with as crimes, or regulated by statute, both of which take them outside the ambit of our discussion. This means that there aren't very many tort cases for us to consider. All in all, public nuisance is very different from both private nuisance and the rule in *Rylands v Fletcher*. Its rules and structure are looser.

12.4.1 What is public nuisance?

The classic definition comes from *Attorney General v PYA Quarries* [1957] 2 QB 169 which concerned quarrying undertaken by the defendants. This caused dust and vibrations which were held to be sufficiently widespread to be a public nuisance. The case defined public nuisance as:

> … acts or omissions of the defendant that materially affect the reasonable comfort and convenience of life of a class of Her Majesty's subjects.

In other words, a public nuisance is:

(a) an act or omission;
(b) that materially affects;
(c) a group of people.

Note that this is a very wide definition, and an array of situations have been held to give rise to a public nuisance action, including the blocking of roads or waterways (very common), picketing on the highway, a music festival and rubbish left in a field after a party.

example

A bridge owned by the defendant is a favourite roosting spot for local pigeons, whose faeces drop onto commuters passing underneath it each day. Could the defendant be liable in public nuisance?

Yes! This example comes from a case called *Wandsworth London Borough Council v Railtrack plc* [2001] All ER 410 in which the defendant was required to pigeon-proof the bridge as a result of the successful public nuisance claim.

Both public nuisance and private nuisance?

Do be aware that some situations can and do give rise to both private and public nuisance actions at the same time. (This might make more sense once you've worked through the structure of a public nuisance claim.) For example, noise or smells or dust might emanate from the defendant's land and have a widespread effect: (i) causing local areas or walkways to be difficult to pass along, in which case a class of pedestrians may bring a public nuisance action, *and* (ii) causing residents in their homes and gardens to be affected too, the basis of a private nuisance claim. Often the issue here is where the claimant is affected by the problem: in their property = private nuisance; in a public area = public nuisance.

12.4.2 Structure of a public nuisance claim

First of all, anyone who is affected by the act or omission can sue. There is no requirement for the claimant to have a legal interest in the land. This makes sense because often the land affected is public, whether that be a field or a road or the area under a bridge, etc.

The only caveat is that the claimant must be part of a group or class, but we'll come to that below.

Sometimes, the action will be brought on behalf of a class (or in its own right) by the local authority and sometimes by the Attorney General under what's called a 'relator action'. This is what happened in *AG v PYA Quarries* (above).

The defendant will simply be the creator of the nuisance or anyone responsible for the nuisance, for example an owner or occupier of land.

12.4.3 Elements of the tort

Act or omission

Claimants can sue for acts or omissions, as with private nuisance, and also for one-off events (unlike private nuisance).

Materially affects, and loss

'Materially' here means more than trivial. Remember that claimants can sue for just about anything in public nuisance, whether that be personal injury, property damage, even pure economic loss, *so long as the loss is 'material'.* (Pure economic loss was claimed for in *Rose v Miles* (1815) 4 M & S 101 in which a blocked riverway caused the claimant extra cost in transporting goods across land.)

The loss must be reasonably foreseeable (*Savage v Fairclough* [2000] Env LR 183).

Class of people

As a starting point, the claimant must show that they belong to a class or group of people affected by the defendant's act or omission. As to the number that constitutes a class, the court has declined to fix this: it will depend on the facts of the case, according to *AG v Hastings Corporation* (1950) SJ 225. In *R v Rimmington* [2005] UKHL 63, the court held that a class meant 'a section of the public' or 'a significant section of the community'. Further, it stated that the class needs to have suffered a common injury, in other words to have been affected more or less at the same time and in the same location.

Can an individual ever sue?

Yes, though only in limited circumstances. Normally, public nuisance is about a class of people bringing the action. However, if an individual from within the class can demonstrate that they have suffered 'special damage', meaning damage different in nature or worse than that suffered by the rest of the class, then that individual may be able to bring an action for their particular loss. In *Colour Quest Ltd v Total Downstream UK Plc* [2009] EWHC 823 (Comm), it was made clear that the 'special damage' must be direct and substantial.

The rule here would be: first, establish that the claimant is part of the class affected. Then, and only then, determine whether the claimant has sustained special damage. If so, the claimant can bring an individual action. Note: if only one individual is affected by the defendant's act or omission then there can be no public nuisance claim (the claimant would have to bring alternative claim, such as in private nuisance or Negligence).

12.4.4 Defences and remedies

The main defences here are as per private nuisance and *Rylands v Fletcher* (though prescription is unique to private nuisance, and default of the claimant seems peculiar to *Rylands v Fletcher*). The most common defence is statutory authority.

As with the other types of nuisance, the remedies are injunctions and damages. Clearly, for a one-off incident, damages would be appropriate rather than an injunction. Interestingly, for actions brought on behalf of a class by the local authority or Attorney General, injunctive relief is the only available remedy.

12.5 Further reading

D Howarth, 'Nuisance, Planning and Human Rights: throwing away the emergency parachute' (2020) 79(3) CLJ 394–97.

M Lee, 'What is Private Nuisance?' (2003) 119 LQR 298.

S Steel, 'The Locality Principle in Private Nuisance' (2017) CLJ 145.

summary

- Nuisance is the generic heading for three torts: private nuisance, public nuisance and the rule in *Rylands v Fletcher*.
- The remedies available are injunctions and damages.
- Private nuisance and the rule in *Rylands v Fletcher* are closely aligned, whereas public nuisance, which is a crime as well as a tort, is the 'odd one out' in a sense.
- All three torts protect use and enjoyment of land, but in slightly different ways.

test your knowledge

Have a go at these multiple-choice questions (MCQs):

Question 1

A woman is claiming for sensible personal discomfort in private nuisance having moved next door to the defendant's factory which pumps out noxious fumes for part of each day.

Which one of the following options best describes the factors that appear relevant and that the court will take into account in determining whether the noxious fumes are an unreasonable interference with the claimant's use and enjoyment of her land?

A   Moving to the area; time and duration.

B   Location/character of the neighbourhood; time and duration; any other factors as relevant.

C   Malice; abnormal sensitivity.

D   Location/character of the neighbourhood won't be relevant as this is sensible personal discomfort; time and duration.

E   Public benefit of the defendant's actions; location/character of the neighbourhood.

Answer

The correct answer is option B. Location/character of the neighbourhood is the key consideration for sensible personal discomfort, along with, in this example, time and duration. The other factors are either not relevant on the facts or else will not be taken into account at this stage, eg moving to the area and public benefit.

Question 2

A man suffers personal injury when pieces of the defendant's scaffolding fall from a height as the man is walking past. Others walking past also sustain injury.

Which one of the following best explains the correct type of nuisance action to bring, and why?

A   A public nuisance action might be possible here as a group of people seem to have been materially affected by the defendant's actions.

B   A private nuisance action might be possible here as the people affected own their own homes.

C   A *Rylands v Fletcher* action might be possible here as the piece of scaffolding escaped from the defendant's land and injured the claimants.

D   A special damage claim in public nuisance might be possible here as the man is one of a class of people affected.

E   A private nuisance action might be possible here despite the fact that the claimants have sustained personal injury.

Answer

The correct answer is option A. As well as a possible Negligence action, there is no reason why this situation couldn't give rise to a public nuisance action, provided enough people were affected to constitute a class. The other options are all incorrect.

Question 3

Some paint spills from tins in D's garage and trickles into C's adjoining garden, killing the grass and other plants in that area. C wants to claim for her property damage.

Which one of the following is accurate as to the legal position?

A   This would be a private nuisance action, and is likely to succeed, as D brought paint onto his land, it escaped and the harm to the plants was foreseeable.

B   This would be a public nuisance action, and is likely to succeed, as D brought paint onto his land, it escaped and the harm to the plants was foreseeable.

C   This would be a *Rylands v Fletcher* action, and is likely to succeed, as D brought paint onto his land, it escaped and the harm to the plants was foreseeable.

D   This would be a *Rylands v Fletcher* action, but is unlikely to succeed because the escape of the paint was not foreseeable.

E   This would be a private nuisance action, but is unlikely to succeed because the escape of the paint was not foreseeable.

Answer

The correct answer is option C. This does fit the classic *Rylands v Fletcher* scenario. Even if a one-off escape, it could succeed, whereas it would need to be continuing for private nuisance. It hasn't affected a class so wouldn't be a public nuisance.

Question 4

Quarrying work is being carried out by the defendant, causing considerable noise and vibrations. A number of people are adversely affected. Some are looking to bring actions in private nuisance, and some in public nuisance.

Which one of the following most accurately describes the possible defences available to the defendant?

A   Prescription and consent.

B   Statutory authority if the quarrying is authorised by statute and being carried out reasonably (and if the nuisance is an inevitable consequence); prescription in private nuisance if the interference has been actionable for at least 20 years for the particular claimants affected.

C   Contributory negligence; statutory authority.

D   Default of the claimant; contributory negligence.

E   Statutory authority if the quarrying is authorised by statute but is being carried out carelessly; prescription but only for the public nuisance claim.

Answer

Option B is the most likely option here, though we'd need more information on the statutory position. The others are either wrong or there is no clear evidence for them.

Trespass to the Person

study
points

After reading this chapter, you will be able to:

- appreciate that trespass to the person is an umbrella term for three separate torts: assault, battery and false imprisonment
- understand the similarities and differences between the three torts
- understand the law relating to each tort and work through the elements of each tort
- explore the related, 'residuary trespass' tort of *Wilkinson v Downton*.

13.1 Introduction and scope

Trespass to the person is a very old tort. In fact, more accurately, it is the collective term for three torts: assault, battery and false imprisonment. All of them concern intentional interferences with the person, and all are crimes as well as torts. We'll also look at a related tort, the tort in *Wilkinson v Downton*, which is having something of a resurgence in recent years.

13.2 Differences between trespass and Negligence

Trespass to the person is different from the tort of Negligence in four key ways:

(1) *History.* Trespass to the person is the much older tort. Negligence didn't really come into being in the form we know it until *Donoghue v Stevenson*, whereas trespass was well established long before.

(2) *Intention or recklessness versus carelessness.* Trespass requires the claimant to prove that the defendant intended or was reckless as to the elements of the trespass. In Negligence, we are not seeking to prove some mental state of mind, but only that the defendant was careless, or fell below the standard we'd expect of them. So, if James pulls a chair away from Penny, just as she goes to sit on it, and she falls to the ground as a result, she may wish to sue him in trespass to the person (probably battery) if she can prove he did this intentionally. But if this was merely careless – he was looking the other way as he did it, not realising Penny was even there – then the better tort would be Negligence. See below at **13.3.2.**

(3) *Actionable per se versus proof of loss.* All trespass to the person claims are actionable per se, ie they are actionable without the claimant having to show they have suffered any loss. Whereas, in Negligence, the claimant cannot

claim unless they have suffered a form of recognisable loss (physical injury, property damage or economic loss). In our example at (2) above, Penny would not need to show she was injured when she fell to the ground to sue in trespass, but she would do in order to sue in Negligence. See below at **13.3.1**.

(4) *Crime and tort versus purely tortious.* The torts covered by trespass to the person are crimes as well as torts (hence many of our cases come from criminal law), and it is necessary to consider intention/recklessness, which go to the mental element of a crime – the *mens rea*. Negligence is purely tortious. See below at **13.3**.

13.3 Trespass to the person overview

All three torts (assault, battery and false imprisonment) are crimes as well as torts, and they will often be dealt with as crimes. This means we use many criminal authorities – though where there is a tort equivalent, you should use that where possible. Certainly, any criminal action would take priority over a tortious one, the rationale being that the court's duty to the public at large is greater than its duty to private individuals. But any evidence used in relation to a criminal matter could then form the basis of a later civil claim, the latter relying on a lower standard of proof (balance of probabilities).

Why might the claimant want to bring a tortious action at all? Well, the Director of Public Prosecutions (DPP) might decline to prosecute, or a criminal case that is brought may be unsuccessful. You may seek compensation as a result of your loss (though this tort is actionable *per se*) in which case the civil route might suit your purpose better than the criminal route.

13.3.1 Actionable *per se*

Assault, battery and false imprisonment are all actionable *per se*, that is, without proof of loss. Having said that, most claimants would not bring an action without some quantifiable loss because of the time and money involved in bringing a claim to court in the first place. (*Wilkinson v Downton* (see **13.7**) is different in that it concerns intention to inflict physical and/or psychiatric harm on a person, with the claimant having to prove that that loss actually occurred, so this tort is not actionable *per se*.)

13.3.2 What links the torts?

What links the torts is that they all require intention (or subjective recklessness), ie the claimant must prove that the defendant intended or was reckless as to the elements of the trespass. (We'll discuss precisely how this plays out below.) They all require a directness and immediacy, and as stated they are all actionable *per se* (with the exception of *Wilkinson*). The defences that apply to each are also the same, as we'll see.

13.4 Assault

Assault is defined as 'an act which causes another person to apprehend the infliction of immediate, unlawful force on his person' (*Collins v Wilcock* [1984] 1 WLR 1172). It's helpful to think of an assault as the threat or anticipation of force, and a battery to be the force itself. So, if I wave my fist at you before punching you, you will probably have experienced an assault (if you reasonably apprehended that I was about to hit you) and then a battery.

Let's break up this definition into its constituent parts. An actionable assault requires that:

(a) the defendant *intends* that the claimant apprehends the application of unlawful force;

(b) the claimant *reasonably apprehends the direct and immediate application of force*; and

(c) the defendant has no lawful justification (ie *no defence*).

example

Simon runs up behind Emcee, intending to push him off his chair. Simon changes his mind at the last moment and does nothing.

Whether or not there is an assault here will depend on whether Emcee apprehended the application of force. If he neither heard nor saw Simon approaching, then there can be no assault, regardless of what Simon intended, and there's no battery because Simon didn't touch Emcee in the end.

13.4.1 Intention or recklessness

The claimant must prove that the defendant acted voluntarily and intended to cause the claimant to apprehend the application of force, *or* was subjectively reckless to the possibility that their action would cause that apprehension in the claimant. Note that the mental state, the intention or recklessness, attaches to the causing of the apprehension in the claimant, not to the touching. In other words, what must be proved is that the defendant intended to cause, or was reckless as to causing the claimant to feel a certain way. It is not necessary to prove that the defendant intended actually to touch the claimant.

Distinguishing between intention and recklessness

The word intention can be problematic, especially in the world of tort where we're so wrapped up in Negligence and carelessness that intention tends to throw us a bit. In *Iqbal v Prison Officers Association* [2009] EWCA Civ 1312, Smith LJ discussed the role of intention, but rather mixed up intention and recklessness, as though they were one and the same or could co-exist. The preferred reading is that we need one or the other, as follows:

(a) the defendant intended to cause the reasonable apprehension in the claimant; *or*

(b) the defendant was subjectively reckless as to causing that apprehension, in other words must have seen it as a possibility but didn't care/went ahead and did it anyway.

13.4.2 Reasonable apprehension

For this element to be made out, we need to determine whether the claimant apprehended application of immediate force, and if so, was that apprehension objectively reasonable? (Which really means putting the reasonable man in the claimant's shoes. How would they have reacted?) In part, this is to protect defendants from oversensitive would-be claimants – see the example below.

example

Oliver points a lime green water pistol at his friend, Manny. Oliver and Manny bought the water pistol together only a few days before. On seeing the water pistol, Manny dives to the ground, sobbing uncontrollably. He says he thought the gun was real and wants to bring an action in assault against Oliver.

In this admittedly rather extreme example, it would seem that Manny's apprehension of immediate physical force is unreasonable. He knows the gun isn't real; it's a lime green water pistol which they bought together. Judged objectively, the claim would fail here.

(Strictly speaking, the gun, if full of water, could have fired water at Manny, which would be a battery, so it's arguably technically correct to say that Manny might reasonably apprehend immediate physical force, but if he thought the force might come only from water, that seems disproportionate.)

Note if the gun had looked real, or been real, and Manny had no knowledge that it wasn't, this would have been a different story, and then Manny's apprehension would have been reasonable, whether or not the gun was capable of firing bullets (*R v St George* [1840] 9 C&P 483).

Stephens v Myers [1830] 4 C&P 349

case example

The claimant was chairing a parish council meeting which had got a little heated. The defendant had already been asked to leave, in response to which he became abusive and leaned across the table towards the claimant with a clenched fist. He was intercepted by the churchwarden and was never close enough to the claimant to actually harm him.

The claimant nevertheless succeeded in his assault action as his apprehension was held to be reasonable. However, the judges were clearly unimpressed as they awarded the claimant a shilling! The court said: 'it is not every threat, when there is no actual violence, that constitutes an assault. There must, in all cases, be the means of carrying that threat into effect.'

We can contrast this with the following case:

Thomas v National Union of Mineworkers (South Wales Area) **[1986] Ch 20**

In this case, the claimant was a miner (a strike-breaker) trying to get across the picket line to work, during the miners' strike in the mid-1980s. He was bussed in every day with other miners wanting to work, and every day faced a jeering, angry crowd of around 50 miners. He brought an action for assault, arguing that he apprehended an immediate application of force, but the court disagreed. It said that the claimant was safe in the van and that the apprehension was therefore unreasonable. The miners could not have committed an immediate, direct battery. The claim failed.

Can words alone constitute an assault?

In a word, yes, so long as the words cause reasonable apprehension of immediate force. It used to be that words could certainly *negate* an assault, as they did in *R v Meade and Belt* [1823] 1 Lew CC 184 in which the defendant, his hand on his sword but the sword sheathed, told the claimant, 'If it were not assizes time, I would not take such language from you!' In other words, 'If the place wasn't full of visiting judges, I'd run you through with this sword.' The Court found that the words negated the action and there was no assault (although query how reassured you'd feel by those words in that situation).

A House of Lords criminal case, *R v Ireland* [1998] 3 WLR 534, confirmed that words alone could amount to an assault in certain circumstances. In this case, three women had suffered psychiatric damage as a result of a long period of harassment by the defendant, including silent telephone calls, often at night. The court was prepared to accept that the women all reasonably apprehended the immediacy of the force – they believed they might be attacked at any moment because they didn't know where the defendant was.

As Lord Steyn said:

> It is easy to understand the terrifying effect of a campaign of telephone calls at night by a silent caller to a woman living on her own. It would be natural for the victim to regard the calls as menacing. What may heighten her fear is that she will not know what the caller may do next. The spectre of the caller arriving at her doorstep bent on inflicting personal violence on her may come to dominate her thinking. After all, as a matter of common sense, what else would she be terrified about?

Immediacy

As mentioned, the apprehension created in the claimant must be of *immediate* physical force, not some force at some time in the future. That's partly why the claim in *Thomas v NUM* failed, because there was immediacy to the threats.

13.4.3 Defences

As the defences (or lawful justification) are the same for all three torts, we'll look at these below at **13.6.2**.

13.5 Battery

Battery is the 'actual infliction of unlawful force on another person' (*Collins v Wilcock*). If assault is the threat of touching, battery is the touch itself. Typically, the touch is an aggressive and direct one. A punch in the face is a classic example of battery. But the touch doesn't need to be aggressive. In theory at least, the slightest touch is an application of force that could be construed as a battery, though in reality the courts have said that would be untenable. All of us expressly or impliedly consent (see below under defences) to a level of touching in our everyday lives, for example being accidentally jostled as we travel on busy public transport. The slightest touch in that situation would therefore not be acceptable as the basis of a battery action; instead the force must exceed 'physical contact which is generally acceptable in the ordinary conduct of daily life' (*Collins v Wilcock*).

The elements of a battery are:

(a) intentional application of force by the defendant;

(b) direct and immediate force;

(c) no defence.

13.5.1 Intentional application of force

Again, the tort requires intention, or alternatively recklessness, on the part of the defendant, and that will be *intention or subjective recklessness*, where the defendant realises their act is highly likely to lead to an application of force and goes ahead with it anyway.

The claimant doesn't need to prove that the defendant intended the degree of force that occurs – perhaps the defendant intended only to push the claimant gently but in fact she falls and bangs her head (in which case that would probably go to the award of damages).

The defendant can be liable where they don't intend any physical harm at all. For example, where a surgeon operating on a patient goes beyond the consent of that patient, the surgeon may find themselves facing a battery action in that they applied force intentionally.

An action may start off accidentally (potentially as negligence, in fact) and turn into a battery as the intention 'kicks in'. This happened in *Fagan v Metropolitan Police Commissioner* [1969] 1 QB 439, in which the defendant accidentally drove his car onto a policeman's foot but then declined to move it even after the policeman shouted at him.

example

Hamish picks up a cricket bat, intending to hit Inigo with it. He misses Inigo, who ducks, and hits Julian instead.

There would still be a battery here, against Julian, even though the intention wasn't to hit Julian. This is by virtue of a doctrine called transferred intent or transferred malice (*Livingstone v Ministry of Defence* [1984] NILR 336).

13.5.2 Direct and immediate force (or indirect force)

The touching must be the direct and immediate result of the defendant's actions. Directness is often easy to prove – a slap in the face. But what about an indirect application of force, for example a gun firing a bullet, a baseball bat used to hit someone, the rump of a horse slapped in order to make the horse rear up so as to tip off the rider? (If that last one sounds very specific, that's because it's exactly what arose in *Dodwell v Burford* (1670) 1 Mod 24.)

The court is willing here to interpret the 'directness' requirement very flexibly, it would seem. In fact, so flexibly that it might seem almost pointless including it as one of the elements. For example, in *Scott v Shepherd* (1773) 2 BI R 892, the defendant threw a lit squib (firework) into a market square. This was caught first by one market trader, and then another, both of them trying to protect themselves and get rid of it. It ended up exploding in the claimant's face, injuring his eye. The defendant was liable for that indirect battery.

Similarly, in *DPP v K (A Minor)* [1990] 1 WLR 1067, a 15-year-old schoolboy was found liable in battery when he poured sulphuric acid into a hand-dryer at the school, which then blew onto the claimant's face, leaving a permanent scar. (In fact the case, in which the boy was convicted of assault occasioning actual bodily harm, was subsequently found to have been wrongly decided on an unrelated ground.)

Requirement of hostility?

It was said, by the Court of Appeal, in *Wilson v Pringle* [1987] QB 237, a case concerning two teenage boys engaged in 'horseplay' in a corridor, during which one inadvertently injured the other when he pulled a bag off the claimant's shoulder, that the claim failed because there was no 'hostility' from the defendant. Battery, therefore, was said to be touching plus hostility. The court declined to define the term hostility, preferring to say that it would be dependent on the facts of each case as to whether it arose.

But of course there are plenty of scenarios that give rise to batteries without hostility, especially in a medical context. Indeed, Goff LJ (as he then was) made clear in *Collins v Wilcock* that a better way to think about battery was not as an action requiring hostility, but as touching without consent. He restated this position in *Re F (Mental Patient: Sterilization)* [1990] 2 AC 1, once he had been appointed to the House of Lords:

> It has recently been said that the touching must be 'hostile' to have that effect [ie to be construed as a battery] ... I respectfully doubt whether that is correct. A prank that gets out of hand; an over-friendly slap on the back; surgical treatment by a surgeon who mistakenly thinks that the patient consented to it – all these things may transcend the bounds of lawfulness, without being characterised as hostile.

13.5.3 Defences

See below at **13.6.2**.

13.6 False imprisonment

The third of our triumvirate, false imprisonment, is 'the unlawful imposition of constraint on another's freedom of movement from a particular place' (*Collins v Wilcock*). In other words, it is an act that directly and intentionally causes the complete restriction of the claimant's liberty.

The elements of false imprisonment are:

(a) the defendant must intend to completely restrict the claimant's liberty;

(b) no defence.

13.6.1 Intention to completely restrict the claimant's liberty

Intention

Like the other torts, intention or recklessness is required to be proven (*Iqbal v Prison Officers Association*). But intention or recklessness as to what? The intention is as to the complete restriction of the claimant's liberty. If I lock a door intending to lock the door but not intending to restrict your liberty, I may well not be liable in false imprisonment (though might be in Negligence).

Let's work this through using the medium of the Portable Loo (a portable camping toilet), frankly because for the purpose of this exercise we want something (a) lockable from the outside, (b) that people might be inside, and (c) that is memorable.

example

Kieran is living the dream, his job being to padlock Portable Loo doors shut at the end of the day:

Loo A   Kieran locks this one, knowing that Harriet is inside = false imprisonment (intention satisfied)

Loo B   Kieran locks this one, knowing that someone might be inside = false imprisonment (applying subjective recklessness)

Loo C   Kieran locks this one, not really thinking about whether anyone is inside. He knew, or ought to have known, that someone was inside, and it would have been easy for him to check by, for example, knocking on the door = Negligence (carelessness but no intention)

Loo D   Kieran checks this one and is sure that no one is inside. Unfortunately for him, there was someone in there, though he had done all he could to check = probably no liability at all

Completely restrict the claimant's liberty

If there is a reasonable means of escape, the liberty of the claimant won't have been restricted completely and the claim would fail (*Bird v Jones* [1845] 7 QB 742). The means of escape must be objectively reasonable, however. A defendant cannot say, 'I locked him in a room on the fifth floor but it's not false imprisonment because I just assumed he'd break a window and abseil to the ground.'

Must the restriction be unlawful?

No, as demonstrated in the following case:

***Esegbona v King's College Hospital Foundation NHS Trust* [2019] EWHC 77 (QB)**

case example

The NHS Trust falsely imprisoned a patient for almost five months. The claimant, Mrs Esegbona, was treated in intensive care for three months after suffering heart failure. She said that she wanted to return home, but due to suffering from cognitive impairment and communication difficulties, the psychiatrists believed her to be confused and ordered an assessment of her mental capacity. The hospital failed to carry this out (and, among other things, breached its duty of care in Negligence), which meant that she was held when she should not have been. The patient was, in the end, transferred to a nursing home and awarded her £15,000 in compensation. Unfortunately, she died a week later.

> ### Must the restriction be for a minimum amount of time to be construed as false imprisonment?
>
> No ('for however short a time'– *Bird v Jones*), although restriction for a short time would ordinarily attract less by way of damages than a longer restriction.

***Walker v The Commissioner of the Police of the Metropolis* [2014] EWCA Civ 897**

case example

The claimant, Walker, was 'technically' falsely imprisoned for a few moments, said the Court of Appeal, in a narrow doorway, by a police officer, immediately before Walker's arrest. The context here was that the police were attending a domestic dispute at Walker's home.

Though the claimant succeeded in this false imprisonment claim against the police, Tomlinson LJ remarked, rather scathingly: 'The detention was indeed trivial, but that can and should be reflected in the measure of damages and does not render lawful that which was unlawful. The judge's assessment of £5 as the appropriate figure was I think generous to Mr Walker, but there is no appeal against that assessment.'

> ### Must the claimant know they are being falsely imprisoned?
>
> No, though again if they are unaware and therefore not distressed, this would be reflected in the amount of damages. (And if they don't at any point become aware, presumably there would be no claim in the first place.)
>
> In *Meering v Grahame-White Aviation* (1919) 122 LT 44, the claimant willingly went and waited in his boss's office, as instructed. Unknown to him, he was suspected of theft, and his colleagues had been asked to guard the door to ensure he didn't escape. There was a false imprisonment here.
>
> This approach was approved (*obiter*) in *Murray v Ministry of Defence* [1988] 2 All ER 521.

13.6.2 Defences

It makes sense to consider defences here as they apply to all three of the torts we have looked at so far. The most important defences to consider are:

(a) statutory authority;

(b) consent;

(c) necessity; and

(d) self-defence.

Statutory authority

This may provide lawful authority for an act that would otherwise be a trespass tort. The Police and Criminal Evidence Act (PACE) 1984 provides an example, as does s 3(1) of the Criminal Law Act 1967, which states:

> A person may use such force as is reasonable in the circumstances in the prevention of crime, or in effecting or assisting in the lawful arrest of offenders or suspected offenders or of persons unlawfully at large.

Consent

This is probably the most widely used defence in the context of trespass to the person claims. Intuitively, most people would understand how it works. In the context of, say, assault and battery, the potential claimant consents where she is an actress working on a domestic abuse scene in which her on-screen husband moves to strike her and then does so. One might well consent if a restaurant owner, under siege, locks customers into a different room so as to protect them from a would-be terrorist (and also that restaurant owner might plead necessity in that situation).

Consent is a live issue in a medical context. A doctor doesn't commit a battery when operating on or treating a patient so long as they have the patient's informed and valid consent. The scope of this was discussed in *Chatterton v Gerson* [1981] QB 432, in which the claimant's consent was said to be valid because she, 'in broad terms', understood the nature of the operation. In that case, the court made clear that, where a patient has not been informed of a risk, redress would more properly lie in a Negligence action rather than a trespass claim.

A battery is most likely to arise where, for example, a surgeon goes beyond that which has been consented to in the course of surgery. Let's say that the surgeon is operating on a patient with cancer. It might be that it's only when that surgeon is operating that they realise the extent of the cancerous tumours and so have to remove more tissue than they had at first envisaged. If this is life-saving surgery, or the surgeon feels there are compelling reasons why they must continue, then necessity would be an appropriate defence (see below). But otherwise the surgeon has two options: they can continue with the surgery and risk a battery action, given they do not have consent for the extended surgery, or they can stop, allow the patient to come round from surgery, explain the position, and get consent to perform further surgery at a later date, thus avoiding tortious liability. Often, consent forms have a provision which allows for the situation outlined above, which might use a form of words such as 'and so on' to indicate that more might have to be done by the surgeon once the patient is in surgery. So long as that has been explained to the patient so that they understand, then that would obviously be the best option.

A doctor can treat a patient without their consent where the patient lacks mental capacity to consent. This is determined by reference to the Mental Capacity Act 2005 and is outside the remit of this book (though very interesting).

Necessity

This is colloquially known as the lesser-of-two-evils defence. For example, I might run towards you and push you hard, but that's to push you out of the path of an oncoming train. In that scenario, the defence of necessity would protect me from potential assault and battery actions.

As mentioned, a doctor may use this defence where they seek to act in the best interests of the patient, especially where the patient's life is at stake. In *Re A (conjoined twins)* [2001] 2 WLR 480, the medical team went to court for permission to separate conjoined twins, Jodie and Mary. It was known that if there was no intervention, both twins would die. Medical evidence showed that Jodie was the strongest and capable of independent living, but Mary was not. Thus by separating the twins to save Jodie, Mary would necessarily die. This case raised legal and ethical questions, but for our purposes is a good example of the necessity defence in action. The court permitted the doctor to separate the twins, utilising the defence of necessity to what would otherwise have been a criminal charge of murder (and a tortious battery of course).

Self-defence

The defendant may be able to show they have acted in self-defence if they have used reasonable force in self-protection. In tort law, they are required to show that their belief as to being attacked was both honest and reasonable, and it must be proportionate to the force exerted against them.

In *Cockroft v Smith* [1705] 11 Mod 43, the defendant's act of biting off part of the claimant's finger was not considered a proportionate response to the claimant's act of running towards the defendant, waggling a finger near the defendant's eyes. In *Lane v Holloway* [1967] 3 WLR 1003, the defendant's blow to the claimant's eye which necessitated stitches was out of proportion to the claimant's initial shoulder punch.

13.7 The tort in *Wilkinson v Downton*

Let's look now at this tort, which is related to but different in nature from the three torts discussed above.

In *Wilkinson v Downton* [1897] EWHC 1 (QB), the defendant, as a joke, falsely told the claimant that her husband had been involved in an accident and been seriously injured. The news caused the claimant to sustain severe physical and psychological reactions. Wright J held that the claimant had a cause of action in tort, outlining the elements of the tort we now know as the tort in *Wilkinson v Downton*: *Where the defendant wilfully did an act 'calculated to cause physical harm' to the claimant and which did cause harm, there arises a good cause of action.*

Wilkinson was followed in the cases of *Janvier v Sweeney* [1919] 2 KB 316 and *Wong v Parkside Health NHS Trust* [2003] 3 All ER 932, but its status as a useful tort was in some doubt after a case called *Wainwright v Home Office* [2003] UKHL 53. This case concerned the claimants, Mrs Wainwright and her son, who were strip-searched by prison officers before being allowed to visit a family member in a Leeds prison. The strip searches were degrading and humiliating for both claimants, and the defendant agreed that the search had not been carried out in accordance with prison rules and regulations. The claimants sought, in part, to claim for their anxiety and distress under *Wilkinson v Downton*.

It was not established on the facts that the officers had intended to cause harm or had been reckless as to causing harm, and this part of the claim failed. Lord Hoffman stated that *Wilkinson v Downton* should have 'no leading role in the modern law of tort' and should 'disappear beneath the surface of the law of negligence'. This was perhaps understandable in relation to *negligently* inflicted psychiatric injury, but what about *intentionally* causing such injury?

Rhodes v OPO (by his litigation friend BHM) and Another [2015] UKSC 32
The claimant in this case was the son of the defendant, or rather the claim was brought by a litigation friend on behalf of the son, OPO, who has ADHD, Asperger's, Dysgraphia and Dyspraxia. The defendant, James Rhodes, a performing artist, wrote a memoir in which he discussed the sexual abuse he suffered at school and his subsequent mental health issues. The claimant sought to prevent publication of the memoir on the grounds that it would cause severe emotional stress. Interestingly, the Court of Appeal held that the claimant had an arguable case in the tort in *Wilkinson v Downton* and granted an interim injunction until trial.
The Supreme Court found for the defendant.

Lady Hale and Lord Toulson, in explaining why there was no tort here, outlined the parameters of *Wilkinson v Downton*. They set out the three elements of this tort, and what needs to be proved for each:

(1) *Conduct element* – requires words or conduct directed to the claimant for which there is no justification or reasonable excuse. (not met in this case)
(2) *Mental element* – intention to cause psychiatric harm, severe mental or emotional distress. (no evidence here)
(3) *Consequence element* – physical harm or a recognised psychiatric injury should be the consequence. (not relevant in this case)

It was also made clear that only intention will do – recklessness was not available as an alternative.

13.8 Further reading

K Patten, 'Defining Harassment' (2010) 160 NLJ 331.
YK Liew, 'The Rule in *Wilkinson v Downton* Revisited' [2015] CLJ 392.
FA Trindale, 'Intentional Torts: Some Thoughts on Assault and Battery' (1982) 2 OJLS 211.

• Assault, battery and false imprisonment are all crimes as well as torts, and all require intention on the part of the defendant, or subjective recklessness.
• All are actionable *per se.*
• The key defences in relation to each are statutory authority, consent, necessity and self-defence.
• *Wilkinson v Downton* is not actionable *per se* but requires a 'consequence', namely physical harm or a recognised psychiatric injury.

Have a go at these multiple-choice questions (MCQs):

Question 1

A man walks up behind a woman, intending to push her off her chair. At the last minute he changes his mind.

Which one of the following options best describes whether this would be an assault?

A   It seems likely this would be an assault, because the woman apprehended the immediate application of force. We would need more information on this.

B   It seems unlikely this would be an assault, unless the woman apprehended the immediate application of force. We would need more information on this, but as the man walked up behind her, this seems unlikely.

C   It seems unlikely this would be an assault, unless the woman apprehended the immediate application of force. It is more likely to be a battery.

D   It seems unlikely this would be an assault, unless the woman apprehended the immediate application of force. It is more likely to be an example of false imprisonment

E   It seems likely this would be an assault, because the woman apprehended the immediate application of force. There may also be a battery here.

Answer

The correct answer is option B. An assault seems unlikely here for these reasons. The other options all contain errors.

Question 2

Two school children are playing in the playground. One attempts to leapfrog the other but lands on the other's head, causing injury.

Which one of the following best describes whether this would be a battery?

A   It seems unlikely this would be a battery, because the leapfrogger would probably be able to plead the defence of consent.

B   It seems unlikely this would be a battery, because the leapfrogger would probably be able to plead the defence of no hostility.

C   It seems unlikely this would be a battery, because the leapfrogger would probably be able to plead the defence of necessity.

D   It seems likely this would be a battery, because the leapfrogger applied physical force.

E   It seems unlikely this would be a battery, because the leapfrogger did not intend to hurt the other child.

Answer

The correct answer is option A. Yes, there is probably implied consent here, as per Goff LJ in *Collins v Wilcock*.

Question 3

A student is studying in the library during a busy day. Unknown to him, the caretaker has locked the library, not bothering to check whether anyone is inside.

Which one of the following is accurate as to false imprisonment?

A   This looks like false imprisonment, on the basis that the student could have exited via another route.

B   This does not look like false imprisonment because the caretaker did not intend to lock the student in.

C   This looks like false imprisonment, on the basis of recklessness by the caretaker. The claimant does not need to know he was imprisoned.

D   This looks like false imprisonment, on the basis of intention by the caretaker. The claimant does not need to know he was imprisoned.

E   This does not look like false imprisonment because the claimant did not know he was imprisoned.

Answer

The correct answer is option C. Yes, this looks like subjective recklessness rather than intention. Any damages may be low here as the student is unaware of the situation.

Question 4

A woman is driven in a locked taxi at speed through a hostile crowd of pedestrians. The crowd shouts at her threateningly and some of them raise their fists at her.

Which one of the following is accurate about whether this would be an assault?

A   It is unlikely to be an assault because any apprehension by the woman as to the immediate and direct application of force would probably be unreasonable here – she is in the relative safety of a locked taxi being driven at speed.

B   It is likely to be an assault because any apprehension by the woman as to the immediate and direct application of force would probably be reasonable here.

C   This would not be an assault because the woman is not subjected to the application of force.

D   This would be an assault because the woman apprehends the immediate and direct application of force.

E   This might be an assault – this would turn on the nature of the threats being shouted at the woman.

Answer

The correct answer is option A. This is unlikely to be an assault for the reasons given (the reasoning being similar to *Thomas v NUM*).

chapter 14 Revision and Consolidation

Having worked through this book, the point of this chapter is to pull all the strands together, and to give you a starting point and an ending point. This is where the book ends, and where you begin to turn your mind towards revising and consolidating. You may find this chapter helpful in that it consolidates and condenses the key points from each topic, and it also offers some guidance on answering questions in exams and more generally on exam technique.

The chapter is set out as follows:

- **Keywords and recaps, summaries and key cases for each topic** – these sections should provide a useful aide memoire as you come to consolidate your learning
- **Guidance**
  - MCQs
  - essay questions
  - problem questions
- **Exam technique**

Chapter 1: Introduction to Tort Law

KEYWORDS AND RECAPS

What is tort?

For legal purposes, a tort is simply a **civil wrong, for which the law provides a remedy.** Not every civil wrong you might be able to think of would be classified as a tort for which the law might provide a remedy.

What is the purpose of tort law?

(1) To compensate those who have been wronged, by awarding damages (money).

(2) To deter others from acting in the way that the defendant acted.

(3) Striking a balance between competing interests and rights.

(4) An alternative to statutory compensation.

What is the significance of policy?

Tort law is decided on the basis of precedent and the application of statute, yet policy has clearly played its part in many landmark judgments. So what is policy? It can best be defined as the non-legal considerations, whether social, political or economic (or a combination), that the court takes into account when having regard to the effect its decision will have. Policy considerations can work for or against either party, and they can narrow or broaden the scope of claims depending on the legal climate at any time.

- A tort is a civil wrong for which the law provides a remedy.
- There is nothing much to connect the torts apart from some overlap as to the interests they protect and the fact that they fit into a residual category of civil wrongs not dealt with by other types of civil law.
- The claimant is the party bringing the action, and the defendant or tortfeasor is the party defending it.
- Most (but not all) torts require some kind of fault to be proven and for the claimant to have suffered recognisable loss.
- Policy underpins much of tort law.

Chapter 2: General Negligence – Loss and Duty of Care

Part I: Loss/Damage and Duty

KEYWORDS AND RECAPS

What is Negligence?

Negligence is really just legal-speak for carelessness. It is a tort – a civil wrong – that provides a remedy (normally damages) where loss or damage is caused to a claimant by the defendant tortfeasor's carelessness, specifically by their breach of a legal duty imposed on them to take care.

The following types of loss are recoverable in Negligence:

(a) **Personal injury.** Personal injury can be both physical and psychiatric, and whilst it's usually relatively straightforward to prove that a duty ought to be imposed on the defendant in relation to personal/physical injury, it's not so straightforward where that loss is psychiatric.

(b) **Property damage.** This might be damage to a vehicle, a watch, an antique vase, a pet (animals are property in tort law), a house – potentially anything damaged as a result of the defendant's breach of their duty.

(c) **Consequential economic loss.** This is financial loss flowing from damage to person or property. It might also include other costs such as physiotherapy fees, equipment required, travel costs to and from treatment, and so on.

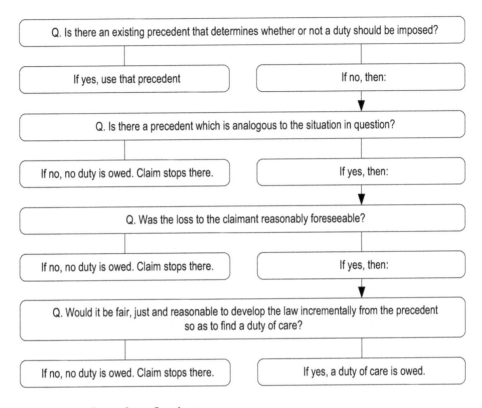

Figure 14.1   Duty of care flowchart

- Damage and duty are the first two elements in the Negligence sequence and should be looked at in that order.
- The leading case on the question of duty is still *Caparo v Dickman*, though there was confusion for a time as to how it should be interpreted.
- The courts will look to existing precedent first and use that to establish the existence or absence of duty. If there is no existing precedent, they will look to analogous cases, and where these exist, ask whether the loss in the present case was reasonably foreseeable, and whether it would be fair, just and reasonable to develop the law incrementally from the precedent.
- There are general rules surrounding the imposition of a duty of care and exceptions to those. For example, generally there is no duty imposed for an omission, but various exceptions to this rule apply.

Part II: Psychiatric Harm

KEYWORDS AND RECAPS

Who is a primary victim/claimant?

A primary victim is someone who is caught up in the incident itself (the car crash, the stadium disaster), who does *not* suffer personal injury (though personal injury is reasonably foreseeable given their proximity to the incident) but who *does* sustain psychiatric harm. We sometimes say that this type of claimant is present in the physical zone of danger. In *White v Chief Constable of South Yorkshire* [1998] UKHL 45, the definition given for a primary victim is a neat one: someone **'objectively exposed to danger [ie physical harm] or reasonably [believing] that [they were]'.**

Who is a secondary victim/claimant?

A secondary victim suffers their loss – psychiatric harm – through having witnessed the incident. Personal injury for the secondary victim is neither sustained nor reasonably foreseeable. Lord Oliver gives us a useful definition (in *Alcock v Chief Constable of South Yorkshire Police* [1992] 1 AC 310): the secondary victim/claimant is 'no more than a passive and unwilling witness of injury caused to others'.

For this category (and remember this is the category about which the court is concerned about floodgates), the House of Lords has put in place a number of hurdles. Claimants wishing to sue as secondary victims must overcome these hurdles to show that they ought to be owed a duty of care, and the hurdles are usually insurmountable. You might think of these hurdles as a strong judicial control mechanism used to 'knock out' as many claims as possible at the duty stage.

Part II: Economic Loss

KEYWORDS AND RECAP

When is a duty owed for pure economic loss? Negligent misstatement

The exception to the rule as to non-recovery for pure economic loss concerns negligent misstatement, which translates as careless or negligent advice provided by the defendant. Where this is relied on by the claimant to their detriment, and they suffer pure economic loss, the court may impose a duty of care, where the circumstances fit those first expounded in the seminal case of *Hedley Byrne & Co Ltd v Heller & Partners Ltd* [1964] AC 465.

Lord Wilson, in *Steel and Another v NRAM Ltd (Scotland)* [2018] UKSC 13, said that *Hedley Byrne v Heller* was the starting point, and that at the heart of that decision was the need for the claimant to have relied, reasonably, on the representation made by the defendant, and for the defendant reasonably to have foreseen that he would do so. He said that, whilst often linked, these were two separate enquiries, and together they amounted to an assumption of responsibility.

- Psychiatric harm is a type of loss in Negligence claims giving rise to particular policy concerns for the court relating to duty.
- The court will categorise claimants as primary or secondary victims, and a duty is rarely imposed in relation to secondary victims, unless all the criteria in *Alcock v Chief Constable of South Yorkshire* are satisfied.
- Pure economic loss is a type of loss in Negligence claims for which a duty of care will not normally be imposed.
- The main exception to this rule concerns pure economic loss caused via negligent misstatements and the key case is *Hedley Byrne v Heller*. Where the claimant can show their circumstances fit those described in *Hedley*, a duty may be imposed.

KEY CASES

There are lots here and it's perhaps easiest to group them, like this:

Duty of care

Donoghue v Stevenson [1932] AC 562
Caparo Industries Ltd v Dickman [1990] 2 AC 605
Hill v Chief Constable of West Yorkshire [1989] AC 53
Michael v Chief Constable of South Wales [2015] UKSC 2
Robinson v Chief Constable of West Yorkshire [2018] UKSC 4

Omissions

Smith v Littlewoods Organisation Ltd [1987] AC 241
Mitchell v Glasgow City Council [2009] 1 AC 874
Home Office v Dorset Yacht Co Ltd [1970] AC 1004

Psychiatric harm

Page v Smith [1996] AC 155
McLoughlin v O'Brian [1983] 1 AC 410
Alcock v Chief Constable of South Yorkshire Police [1992] 1 AC 310

Pure economic loss and negligent misstatement

Hedley Byrne & Co Ltd v Heller & Partners Ltd [1964] AC 465
Smith v Eric S Bush [1990] 1 AC 831
Steel and Another v NRAM Ltd (Scotland) [2018] UKSC 13
Banca Nazionale del Lavaro SPA v Playboy Club London Ltd [2018] UKSC 43

Chapter 3: General Negligence – Breach

KEYWORDS AND RECAP

How many stages to breach?

Breach is a two-stage test:

(1) First, we set the standard expected of the defendant, and we do that by reference to the law. This is the part where we are effectively suggesting how the defendant ought to have conducted themselves.

(2) Next, we try to decide whether the defendant has fallen below that standard, and we say that that is a question of fact rather than law, because the court will look at the factual circumstances of the case to help it determine whether there has actually been a breach or not. This is the part where we ask what actually happened and why.

- Breach is made up of two stages.
- We first of all set the standard expected of the defendant objectively and by reference to the task or activity the defendant is undertaking.
- The second stage is to look at the facts to establish breach. This is where we ask the question what went wrong and, importantly, why.
- Occasionally, claimants may be able to use the doctrine of *res ipsa loquitur* which means 'the thing speaks for itself', rather than having to prove breach, but only where there has been negligence on the defendant's part but the facts are unascertainable.

KEY CASES

Wilsher v Essex Area Health Authority [1988] 1 AC 1074
Nettleship v Weston [1971] 2 QB 691
Bolam v Friern Hospital Management Committee [1957] 1 WLR 583
Bolton v Stone [1951] AC 850
Bolitho v City and Hackney Health Authority [1998] AC 232

Chapter 4: General Negligence – Causation

KEYWORDS AND RECAP

Where do we start with causation?

The place to start with factual causation is always the 'but for' test. The claimant must prove that but for (had it not been for) the defendant's breach, the loss to the claimant would not have happened at that time and in that way.

What is legal causation?

Having established factual causation – and we sometimes think of factual causation as the chain that links the breach with the damage to the claimant – we now look to see whether that chain has been broken or affected by a subsequent intervening act. This is called legal causation and is really a consideration of whether, in law, the defendant ought to be responsible for all that follows their breach.

- Causation is looked at in two parts – factual causation and legal causation.
- Factual causation always begins with the but for test and claims may fail at that stage.
- There are exceptions to the but for test, but these are truly exceptional and apply only to specific types of case.
- Legal causation asks whether there has been a *novus actus interveniens* that breaks the factual chain of causation.
- Events that can break the chain are acts of the claimant, acts of third parties and acts of God/natural events.
- These events will only break the chain where they are unreasonable and/or unforeseeable.

KEY CASES

Barnett v Chelsea and Kensington Hospital [1969] 1 QB 428
Wilsher v Essex Area Health Authority [1988] AC 1074
Bonnington Castings Ltd v Wardlaw [1956] AC 613
McGhee v National Coal Board [1973] 1 WLR 1
Fairchild v Glenhaven Funeral Services Ltd [2003] 1 AC 32

Chapter 5: General Negligence – Remoteness

KEYWORDS AND RECAP

What is remoteness?

The claimant must prove that their loss was reasonably foreseeable from the breach, and not too remote from it. Whether something is too remote from the breach or not is judged by the standards as they existed at the time of the breach, rather than by the standards that might exist by the time of trial.

What is the test?

Was the type of damage suffered by the claimant reasonably foreseeable at the time the breach occurred? This comes from *The Wagon Mound (No 1)*.

- Remoteness is the means by which the court determines the type and extent of liability towards the claimant.
- It is based on a test of the type of harm being reasonably foreseeable.
- It's an element heavily driven by policy, though the general rules are usually followed.
- The court will take into account the claimant's egg-shell skull where appropriate, and that extends to their 'thin wallet' (impecuniosity).

KEY CASES

Overseas Tankship (UK) Ltd v Morts Dock and Engineering Co (The Wagon Mound No 1) [1961] UKPC 2
Vacwell Engineering Co Ltd v BDH Chemicals Ltd [1971] 1 QB 88

Smith v Leech Brain and Co Ltd [1962] 2 QB 405
Hughes v Lord Advocate [1963] AC 837
Doughty v Turner Manufacturing Co Ltd [1964] 1 QB 518
Lagden v O'Connor [2004] 1 AC 1067

Chapter 6: General Negligence – Defences and Remedies

KEYWORDS AND RECAP

What are the three key defences?

The three key defences in Negligence are *volenti* (or consent), *ex turpi* (or illegality) and contributory negligence.

What is volenti?

The rationale of *volenti non fit injuria* (meaning 'no wrong will be done to the willing') or consent is that 'one who has invited or assented to an act being done towards him cannot, when he suffers it, complain of it as a wrong' (from *Smith v Charles Baker & Sons* [1891] AC 325). In other words, if a claimant has expressly or impliedly consented to be injured, or to run the risk of the injury they then sustain, the defendant may be able to utilise this defence to sidestep liability. It is a full defence and heavily policy driven.

What is ex turpi?

Ex turpi causa non oritur actio means that no action may be founded on an illegal or immoral act, and its rationale is to prevent a claimant profiting where they themselves are involved in an illegal act. It is a full defence and heavily policy driven.

What is contributory negligence?

Contributory negligence is a partial defence that serves to reduce but not extinguish the defendant's liability. It's highly pragmatic in that it takes account of the culpability of both defendant and claimant, and it's governed by statute. Section 1(1) of the Law Reform (Contributory Negligence) Act 1945 states that the court can reduce the claimant's damages in accordance with what it considers just and equitable. This is the most common defence in negligence.

summary

- There are three key defences within the tort of Negligence: *volenti*, *ex turpi* and contributory negligence.
- *Volenti* and *ex turpi* are full defences, heavily driven by policy, and often difficult to predict with any degree of consistency.
- Contributory negligence is a partial defence, governed by statute. It's the most common defence of the three.

KEY CASES

Dann v Hamilton [1939] 1 KB 509
Morris v Murray [1991] 2 WLR 195

Pitts v Hunt [1991] 1 QB 24
Gray v Thames Trains Ltd [2009] UKHL 33
Patel v Mirza [2016] UKSC 42
Froom v Butcher [1976] 1 QB 286

Chapter 7: Clinical Negligence

KEYWORDS AND RECAP

What is Clinical Negligence?

Clinical (or professional) Negligence is just Negligence in a clinical context. Most of the same rules apply here as apply to Negligence but there are some specific cases to consider.

What is the standard of care for professionals such as doctors?

For professionals acting in their professional capacity, the standard (which is objective) comes from *Bolam v Friern Hospital Management Committee* [1957] 1 WLR 583. The court will expect the professional to demonstrate that they met the standard of the reasonably competent professional carrying out that particular art. Remember that the standard attaches to the task, not the person doing it ('the act not the actor'), so, for example, if a junior doctor is doing a task that requires more skill than perhaps they have yet attained, that won't serve to lower the objective standard expected of them. (This was the position in *Wilsher v Essex Area Health Authority* [1988] 1 AC 1074.)

How was the possible breach by omission dealt with in Bolitho?

The House of Lords in *Bolitho v City and Hackney Health Authority* [1998] AC 232 made clear that there were two questions to ask in that case itself: first, what would the doctor have recommended had she attended the boy? If the answer was that she would had recommended intubation, then that would have been evidence of a breach, with that breach causing the loss because she failed to do something which she knew she ought to have done. (Note that this involves breach *and* causation.) The doctor said she would not have intubated, so the second question was: had she attended and not intubated, would that failure to intubate have been negligent? On the facts, it was found that that decision not to intubate would not have been a breach, given the risks of intubation in a child that young (and that the failure to intubate was not the cause of death).

What is the leading case where there has been a failure to warn of risk?

Montgomery v Lanarkshire Health Board [2015] UKSC 11 has undoubtedly changed the emphasis where failure to warn of risk is concerned in the context of breach.

- Clinical Negligence follows the General Negligence structure and is based on the same principles.
- The focus tends to be on complex areas, especially breach (and causation).
- *Bolam* is the key case when assessing the standard required of professionals acting in their professional capacity at the first stage of breach. It's often very important at the second stage, too, where the potential breach concerns a choice made by the defendant as to, say, treatment, or techniques.
- In respect of breach issues arising where there has been a failure to warn of risk, the key case is now *Montgomery*.

KEY CASES

Bolam v Friern Hospital Management Committee [1957] 1 WLR 583

Bolitho v City and Hackney Health Authority [1998] AC 232

Montgomery v Lanarkshire Health Board [2015] UKSC 11

Pearce v United Bristol Healthcare NHS Trust [1999] EWCA Civ 865

Chester v Afshar [2005] 1 AC 134

Chapter 8: Employers' Primary Liability and Vicarious Liability

KEYWORDS AND RECAP

What is employers' primary liability?

The common law recognises the need to protect employees at work, and the tort of employers' liability reflects that. It is really just Negligence in a specific context, namely, in the workplace.

This is an area heavily governed by statute and numerous, ever-evolving regulations, but the common law duties exist alongside this. Employers owe a duty of care to take care of their employees, and this is a primary duty, meaning that, just as with General Negligence, a claimant (employee) can sue their employer for that employer's negligence.

What is secondary or vicarious liability?

Vicarious liability simply means 'on behalf of', and typically this will involve the employer of the tortfeasor being vicariously financially liable for the **torts** of that tortfeasor employee, even though the employer has not committed the tort. Vicarious liability is not a tort; it's a mechanism or device designed to shift the financial burden across to the defendant employer, where that employer has compulsory insurance to deal with any claims arising.

- Employers' primary liability is Negligence in a specific context, namely a claim brought by an employee against their employer.
- The structure is the same as for General Negligence, though some of the authorities are different.
- Secondary or vicarious liability renders the defendant employer financially liable for the torts of that employer's employee (the tortfeasor).
- Vicarious liability is not a tort – its effect is to make the employer strictly liable once three elements are established.

KEY CASES

Wilsons and Clyde Coal Co Ltd v English [1938] AC 57
Ready Mixed Concrete Ltd v Minister of Pensions [1968] 2 QB 497
McWilliams v Sir William Arrol [1962] 1 WLR 295
ICI Ltd v Shatwell [1965] AC 656
Lister v Hesley Hall [2002] 1 AC 215
WM Morrisons Supermarkets plc v Various Claimants [2020] UKSC 12

Chapter 9: Product Liability

KEYWORDS AND RECAP

Product liability covers the law relating to loss caused by products. Its rationale is to hold manufacturers accountable for unsafe goods. Manufacturers, distributers, suppliers and retailers can all be held responsible, where a product or any of its component parts are defective, and that liability can arise under the Consumer Protection Act (CPA) 1987 or the common law of Negligence.

Why would a claimant choose to bring an action under the CPA 1987 for defective products?

The CPA 1987 makes the manufacturer of a product, and everyone else dealing with that product through the supply chain, **strictly liable** for damage caused to a claimant. That means there's no need to prove fault, unlike with a common law Negligence claim where the fault stage is breach – the part where we look at whether the defendant was at fault. This might make a claim through the CPA 1987 more attractive to claimants in some circumstances. That damage might be personal injury or property damage, and it needs to have been caused 'wholly or partly' by a defect in the product.

- Product liability is a statute-based tort, but a common law claim is also available.
- The CPA 1987 is a strict liability regime, whereby fault on the part of the defendant should not be relevant.
- Whether a product is defective turns on its safety, and what persons are entitled to expect as regards the safety of a product.
- Much turns on s 3(2)(a)–(c) of the CPA 1987 and there are also various defences available.

KEY CASES

Richardson v London Rubber Company Products Ltd [2000] Lloyd's Rep Med 280
Abouzaid v Mothercare (UK) Ltd [2000] EWCA Civ 348
A and Others v National Blood Authority [2001] 3 All ER 289
Gee & Others v DePuy International Ltd [2018] EWHC 1208 (QB)

Chapter 10: Occupiers' Liability

KEYWORDS AND RECAP

What is occupiers' liability

Whilst the General Negligence principles apply, this tort is distinctive in that it is largely governed by statute: the Occupiers' Liability Act (OLA) 1957 for visitors and the Occupiers' Liability Act (OLA) 1984 for non-visitors.

What are the key terms we need to define?

The three key terms are:

- occupier
- visitor
- premises.

Once defined, we know whether the claimant will bring a claim under the OLA 1957 or the OLA 1984.

How is this different from a Negligence claim?

The claim is statute based, and it focuses on damage occurring as a result of the state of the premises rather than as a result of some activity done. The statutes themselves formalise the duty, breach and defence stages, but there is no mention of causation or remoteness.

What are the key differences between the statutes?

It's much easier for a visitor to bring an action than a non-visitor, because the visitor starts from a place of permission, whereas the non-visitor/trespasser has to work hard at every stage to succeed, from duty to breach.

There are some specific differences; for example, you can't claim for property damage under the OLA 1984.

- Occupiers' liability is a form of statute-based Negligence but that also looks to case law.
- Visitors are afforded a high degree of protection when injured on premises as a result of the OLA 1957.
- Non-visitors or trespassers have some limited protection as a result of the OLA 1984.
- Most cases brought under the OLA 1984 fail at the duty stage.

Chapter 11: Defamation

KEYWORDS AND RECAP

What is defamation?

Defamation protects a claimant's reputation. Specifically, it protects a claimant's reputation from *untrue* statements that would harm them in the eyes of others.

What is libel?

Libel is the publication of a defamatory statement in a permanent form.

What is slander?

Slander, in contrast to libel, is defamation in a temporary or transitory form. The most obvious example would be speech (that hasn't been recorded), but it could include sound, gestures or anything regarded as transitory in nature.

What must the claimant prove?

A claimant must prove three elements: that the statement was defamatory, referred to the claimant and was communicated/published to a third party.

What defences are available?

The key defences are found in statute form, though they still rely on or borrow from the common law. They are truth, honest opinion, privilege (there are various forms) and publication on a matter of public interest. There are other more minor defences plus 'offer of amends', which isn't so much a defence as an offer to settle made pre-trial, which, if rejected, can be utilised as a form of defence at trial.

- Defamation is the generic term for two torts: libel (for defamatory statements in permanent form) and slander (for defamatory statement in temporary form).
- Defamation protects reputation against untrue statements.
- A claimant must prove three elements: that the statement was defamatory, referred to the claimant and was published.
- Defamation is a complicated tort that requires understanding of both statute, in particular the Defamation Act 2013, and common law.

KEY CASES

Sim v Stretch [1936] 2 All ER 1237

Monson v Madame Tussauds Ltd [1894] 1 QB 671
Berkoff v Burchill [1996] 4 All ER 1008
Monroe v Hopkins [2017] EWHC 433 (QB)
Stocker v Stocker [2019] UKSC 17
Charleston v Newsgroup Newspapers Ltd [1995] 2 All ER 313
Tolley v JS Fry & Sons Ltd [1931] AC 33
Knupffer v London Express Newspaper Ltd [1944] AC 116
Grobbelaar v News Group Newspapers Ltd [2002] UKHL 40
Reynolds v Times Newspapers Ltd [2001] 2 AC 127

Chapter 12: Nuisance and the Rule in *Rylands v Fletcher*

KEYWORDS AND RECAP

What is nuisance?

Nuisance is actually an umbrella or generic term for three separate torts, and these are private nuisance, public nuisance and the rule in *Rylands v Fletcher* (1868) LR 3 HL 330, the latter tort being named after the case itself.

What is private nuisance?

Private nuisance is unlawful interference with a person's use or enjoyment of land. 'Interference' will usually mean some indirect and continuous activity or state of affairs, be it noise, fumes, smells, vibrations and so on.

How is private nuisance related to Rylands v Fletcher?

If the basis of private nuisance is that the defendant has caused interference with the claimant's use and enjoyment of their land, then the basis of *Rylands v Fletcher* is similar, albeit that the 'thing' causing damage to the claimant's land will have escaped from the defendant's land and caused property damage. *Rylands v Fletcher* actions tend to concern isolated escapes rather than an ongoing state of affairs, and they arose as a result of, and in response to, the increasingly industrial landscape of the mid-19th century.

What is public nuisance?

Public nuisance is very different from the other two types of nuisance. For a start, it's a crime as well as a tort and it breaks down as:

- an act or omission
- that materially affects
- a group of people.

- Nuisance is the generic heading for three torts: private nuisance, public nuisance and the rule in *Rylands v Fletcher*.
- The remedies available are injunctions and damages.
- Private nuisance and *Rylands v Fletcher* are closely aligned, whereas public nuisance, which is a crime as well as a tort, is something of the 'odd one out'.
- All three types of nuisance protect use and enjoyment of land, but in slightly different ways.

KEY CASES

Transco v Stockport MBC [2003] UKHL 61
Network Rail Infrastructure Ltd v Williams [2019] QB 601
Coventry v Lawrence [2014] UKSC 46
Sturges v Bridgman (1879) 11 Ch D 852
Network Rail Infrastructure Ltd v Morris [2004] EWCA Civ 172
Rylands v Fletcher (1868) LR 3 HL 330
Cambridge Water Co Ltd v Eastern Counties Leather Plc [1994] 2 AC 264
Attorney General v PYA Quarries [1957] 2 QB 169

Chapter 13: Trespass to the Person

KEYWORDS AND RECAP

What is trespass to the person?

Trespass to the person is the collective term for three torts: assault, battery and false imprisonment. All of them concern intentional interferences with the person, and all are crimes as well as torts. There is a further trespass tort called *Wilkinson v Downton* which concerns the defendant inflicting psychiatric harm on the claimant.

How does trespass to the person differ from Negligence?

There are overlaps in that both protect your bodily integrity. But trespass to the person concerns the intentional (or subjectively reckless) act of the defendant, whereas Negligence has no '*mens rea*' requirement, its equivalent being carelessness on the part of the defendant.

What is assault and what is battery?

In simple terms, assault relates to the anticipation of force, and battery relates to the application of force.

What is false imprisonment?

This is a tort whereby a defendant intentionally or recklessly restricts a claimant's liberty.

What are the main defences to trespass torts?

These are statutory authority, consent, necessity and self-defence

- Assault, battery and false imprisonment are all crimes as well as torts, and all require intention or subjective recklessness on the part of the defendant.
- All are actionable *per se*.
- The key defences in relation to each are statutory authority, consent, necessity and self-defence.
- *Wilkinson v Downton* is not actionable *per se* but requires a 'consequence', namely physical harm or a recognised psychiatric injury.

KEY CASES

Collins v Wilcock [1984] 1 WLR 1172
Iqbal v Prison Officers Association [2009] EWCA Civ 1312
Scott v Shepherd (1773) 2 Bl R 892
Wilson v Pringle [1987] QB 237
Wilkinson v Downton [1897] EWHC 1 (QB)
Rhodes v OPO (by his litigation friend BHM) and Another [2015] UKSC 32

Guidance on Answering MCQs, Essay Questions and Problem Questions

This section offers point-by-point guidance on answering different types of question. It's necessarily generic but should provide a helpful template. As you gain experience and confidence in answering MCQs, essay questions and problem questions, you might find it useful to devise your own guidance that builds on what's here but is tailor-made for you.

GUIDANCE ON ANSWERING MCQS

(1) Read the question **carefully** as many times as you need to. Think of what your answer might be and look for that first, and then check your preferred answer against the others, rather than scanning the possible answers from the outset to find the 'best'.

(2) Try and understand the topic as fully as you can, and learn about it as though you're not being tested on it via an MCQ. MCQs are not an easy option, though they might appear so at first glance.

(3) Be aware of questions containing must/may/never/always – read these carefully and sense check them.

(4) MCQs tend to test general rules not exceptions, so try to learn the core principles and how these might apply.

(5) Look out for questions that ask about what a court might or must do. Does it have discretion to do something, or must it do something?

(6) Practise doing MCQs and practise doing them at the speed you'll have in the exam.

(7) Choose an answer – don't leave a blank.

(8) Check feedback for questions you get wrong. Why was it wrong? The more you understand the topic, the less an MCQ feels like sticking in a pin at random.

GUIDANCE ON ANSWERING ESSAY QUESTIONS

(1) Read the question carefully and try to actually answer it – weaker scripts tend to forget to do this, or else present an answer to a question that wasn't asked.

(2) Check that each paragraph deals with one idea/issue and that it relates to the question set.

(3) Inform your arguments with authority throughout. This is the difference between an informal discussion and a legal argument.

(4) Write your introduction last, once you know what you want to say and have a clear view.

(5) Your introduction should give the examiner confidence that you understand the question and give some insight into how you intend to answer it.

(6) If the question asks for critical evaluation or discussion, make sure you provide that: that means giving your verdict – showing you agree or disagree/ to what extent/why? – having weighed up both sides of the argument.

(7) Think analysis not narrative. Narrative is more like copying and pasting the content of an article on the page, whereas analysis is using that content in a way that informs your argument in some way, by strengthening it or challenging it. If you have a view, can you find an authority that gives a different or the opposite view? How will you reflect that in your essay?

(8) If there is more than one component to an essay question, ensure you have answered all of them.

(9) Remember to conclude in some logical way rather than just stopping. Does your conclusion pull the strands of your argument together? This is probably not the time to contradict your own arguments that you will have set up and followed through to reach your conclusion.

(10) Watch your time management. Better to stop and move on if you are under time pressure. You may have time at the end to return to anything left out.

GUIDANCE ON ANSWERING PROBLEM QUESTIONS

(1) Read the question carefully and be clear on what you're being asked to do.

(2) Be specific with your advice, not generic. To focus your mind as to what this means, try imagining a real client sitting opposite you and waiting for your advice (and checking their watch). They don't want to hear about the history of Negligence, exciting as that might be; they want to know whether they are owed a duty of care here. Be as specific as possible.

(3) Save all your knowledge and understanding for the specifics of your advice, and don't be tempted simply to write down everything you know.

(4) Have a clear and logical structure and follow it.

(5) Deal with every part of every claim and don't miss parts out.

(6) Inform your arguments with authority throughout. Apply the law to help you take a view. Show you are applying the law by signposting this – use phrases such as 'applying that here, we can see that…' or 'unlike in [insert case], the claimant in this scenario will not be able to bring a claim because …'.

(7) Avoid narrative – no need to repeat the wording of the question.

(8) Superficial answers are those that lack any depth – this is usually because there is no law applied, or else the student has used a scattergun approach with lots of cases but no or limited application.

(9) Examiners are not trying to trip you up; they want to award you credit wherever possible.

General Exam Guidance Top Tips

- Check the format of your exam and work to that. Is it an MCQ, essay question, problem question, something else, or a mixture?
- Will it be closed or open book? How will that affect the way you revise?
- Try to find past papers provided by your institution and practise. If mocks are offered, do them.
- Practise properly by limiting yourself on time and not cribbing! Get things wrong now, learn why that happened and go again.
- When you're revising, start with the basics. Do you understand the topic? Could you explain what it's all about in a few lines to a layperson with no legal knowledge? If not, why not? What is tripping you up? Try explaining out loud and noticing where you get stuck.
- From there, try some of the trickier concepts. Can you explain them simply? (This isn't the same as giving a simplistic answer.)
- It's much easier to learn case names if you actually read and understand the cases (or at least a good explanation/summary of the cases). Once you understand them, the facts are more memorable.
- Try and learn key cases, not every case.
- Useful cases are the ones that do more than one job for you. For example, *Wilsher v Essex AHA* can be used at the breach and causation stage of Negligence questions, as well as specifically in a clinical context, so it's a high-value case. Other cases might be more niche – useful if you have them in your armoury but perhaps lower value in terms of their use to you.
- This may be of less concern if the exam is open book, but even so, the more cases and authorities you can commit to memory beforehand, the less 'scrabbling around' you have to do in the assessment, trying to find them!

And finally – good luck with your study of tort law. Enjoy it!

INDEX

assault 225
   defences 227, 231–3
   intention 225
   reasonable apprehension 226–7
      immediacy 227
      words alone? 227
   recklessness 225

battery 228
   defences 229, 231–3
   direct and immediate force (or indirect force) 229
      hostility? 229
   intentional application of force 228
breach of duty 53
   Clinical Negligence 109–16
   employers' liability 130
   factors the court may take into account
      balancing the factors 61
      common practice 59
      foresight not hindsight 60
      likelihood of harm 58
      potential seriousness of injury 58–9
      practicality of taking precautions 60
      social utility 61
   occupiers' liability 163–9, 173–4
   question of fact 58
   res ipsa loquitur 62–3
   setting the standard ('the reasonable person') 54
      modified 55–6
      objective 54–5
      professionals 57, 109
'but for' test 68–9
   exceptions
      failure to warn of risks 74, 115–16
      multiple potential causes 70–4

'but for' test– *continued*
      material contribution to harm 71–2
      material increase in risk of harm 72–3

causation 68–9
   Clinical Negligence 117
   employers' liability 131
   factual causation 68–76, 117
      'but for' test 68–9
      determining 75
      exceptions to the 'but for' test 70–5
   intervening events (*novus actus interveniens*) 77–80
      acts of God/natural events 80
      acts of the claimant 77–9
      acts of third parties 79–80
   legal causation 77, 117
      vs remoteness 77
   product liability 148–9
children 165, 175–6
Clinical Negligence 107
   apportionment of damages 118
   breach of duty 109
      breach of the standard 109–116
      setting the standard 109
   causation 117
   duty of care 108–9
   loss/damage 108
   overlaps with criminal law 107–8
consent *see volenti*
contributory negligence 100–102, 213
   elements 101
   failure to exercise reasonable care 101–2

damage *see* loss/damage
damages 8
   apportionment 118

damages – *continued*
 defamation 201–2
defamation 181–2
 defences 193–201
  distributors 199–200
  honest opinion 194–5
  matter of public interest 197
  more than one statement made 194
  offer of amends 200–1
  privilege 195–7
  truth 193–4
 distinction between libel and slander 183
 elements
  defamatory statement made 186–7
  statement referred to the claimant 190–2
  statement published to third party 192–3
 libel 182
 meaning of statement 186–90
  context 188
  defamatory to that claimant 190
  innuendo 188–90
  literal meaning unclear 187–8
 remedies 201–2
  damages 201–2
  injunctions 202
 slander 183
 structure of claim
  requirement of serious harm 185–6
  who can and cannot sue 184–5
 vs mere abuse 183–4
defences
 defamation 193–201
 employers' liability 131
 Negligence 95–102
  contributory negligence 100–102
  ex turpi (illegality) 98–100
  volenti (consent) 96–8
 occupiers' liability 169–70, 174–5
 private nuisance 212–14
 product liability 149–50
 rule in *Rylands v Fletcher* 217
 trespass to the person 231–3
duty of care 15–16
 breach *see* breach of duty
 Caparo v Dickman 17–18
 Clinical Negligence 108–9
 employers' liability 124–30
 expansion and contraction 16

duty of care – *continued*
 Michael and *Robinson* 19–20
 occupiers' liability 163, 171–3
 precedent 20–1
 psychiatric harm 36
 pure economic loss 44–5
 special duty situations 21
  liability for acts of third parties 24–7
  omissions 21–4
  public bodies 27–33

employee 123
 multiple or economic reality test 123–4
 relationship of, or akin to, employment 134–5
employers' liability 121–2
 breach of duty 130
 causation 130–1
 damage/loss 122
 defences 131–2
  contributory negligence 131–2
  volenti (consent) 131
 duty of care 124–30
  'reasonable' care 129–30
  safe and competent staff 125–7
  safe place of work 127–8
  safe system of work 128–9
 'employee' 123–4
 scope 121–2
 structure of a claim 122
employment
 'in the course of' 136–8
  close connection test 136–8
ex turpi (illegality) 98–100
 circumstances 99–100
 elements 98–9
 evolution 100

false imprisonment 230
 defences 231–3
  consent 232–3
  necessity 233
  self-defence 233
  statutory authority 232
 intention to completely restrict claimant's
  liberty 230–1
  completely restrict 230–1
  intention 230
floodgates 6

illegality *see ex turpi*
injunctions 202
intervening events (*novus actus interveniens*)
  77–80
    acts of God/natural events 80
    acts of the claimant 77–9
    acts of third parties 79–80

liability for acts of third parties 24–7
loss/damage 12
    Clinical Negligence 108
    defamation 179
    employers' liability 122
    may not be recoverable
        psychiatric harm 14, 36–43
        pure economic loss 14–15, 44–45
    private nuisance 207, 210
    public nuisance 219
    recoverable or recognisable 12–13
        consequential economic loss 13–14
        personal injury 13
        property damage 13
    rule in *Rylands v Fletcher* 215

Negligence
    breach of duty *see* breach of duty
    causation *see* causation
    clinical *see* Clinical Negligence
    defences *see* defences, Negligence
    definition 11–12
    duty of care *see* duty of care
    loss/damage *see* loss/damage
    product liability *see* product liability,
        Negligence claims
    remoteness *see* remoteness
    remedies *see* remedies, Negligence
nuisance
    definition 205
    interests protected 205
    private nuisance *see* private nuisance
    public nuisance *see* public nuisance
    remedies 206
    rule in *Rylands v Fletcher see* rule in *Rylands v
        Fletcher*

occupiers' liability 157–8
    differences between 1957 and 1984 Acts
        176–7
    'occupier' 159–60

occupiers' liability – *continued*
    Occupiers' Liability Act 1957 *see* Occupiers'
        Liability Act 1957
    Occupiers' Liability Act 1984 *see* Occupiers'
        Liability Act 1984
    'premises' 162–3
    'visitor' 160–2
        express permission 161–2
        implied permission 162
        lawful 159
        unlawful 159
    vs Negligence 158–9
Occupiers' Liability Act 1957
    breach 163–9
        children 165
        person in exercise of their calling 165–6
        standard expected of the occupier 163–4
        subcontractors 167–8
        warning notices 166–7
    defences 169–70
        contributory negligence 169–70
        volenti 169
    duty of care 163
    exclusion 170
Occupiers' Liability Act 1984
    background 171
    breach 173–4
        warnings 173
    duty of care 171–3
    exclusion of liability 175
    likelihood of successful claim 175
        children 175–6
    non-visitor or trespasser 170–1
omissions 21–4, 114–15, 218
    Clinical Negligence 114

policy 5
    causation 68
    crushing liability 7
    defensive practices 7
    floodgates 6
    insurance 7
    remoteness 85
private nuisance 206
    damage
        property damage 208
        sensible personal discomfort 207
    defences 212–14

private nuisance – *continued*
    contributory negligence 213
    no defence? 213–14
    prescription 212
    statutory authority 213
    volenti (consent) 213
    elements
        indirect interference 210
        reasonably foreseeable damage of a
            recognised kind 210
        unlawful/unreasonable interference
            210–12
    public and private nuisance? 218
    remedies
        damages 214
        injunction 214
    who can sue and be sued? 208–9
privilege 195–7
    absolute 195–6
    qualified 196
    statutory qualified 196–7
product liability 141–2
    Consumer Protection Act 1987 142–51
        causation 148–9
        'defect' 145–8
        defences 149–50
        development risks 150
        limitation period 149
        'product' 144–5
        what damage can be claimed? 144
        who can sue and be sued? 142–4
    Negligence claim 151
        breach 152
        damage 151
        design defects 152–3
        duty 151–2
    other forms of liability
        contract 141–2
        criminal law 141
        Fatal Accidents Act 1976 142
psychiatric harm 14, 36–43
    definition 36
    primary victims 38–40
        rescuers 38–40
    secondary victims 40–3
public bodies 27–33

public nuisance 217
    defences 219
    definition 217–8
    elements
        act or omission 218
        class of people 219
        individual? 219
        loss 219
        'materially affects' 219
    public and private nuisance? 218
    remedies 219
    who can sue? 218
pure economic loss 44–8, 219
    negligent misstatement 44–7
    negligent provision of services 48

remedies
    damages 8
    defamation 205
    injunctions 202
    Negligence 102
    private nuisance 206, 214
    public nuisance 219
    rule in *Rylands v Fletcher* 206, 215
remoteness 85–6
    claimant's impecuniosity 90
    employers' liability 131
    reasonable foreseeability 86–7
        extent need not be foreseen 88
        no need to foresee precise way in which
            damage occurs 89–90
        test 86–7
    same kind or type of harm 87
        narrow and wide view 88–9
        procedure 87–8
revision and consolidation 239–56
    guidance
        essay questions 255
        exam tips 256
        MCQs 254–5
        problem questions 255–6
    revision 239–54
rule in *Rylands v Fletcher* 214–15
    defences 217
        act or default of claimant 217
        act of God 217

rule in *Rylands v Fletcher – continued*
    act of third party 217
    elements
        'anything likely to do mischief if it escapes'
            215
        'brings on his land and collects there' 215
        escape 216
        non-natural use of land 216
        reasonably foreseeable harm 214–15
    loss/damage 215
    strict liability 215
    remedies 215
    who can sue and be sued? 215

strict liability 215

tort
    definition 1
    in outline 4–5
    policy 5
    what is tort not?
        contract law 3
        criminal law 2–3
        land law 3
    terminology
        actionable *per se* 8–9, 223–4

tort – *continued*
    claimant/defendant 7
    fault liability and strict liability 8
    loss/damage/damages 8
tort in *Wilkinson v Downton* 233–4
trespass to the person 223–4
    actionable *per se* 224
    assault *see* assault
    battery *see* battery
    false imprisonment *see* false imprisonment
    tort in *Wilkinson v Downton* see tort in
        Wilkinson v Downton
    vs negligence 223
    what links the torts? 224

vicarious liability 132
    elements 133
        tort has been committed 133
        by the employee of the defendant
            134–6
        in the course of employment 136–8
    rationale 132
    who can sue? 133
volenti (consent) 96–8, 215
    example 97–8
    elements 96–7

Lightning Source UK Ltd.
Milton Keynes UK
UKHW030430260821
389503UK00003B/18